From its enthusiastic reception in 19 *Lochs of Scotland* has established itself as a reliable and much valued reference work for the game fisherman. It has inspired its readers to cast their flies on trout waters in some of Scotland's most beautiful scenery and to fish them for wild trout with all the confidence that a little background information can bring. This, the third edition, is completely revised and updated and has the added value of providing detailed information on 150 new lochs. For the many regular trout fishermen in Scotland and for the thousands of visiting anglers each year, this enlarged third edition of *Trout Lochs of Scotland* will provide all basic information required in planning fishing expeditions. It includes:

❊ *The trout lochs*
   over 800 highland and lowland lochs detailed, mapped and indexed

❊ *Where they are*
   all the lochs are shown on location maps, Ordnance Survey grid references given, and good advice on how to get there by car and on foot

❊ *Permits and permissions*
   who you need to ask, where they live, telephone numbers, fishing restrictions and stipulations

❊ *Local information*
   how to reach the lochs, best times to fish, topographical peculiarities, boat or no boat

❊ *Fishing tips*
   recommended tactics and flies, average catches, record weights

Bruce Sandison, well known for his regular contributions to *The Scotsman*, *Trout and Salmon* and for his Radio Scotland broadcasts 'Tales from the Loch', has spent a large part of his life in pursuit of Scottish trout. His enthusiasm for fly fishing has taken him to many remote and obscure lochs as well as to the more famous fishing places in Scotland; his accumulated knowledge of them is second to none. He lives in Caithness, almost within casting distance of Loch Watten, in the heart of what he considers to be some of the best trout fishing in the world.

TROUT LOCHS OF SCOTLAND
A Fisherman's Guide
SECOND EDITION

TROUT LOCHS OF SCOTLAND
A Fisherman's Guide
SECOND EDITION
FULLY UPDATED AND WITH NEW ENTRIES

Bruce Sandison

UNWIN
PAPERBACKS

LONDON SYDNEY WELLINGTON

First published in Great Britain by Allen and Unwin, 1983
Second edition, revised and enlarged 1987

First published in paperback by Unwin® Paperbacks, an imprint
of Unwin Hyman Limited in 1988

UNWIN HYMAN LIMITED
15–17 Broadwick Street,
London W1V 1FP

Allen & Unwin Australia Pty Ltd.
8 Napier Street, North Sydney, NSW 2060, Australia

Allen & Unwin New Zealand Pty Ltd. with the Port Nicholson Press
60 Cambridge Terrace, Wellington, New Zealand

British Library Cataloguing in Publication Data

Sandison, Bruce
    The trout lochs of Scotland
1. Trout fishing – Scotland
I. Title
799.1′755   SH687
ISBN 0–04–799017–1

Set in 10 on 11 point Bembo by Nene Phototypesetters Ltd,
Northampton
Printed and bound in Great Britain by
William Clowes Ltd, Beccles and London

This book is dedicated to my wife Ann, without whose encouragement it would never have been started and without whose patience it would never have been finished.

Contents

Illustrations

Maps

The map reference after the name of each loch denotes the Ordnance Survey sheet number followed by the grid reference.

Acknowledgments

D. Anderson, Kilsyth
P. B. Anderson, Locheport, North Uist
F. N. Andrews, Blackwaterfoot, Arran
M. Andrews, Girvan
Assistant Head of Estates, Strathclyde Regional Council, Glasgow
M. Atkinson, Kings House Hotel, Glencoe
Mrs M. Baird, Forsinard Hotel, Strath Halladale
Ballathie Estates, Stanley
Eric Begbie, Tillicoultry
Douglas Bertram, Shieldaig Lodge Hotel, Gairloch
S. R. Biggar, Leslie, Glenrothes
J. Black, Upper Annandale Angling Association
J. T. Boscawan, Strathtay Estate Office, Aberfeldy
J. Boyd, Kirkintilloch
R. Breingan, Redwell Place, Alloa
H. Brown, Nature Conservancy Council, Kinlochewe.
J. Brown, Kinloch, Rannoch
W. Brown (Rogie), Strathpeffer
G. S. Buchanan-Smith, Burntisland, Fife
Buccleuch Estates, Thornhill, Dumfries-shire
K. Byrne, Isle of Colonsay Hotel, Argyll
Cally Hotel, Gatehouse of Fleet
M. A. Cameron, Post Office, Lochgilphead
R. Cameron, Acharacle, Argyll
I. Campbell, Langside Drive, Glasgow
N. Campbell, Nature Conservancy Council, Inverness
Major R. A. Carnegie, Lonmay, Aberdeenshire

Chief Forester, Aberfoyle, Stirlingshire
Chief Forester, Dunoon, Argyll
Chief Forester, Galloway Forest Park, Dumfries-shire
Chief Forester, Portree, Skye
Chief Forester, Taynuilt, Argyll
J. M. Christie, Broughty Ferry, Dundee
T. Clark, Hannahston Avenue, Drungan
R. A. Clement, Ingram St, Glasgow
Cologin Homes, Leragas, Oban
A. Colquhoun, Foyers, Inverness-shire
R. A. M. Coyne, Leckmelm, Garve, Ross-shire
D. H. Craig, Linsidecrag, Lairg
M. M. Crowe, Glenconner Drive, Dundee
Culag Hotel, Lochinver, Sutherland
Mrs S. Cull, Navidale House Hotel, Helmsdale
W. Cuthbert, Fleurs Cresent, Forres
Dalbeattie Angling Association, Kirkcudbrightshire
The Dalry Angling Association
R. C. Davies, Uig Lodge, Stornoway
Department of Leisure and Recreation, Lothian Regional Council, Edinburgh
Deputy Chief Executive, Protective and Basic Services, Strathclyde Regional Council, Glasgow
W. L. Dick-Smith, Council Offices, Kirkcudbrightshire
A. W. Dickison, Violet Bank, Peebles

Director of Administration,
Council Offices, Lugar,
Cumnock
Director of Recreation, Moray
District Council, Elgin
Mrs H. Dobie, Abbey St Bathans,
Berwickshire
J. Donald, Currie, Midlothian
A. M. Dougall, Fort William,
Inverness-shire
M. Douglas, Tarvie, Ross-shire
A. J. Dowman, Crawford Priory
Estate, Cupar, Fife
R. S. Duncan, Grampian Regional
Council, Fraserburgh
Dumfries and Galloway Angling
Association, Dumfries
Dumfries and Galloway Tourist
Association, Newton Stewart
Dunsky Estate, Portpatrick,
Wigtownshire
L. W. G. Elliot, High Street,
Hawick
The Enderline Estate, Ford,
Lochgilphead
The Factor, Dalhousie Estate,
Brechin
The Factor, South Esk Estate,
Brechin
The Factor, Stornoway Trust
Estate Office, Lewis
The Factor, Strathspey Estate
Office, Grantown-on-Spey
R. F. Fairburns, Quinish Estate,
Mull
P. M. Fairweather, Cherry Park,
Inveraray, Argyll
Fernhill Hotel, Portpatrick,
Wigtownshire
B. M. Flower, North Beach
Street, Stornoway
A. D. Forgan, West Ferry,
Dundee
D. Fraser, Bridge House, Islay
J. Fraser, Tomich Beauly,
Inverness-shire
Dr K. H. Freshwater, The Wyck,
Dundee

Mr J. Fyfe
J. Galbraith, Well Park, Stirling
Galloway Arms Hotel,
Crocketford
C. Gartor, Loch Merkland, Lairg
J. B. Gibson, Seaforth Road, Ayr
I. Gillies, Scarinish, Tiree
S. Gillies, Kilsyth Fish Protection
Association, Kilsyth
P. Gladstone, Laurencekirk,
Kincardineshire
Fife Tourist Organisation,
Glenrothes
Gleneagles Hotel, Auchterarder
D. Gordon, Glenshee, Golspie
F. Gourley, Barend, Sandyhills,
Dalbeattie
R. Gowans, Brier Cottage, Forfar
W. Graham, Hightoe, Locherbie
I. F. H. Grant, Glenmoriston
Estates, Glenmoriston
J. Grant, Crask Inn, Lairg
D. K. Greaves, Overscaig, Loch
Shin, Lairg
W. J. Hamilton, Loch Leven,
Scotlandwells
A. Hamish-Scott, Acre Place,
Wigtown
R. Harriman, Sunnyknowe,
Pitlochry
G. R. Hatfield, Forestry
Commission, Fort William
G. Hawkins, Dingwall, Ross-shire
Ian Hay, Scourie Hotel, Sutherland
W. Hay, Assynt Estate Office,
Lochinver, Sutherland
Col Hector, Lyndhurst, Fleet,
Hants
W. H. Hedley, Invershin Hotel,
Sutherland
P. Helm, Annan, Dumfries
J. Henderson, Callay Estate Office,
Gatehouse of Fleet
T. Henry, Collingwood, Innellan
Highland Coastal Trading Co.,
Estate Office, Kessock
J. L. Hogg, Forest Office,
Glentrool, Newtown Stewart

Mrs E. Huggett, Dornie, Ross-shire

R. G. Hulbrook, Carraig-Thura Hotel, Loch Awe, Dalmally

Inverbeg Inn, Luss, Loch Lomand

Inverpolly Estates, Achiltibuie, Lochinver, Sutherland

R. Irvine, Summer Isles Hotel, Achiltibuie, Ullapool

D. W. Jack, Fife Regional Council, Glenrothes

J. J. Jaimieson, Wedderburn Street, Dunfermline

Drew Jamieson, Torphicen Street, Edinburgh

J. V. M. Jamieson, King Street, Castle Douglas

H. R. Jenkins, Loch Morar Sailing School, Bracora, Mallaig

W. Johnston, Erbusaig, Kyle, Ross-shire

J. Johnston-Mann, Creel Cottage, Acharacle, Argyll

M. Jones, Fairliehopes Farm, Carlops

R. T. Jones, Forest Office, Girvan

A. A. Jordan, Meanston, Ilkley, Yorkshire

A. Justice, Charleston Drive, Dundee

Mrs E. Kemp, Newton Stewart, Wigtownshire

F. R. Khan, Area Engineer, Strathclyde Regional Council, Glasgow

D. King, Dalgety Avenue, Edinburgh

R. Knight, Butterstone, Dunkeld

D. L. Laird, Airlie Estate Office, Cortachy, Kirriemuir

Lammington & District Angling Improvement Association, Biggar

A. Lamont, Ben View Hotel, Strontian

Ledcreich Hotel, Balquhidder, Perthshire

Messrs Lidderdale & Gillespie, Castle Douglas

J. G. Lindsay-Pate, Woodbine Cottage, Dunoon, Argyll

Loch Achray Hotel

Lochnaw Castle Hotel, Stranraer

C. T. Lucas, Horsham, Sussex

J. Lucas, New Barnet, Herts

Miss E. G. Luke, West Craigs Crescent, Edinburgh

A. MacArthur, Lairg, Altnaharra, Sutherland

J. S. McChesney, Main Street, Dalrymple, Ayr

Mrs M. McCorkindale, Kilninver, Oban

J. F. McCreath, Bali-Hi, Helensburgh

W. S. McCulloch, Dunfermline

H. McDonald, Keppers Cottage, Leckmelm Estate, Ullapool

Mrs P. MacDonald, Eilean Iarmain, Ornsay, Skye

D. MacDougall, Lochgilphead & District Angling Association

N. M. S. MacDougall, Foyers Hotel, Loch Ness, Inverness-shire

R. W. McDowal, Arthur Street, Newton Stewart

J. MacFarlane, Logierait Hotel, Ballinluig, Perthshire

W. S. McFarlane, Aillivoe, Yell, Shetland

Mr J. MacGillivary

B. G. McGlennan, Balmacara Hotel, Kyle of Lochalsh

M. MacGregor, Acharacle, Argyll

A. MacKay, Drumbeg Hotel, Assynt, Sutherland

Major J. A. McKay-Forbes, Ballygrant, Mull

J. M. McKeand, Scoor House, Mull

M. R. P. McKenzie, Kinbrace, Sutherland

R. J. MacKinnon, Lochgair Hotel, Lochgilphead

H. MacKintosh, Allness, Lairg

Dr I. K. McKintosh, Gleann Mor, Lewis

Charles McLaren, Altnaharra Fishings, Lairg, Sutherland

D. MacLennan, Post Office, Laide, Ross-shire

J. MacPherson, St Fillans & Loch Earn Angling Association, St Fillans

D. MacRitchie, Strathpeffer, Ross-shire

Mr Maddison, Baltasound, Unst, Shetland

A. Mair, Carnoustie Gardens, Glenrothes

The Manager, Dalwhinnie Distillery, Dalwhinnie, Inverness-shire

The Manager, Loch Fitty, Dunfermline, Fife

The Managing Director, Aviemore Centre, Inverness-shire

E. Mann, Sheriff Park Gardens, Forfar

E. J. P. Mason, Estate Office, Golspie

Mrs Maxwell, Bettyhill Hotel, Sutherland

J. Meldrum, Scardroy Estates, Muir of Ord, Ross-shire

The Merkister Hotel, Harray, Orkney

Midland Counties Angling Association

A. J. Miller, Shetland Angling Association, Lerwick

C. Miller, Tweedvalley Hotel, Walkerburn, Peebles

J. Miller, Greenbank Loan, Edinburgh

A. Miller-Mundy, Garynahine Estate, Lewis

Milton Park Hotel, Dalry, New Galloway

T. S. Mitchell, Morvern Crafts, Lochaline, Inverness-shire

Mrs Moffat, Forest Farm, Ardgay, Ross-shire

Mrs Montgomery, Cape Wrath Hotel, Sutherland

T. Moran, Riverside Mills, Kirkcudbrightshire

W. Mossie, Sundrum Park, Joppa

J. C. Mowat, Smithfield Hotel, Dounby, Orkney

A. Muir, Castle Douglas, Kirkcudbrightshire

D. Munro, Roy Bridge, Inverness-shire

Murray Arms Hotel, Gatehouse of Fleet

A. Murray, Whinnyhill, Dumfries

J. H. Murray, Dalrymple St, Girvan

I. Neale, Glenbellart House, Darvaig, Mull

J. Neilly, Cornish Court, Coatbridge, Lanarkshire

Newton Stewart Angling Association, Newton Stewart, Wigtownshire

R. Noble, Orkney Field Arts Centre, Birsay, Orkney

Novar Estates, Evanton, Ross-shire

J. A. Ogilvie, Chief Forester, Strathmaskie Forest, Inverness-shire

The Ord House Hotel, Muir of Ord, Ross-shire

Orkney Trout Fishing Association, Kirkwall, Orkney

J. Paton, Prestwick, Aryshire

D. Petrie, Invercauld Estate Office, Braemar, Aberdeenshire

Port Arkaig Hotel, Islay, Argyll

Portree Angling Association, Portree, Skye

M. T. Prior, Duisdale Hotel, Ornsay, Skye

A. Pryce, Area Engineer, Strathclyde Regional Council, Ayr

Major N. Ramsay, Farleyer,
Aberfeldy, Perthshire
H. Ratcliffe, Knott House,
Rawdon, Leeds.
A. W. Reid, Edinburgh
D. Reid, Cupar, Fife
J. Reid, Invergowrie, Saltcoats,
Ayrshire
Dr J. H. M. Rennie, Bourtree
Place, Hawick
Mrs R. Ritchie, Rousay, Orkney
P. J. Rodgers, Divisional Manager,
Strathclyde Regional Council
Offices, Ayr
Rogart Angling Association,
Rogart, Sutherland
Mrs R. Ross, West End Guest
House, Durness, Sutherland
W. Ross, Broomlands Drive,
Dumfries
Ross & Cromarty Tourist
Organisaton, Muir of Ord,
Ross-shire
Rowardennan Hotel, Drymen,
Dunbartonshire
St Mirren Angling Association,
Busby
P. S. Sandilands, Lagganmore,
Oban
A. Scherr, Borve Lodge Estate,
Harris
H. Schoffield, Cumnock,
Ayrshire
R. McD. Seligman, National Trust
for Scotland, Inverness
F. & D. Simpson, West Preston
Street, Edinburgh
J. R. Simpson, Bute Estate Office,
Rothesay
W. Smellie, Ardkinglas Estate
Office, Argyll
J. Sommers & Son, Thistle Street,
Aberdeen
R. J. B. Stevenson, Langholm,
Dumfries
B. D. Stewart, Leven, Fife
F. J. Stewart, Lochgilphead
G. Stewart, Arisaig Hotel, Arisaig,
Inverness-shire

R. W. K. Stirling, Fairburn
Estates, Muir of Ord,
Ross-shire
A. Sutherland, Helmsdale,
Sutherland
Sutherland Tourist Organisation,
Dornoch
R. Taylor, Dumfries & Galloway
Regional Council
A. G. Thom, Drumluchty Arms,
Auchenblae
H. Thomson, Campbelltown,
Argyll
Col J. F. Todhunter, Dunstead,
Suffolk
M. G. Trefusis-Paynter, Allanbank
Hotel, Dunblane
Troon Angling Club, Barassie,
Troon
J. Trotter, Brin Estate,
Inverness-shire
M. S. Tudthrope, Kilwinning,
Ayrshire
W. S. Tuer, Castle Street,
Dornoch
I. Tunnah, Campbelltown, Argyll
S. Wallace, Mauchline, Ayrshire
M. Waller, Inverness
Mrs J. Waller, Aviemore
A. McKellar Watt, Giffnock,
Glasgow
Whitebridge Hotel, Inverness-shire
D. Whiteford, Jaimeson Drive,
Stornoway
A. B. Wiles, Bridgend, Islay
P. Williamson, Newburgh, Fife
B. Wilson, Lochore Meadows
County Park, Lochgelly
K. Wilson, Department of
Agriculture, Benbecula
Rob Wilson, Brora, Sutherland
T. L. Wilson, Church Square,
Girvan
Sir Hugh Wontner, Barscombe,
New Galloway
H. E. Woodman, Cologin, Lerags,
Oban
J. Yule, South Lodge, Reswallie.
Forfar

Introduction to the First Edition

When I was asked to write this book two years ago I agreed with alacrity. It was something I had always wanted to do since I felt there was a real need for a single volume to cover as many of Scotland's trout lochs as possible. There are a number of excellent publications concerning specific areas, but no one work covering the whole of the country. This, I thought, was the opportunity I had been waiting for. At last I could combine my two great loves, writing and fishing. I realise now that I had no conception of the amount of work involved and no idea of the sheer volume of information, facts and detail I would have to gather before I could write 'the end'. As we say in Scotland, 'Weel, ye ken noo!'

Compiling the information contained in the book has involved a correspondence amounting to nearly two thousand letters, countless telephone calls, several thousand miles of driving, climbing and photography and endless hours spent pouring over maps checking details. My greatest disappointment was that there was not enough time to cover more lochs; my greatest pleasure, the kindness, courtesy and help I received from hundreds of fellow anglers. Without their assistance this volume could never have been written and the book is as much theirs as it is mine. I would like to thank them all again, for giving so freely of their time and experience and I acknowledge my indebtedness and gratitude. I hope that the results of our efforts will be of use to all anglers.

I would also like to express my sincere thanks to Roy Eaton, editor of *Trout and Salmon*, for permission to use so many of his excellent photographs. They enliven the text and enhance the book mightily, and I am most grateful for them; but even more so I am grateful for his advice and encouragement over the past eight years – may all his trout be big ones.

My thanks are due also to Merlin Unwin of George Allen & Unwin for giving me the opportunity of fulfilling a long held desire in writing *The Trout Lochs of Scotland*, and for his quiet and friendly guidance throughout the preparation of the manuscript – may his casts never break nor blood knots slip.

You will appreciate that in deciding which lochs to write about I have had to be highly selective and I am sure that I have 'missed' many which should have been included. For these omissions, my apologies. Likewise, if some of the details are at variance with your own knowledge, my apologies again. However, I feel that within the covers of this book the visiting angler will find most of the information he requires in order to make a well planned and

1 *Everything ready? Then let's begin.*

interesting fishing holiday. The information it contains will point you in the right direction and, I hope, give you added confidence when you cast that first fly.

One thing the book cannot do is tell you how to catch them. That, dear friends, is up to you and whatever gods you put your trust in. Nevertheless, throughout the book you will notice that I talk of standard pattern loch flies and it has become apparent to me that the same group of flies are as effective in the Outer Hebrides as they are in Galloway and Dumfries. With unfailing regularity, nationwide, my correspondents have reported that the most successful flies are Black Pennell, Black Zulu, Blue Zulu, Invicta, Soldier Palmer, Grouse and Claret, Wickham's Fancy, Greenwell's Glory, March Brown, Alexandra, Peter Ross and Butchers. Therefore, when I talk about standard pattern loch flies, these are the ones I mean. Where other patterns do well, Ke-He, Dunkeld, Woodcock and Green and so on, I have mentioned them and also the various types of reservoir lures which are being used with increasing frequency throughout Scotland. As for me, I'm lazy. I started fishing thirty-five years ago with three size 14 pattern loch flies and have continued in the same style ever since. During the course of the season I rarely change either size or pattern and have had no cause for complaint. No doubt you will have your own favourites as well, but the list I have given should cover most eventualities.

I haven't included details of charges. They vary widely

throughout Scotland and the visitor can obtain that information when booking. It is possible, however, to generalise and on average you may expect to pay between £5.00 and £8.00 per day for boat and two rods. Bank fishing will cost you considerably less; fishing a 'commercialised' water such as Loch Fitty or Butterstone, considerably more. What you will get is value for money and Scotland is unique in that respect, offering the visiting angler hundreds of excellent waters at a low cost.

Come and visit us. Walk in our magnificent hills and mountains and fish in our trout-filled lochs and lochans. As long as you respect the rights of the riparian owners and hardworking angling clubs and associations, and fish in a fair and sportsmanlike fashion, you will find a warm welcome – always.

Finally, I would like to pay tribute to the members of my long suffering family who have had to put up with my tantrums and tempests during the preparation of this book. Their support, advice and practical help has been superb and I'll never complain again when they raid my fly boxes and misappropriate my landing nets and nylon – I promise. Now, if you will excuse me, I have a long overdue date with some brown trout on Loch Watten. I hope very much that my book will both please and help you. In the meantime, have a good season and tight lines.

Introduction to the Second Edition

I would like to thank the friends and fishermen who helped me revise *The Trout Lochs of Scotland*; without their patience, courtesy and consideration, the new volume would never have appeared. May I also thank my long-suffering wife and family for tolerating six months of tantrums. I promise to be better behaved in future – at least until a third edition is required.

The new book contains details of 800 Scottish trout lochs. Armed with a copy, you will be able to find your kind of fishing, be it half way up a northern mountain or amidst accessible lowland tranquillity. But the notion that Scottish trout fishing is free is a myth: you must have proper permission. I believe that most anglers seek such permission and that my book will make it easier for them to find it. As to the scoundrels who don't bother – a curse upon their tackle; they damage us all.

For sins and omissions, fullest apologies. No one is perfect – a fact my nearest and dearest remind me of constantly. I wish you joy in your fishing and happiness in your companions. 'Deus nobis haec otia fecit' – A god gave us this leisure.

Ruther House
Watten, Caithness

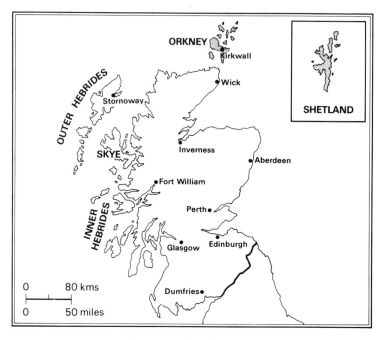

Map   1   *Northern Isles*

1 Northern Isles

The Orkney and Shetland Isles offer the visiting angler superb trout fishing amidst beautiful surroundings. Whether you arrive by sea or air you will experience an immediate sense of being 'away from it all', of having arrived almost in a different world. The short sea passage from Scrabster to Stromness is probably the most dramatic way of arriving in Orkney. As the *St Ola* passes the Old Man of Hoy, few, least of all anglers, could fail to feel a sense of mounting excitement. Orkney is a gentle, restful place. Apart from trout-filled lochs there are empty beaches of shining sand washed by green, foam-fringed waves, ancient villages, the magnificent twelfth century cathedral of St Magnus in Kirkwall, and the islands themselves cast a spell over the visitor which makes it very difficult to leave. To the north the Shetland Islands are, in fact, closer to Norway than to mainland Scotland. There are over one hundred islands in a wild scatter of sunlight, sea and moorland, and literally hundreds of trout lochs. It would be impossible to describe them all but what I have done is to give a representative picture of the principal waters and the best areas to fish. As far as Shetland is concerned, that's almost everywhere. In spite of the development of the oil industry, Shetland has managed to retain its essential character, space, light and friendly, welcoming people. Fishing on the islands is theoretically free. In practice, the superlative quality of the trout fishing is due to the hard work and good management of the two local angling clubs. Become a member during your visit and, for a small charge, you will obtain the use of all the clubs' facilities and at the same time be helping in the work of preserving and maintaining the priceless asset of the fishing.

LOCH OF SNARRAVOE 1/570016
Permission: J. Hunter, Garage, Baltasound, Unst.
Tel: Baltasound (095781) 306

This is the best loch on Unst and is easily accessible being near to the road at Belmont. The loch has been stocked with Loch Leven trout in the past and these fish have developed into a beautifully marked golden fish which fight very well indeed. Average weight is ¾-1lb. Bank fishing only and the trout come close in to the margins to feed so fish this area very carefully. Skill and cunning

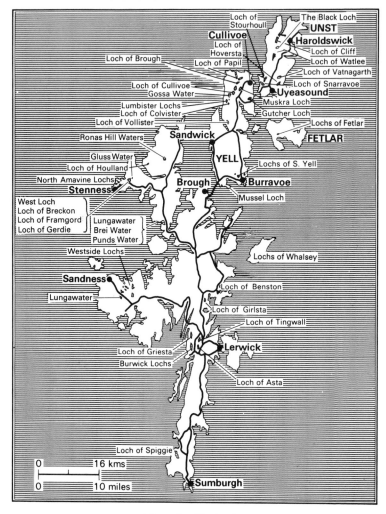

Map 2 *Shetland*

is required to tempt them since the water is clear but when the
trout are rising fish of up to 4½ lb. have been caught, and trout
rise all round the shore line. Sea trout appear during the 'back end'
and they average 2 lb. in weight. Flies to use include Black
Pennell, Kingfisher Butcher and Silver Butcher in size 8–10
dressings.

LOCH OF STOURHOULL
1/578028

Permission: Not required

First left north of the pier at Belmont on the A968 and a short
walk south. Stourhoull is a dour loch with a reputation for
holding large trout. In August 1981 it produced a fish of 3½ lb.
and many years ago was stocked with Loch Leven fish like its near
neighbour Snarravoe. Use similar pattern flies and take a lot of
hope.

LOCH OF VATNAGARTH
1/609028
LOCH OF HOVERSTA
1/608026

Permission: Not required

These lochs lie to the north of Mailand near Uyeasound and the
A968. Hoversta is the largest and contains the best trout. Fish of
up to 2½ lb. have been caught and the average is ¾ lb. A basket
of 3–5 trout would be considered good for this loch and the fish
are hard to catch. Loch of Vatnagarth also holds excellent trout
but becomes very weedy as the season passes. Wading
is dangerous due to soft, muddy bottom. Fish both lochs
from the bank and try Greenwell's Glory and Grouse and Claret
first.

LOCH OF CLIFF
1/600120

Permission: Not required

This is the largest loch on Unst and most frequently fished, and
gets its name from Houllna Gruna and Libbers Hill which rise
from the west shore. Approach from the B9086. It is a peaty loch
and the trout average ½–¾ lb. Fishing is from the bank only and
the best areas are down the east and west shores. Flies to use
include Greenwell's Glory, Grouse and Claret, Black Pennell, Teal
and Blue, Wickham's Fancy and Butchers, all in size 12–14
dressings. Sea trout arrive in September. An average basket
should bring you up to 5 trout but baskets of 10–15 trout are
often taken. The heaviest fish taken during the 1981 season
weighed 1¼ lb. though there are reports of a 10 lb. trout being
caught some years ago. A good loch for beginner and expert
alike. Trout will rise well to the fly and often several fish compete
for the same fly.

LOCH OF WATLEE   1/595055
Permission: Not required

Although linked to the Loch of Cliff by a good sized burn, Watlee lies 3 miles to the south and access is from the A968 3½ miles north of the pier at Belmont on Unst. A good track leads to the southern end of the loch. Watlee is peaty and the trout average ½–¾ lb. There are much larger fish and trout of 3–4 lb. have been caught. Best flies include Black Pennell and Butchers. Fish rise all round the loch and it is a very pleasant water to fish complete with island and classic headland on the east shore.

THE BLACK LOCH   1/598064
Permission: Not required

A small, peaty loch, to the north of Loch of Watlee in the valley of the Burn of Caldback. The Black Loch produces surprises from time to time when really large fish are caught; they are few and far between but it is worth a few casts if things are quiet on Watlee.

LOCH OF GARTH   1/545006
KIRK LOCH   1/532050

They look good and you may well be tempted to stop and fish – don't, since there are no fish in them.

LOCH OF PAPIL   1/541042
Permission: Yell Anglers Association, Ian Nisbet, Gairdie, Mid Yell, Shetland.
Tel: (0957) 2204

The Loch of Papil on North Yell lies to the east of Greenbank, north of Cullivoe on the B9803. It is on the cliffs between Papil Bay and the Bay of Brough. The trout average ½ lb., fight hard and rise well to the fly. Although weedy at times, there is an area along the north shore which always remains clear. Bank fishing only and take care, there's a bad hole at the north end by the stony beach. Use standard loch fly patterns.

LOCH OF BROUGH   1/530030
Permission: Yell Anglers Association, Ian Nisbet, Gairdie, Mid Yell, Shetland.
Tel: (0957) 2204

Approach from the stony road west of Cullivoe. This loch

provides the water supply for North Yell and the building of the dam has not helped the fishing. However, things are now getting back to normal and good baskets of trout can be caught. Fish average ¾ lb. and recently some weighing 2–3 lb. have been taken. Bank fishing only and take care on soft margins.

LOCH OF CULLIVOE 1/534023

Permission: Yell Anglers Association, Ian Nisbet, Gairdie, Mid Yell, Shetland.
Tel: (0957) 2204

Park at the Loch of Brough west of Cullivoe and walk south-east over the moor. Cullivoe is a small loch containing good trout averaging ½–¾ lb. It is the best loch in the area and fish of up to 2 lb. are caught. Bank fishing only and wading requires care. Beware of the large stones just below the surface in the north-west corner. Standard pattern loch flies.

MUSKRA LOCH 1/522021

Permission: Yell Anglers Association, Ian Nisbet, Gairdie, Mid Yell, Shetland.
Tel: (0957) 2204

A small loch to the south of lochs Cullivoe and Brough. A reputation for being dour but easily accessible and often producing excellent results. Large fish can be caught and it is worth trying for a few hours. Standard pattern flies.

GOSSA WATER 1/490000

Permission: Yell Anglers Association, Ian Nisbet, Gairdie, Mid Yell, Shetland.
Tel: (0957) 2204

Gossa Water is the largest loch on Yell. West of the A968 it is best approached by following the Burn of Gossawater up from the road. There are excellent trout in Gossa Water and fish of 3 lb. are caught. The average weight is ¾–1 lb. and it is bank fishing only. Depending upon the weather, sea trout arrive in the loch during the latter months of the season and this very pleasant loch is worth the effort of the walk out. Standard pattern flies will do fine.

LOCH OF COLVISTER   1/500970
Permission: Yell Anglers Association, Ian Nisbet, Gairdie, Mid Yell, Shetland.
Tel: (0957) 2204

Lies to the west of the A968 north of Camb and approached from Colvister by following up the outlet burn. A dour loch and not much fished with trout averaging three to the pound. Some larger fish and worth a few casts on your way west over the moor. Don't spend too much time, there's much better to come.

LOCH OF LUMBISTER   1/485965
Permission: Yell Anglers Association, Ian Nisbet, Gairdie, Mid Yell, Shetland.
Tel: (0957) 2204

This series of lochs lies 2 miles west of the A968. Approach from Colvister. The trout average ¾–1 lb. and all these lochs offer excellent sport in very lovely surroundings. Don't miss the spectacular cliffscape near Gorset Hill. Standard loch fly patterns.

LOCH OF GUTCHER   1/548993
Permission: Yell Anglers Association, Ian Nisbet, Gairdie, Mid Yell, Shetland.
Tel: (0957) 2204

A small loch at the end of the A968 on North Yell. Good fishing with trout averaging ¾ lb. Bank fishing only and wading is comfortable. Perfect for an evening's fishing. Lovely views of Fetlar and Unst. Standard pattern flies will do.

LOCH OF VOLLISTER   1/478943
Permission: Yell Anglers Association, Ian Nisbet, Gairdie, Mid Yell, Shetland.
Tel: (0957) 2204

Vollister is an RSPB reserve and anglers should take great care to avoid disturbing nesting species. The loch lies on the north shore of Whale Firth and is approached from Windhouse. Follow the shoreline for 1¾ miles to reach Vollister. Good quality brown trout averaging ¾ lb. with fish of up to 2 lb. taken most season.

LOCHS OF SOUTH YELL

LOCH OF KETTLESTER	2/513805
LOCH OF LITTLESTER	2/513797
LOCH OF ULSTA	2/472812

Permission:
Burravoe Post Office, South Yell.
Tel: Burravoe (095784) 237

Yell Anglers Association, Ian Nisbet, Gairdie, Mid Yell, Shetland.
Tel: (0957) 2204

These lochs all contain trout and are accessible from the B9081. Littlester is the best and contains trout of up to 4 lb. Ulsta is ideal for learners and is full of small trout averaging three to the pound. Bank fishing only and all standard loch fly patterns work well.

MUSSEL LOCH	1/472788

Permission: Yell Anglers Association, Ian Nisbet, Gairdie, Mid Yell, Shetland.
Tel: (0957) 2204

Mussel Loch lies at the southern end of South Yell above the Wester Wick of Copister and the sound of Brough. Follow the minor road that runs west from the pier, then southwards, along the line of Saidlas Burn. The trout average ½–¾ lb. but are of good quality and fight well. Bank fishing only.

LOCHS OF FETLAR

PAPIL WATER	2/605905
SKUTES WATER	2/623981
WINYADEPLA	2/640930

Permission: Not required

Three excellent lochs on one of the most lovely of the Shetland Isles. Papil is the most easily accessible and it contains good trout of up to 2 lb. Skutes is the public water supply for the island and has brown trout of ½ lb. along with some stocked rainbow trout. Winyadepla is the most remote water and getting to it involves a two-mile hike over the moors to the Hill of Mongirsdale; the scenery along the way is spectacular – so is the fishing. But it is a dour loch and you will have to work hard for results. Hope for trout of up to 3 lb.

LOCHS OF WHALSAY

LOCH OF HUXTER	2/558623
LOCH OF LIVISTER	2/558631
LOCH OF ISBISTER	2/577643
LOCH OF VATSHOULL	2/571658

Permission: Whalsay Anglers Association, B. Polson, 3 Saeter, Symbister, Whalsay.
Tel: (08066) 472

Regular ferries ply between Mainland and Whalsay and it is possible to spend a day fishing and still be back on Mainland in time for supper. But you will find it hard to leave for both the trout fishing and the island soon have you enthralled. Top-quality, pink-fleshed brown trout in all lochs. The average weight is in the order of ½–¾ lb. with a good chance of heavier fish of up to 3 lb. The best fish taken in recent years, however, weighed 9 lb. 9 oz. and was caught in 1983 by expert Whalsay angler, George Irvine on the Loch of Huxter. Go thou and do likewise.

LOCH OF HOULLAND   3/215790

Permission: Shetland Anglers Association, A. J. Miller, 3 Gladstone Terrace, Lerwick.
Tel: Lerwick (0595) 3729

The lochs in this area provide the most consistently good fishing in the Shetlands. Many are limestone lochs, such as Houlland. A 7 lb. trout was caught on this first-class loch during the 1980 season and each year these lochs produce numbers of trout in the order of 4 lb.

WEST LOCH	3/217779
LOCH OF BRECKON	3/214779
LOCH OF FRAMGORD	3/209785
LOCH OF GERDIE	3/206782

Permission: Shetland Anglers Association, A. J. Miller, 3 Gladstone Terrace, Lerwick.
Tel: Lerwick (0595) 3729

These lochs lie in Eshaness, close to Loch of Houlland, and all offer first-class sport – in the right conditions. Access is easy –

taking out trout is not, since they are clear-water lochs. But it is well worth trying and fish of up to 2 lb. are taken most seasons.

GLUSS WATER   3/256814

Permission: Shetland Anglers Association, A. J. Miller, 3 Gladstone Terrace, Lerwick.
Tel: Lerwick (0595) 3729

Follow the B9078 to Braewick and then turn north on the minor road. Park near the Giants Stones. Gluss Water lies at the end of a rough track in Scora Field. This is a difficult water, with a well deserved reputation for being dour. Persevere – trout of up to 3 lb. are occasionally caught, although you are most likely to encounter their smaller cousins which are in the order of 12 oz.

RONAS HILL WATERS
SANDY WATER   3/305865
LOCH OF MANY CROOKS   3/314864
TONGA WATER   2/333875
ROER WATER   2/336863
BIRKA WATER   1/316875

Permission: Shetland Anglers Association, A. J. Miller, 3 Gladstone Terrace, Lerwick.
Tel: Lerwick (0595) 3729

Once fished, never forgotten. For a memorable day out, park the car at grid reference 363863, near Midastew, and follow the gully up on to the moor. Sooty Alan, the Shetland name for the arctic skua, follow you over the hill; golden plover pipe from spagnum tussocks – all that is best in wild brown trout fishing. There are dozens of lochs and lochans scattered over Ronas Hill and I have noted the principal ones above. All contain excellent trout which vary in size from a modest ½ lb. to fish of up to 4 lb. My favourite is Birka Water, where a dramatic waterfall cascades into the loch in a sheet of silver. Above this waterfall there is an unnamed loch which is also well worth fishing. I had a lovely fish of 1 lb. 12 oz. from it and there are more, waiting, for your well presented fly. A compass and map are essential since it is easy to become disoriented. One of the finest fishing areas in Scotland and highly recommended.

LUNGAWATER	3/319708
BREI WATER	3/318712
PUNDS WATER	3/325715

Permission: Shetland Anglers Association, A. J. Miller, 3 Gladstone Terrace, Lerwick.
Tel: Lerwick (0595) 3729

A mile north from Klev on the A970 road to Hillswick, turn left towards Mangaster. There are a series of lochs here which may be fished in circuit and you should allow a full day to explore them. Wading is not required and, indeed, is downright dangerous on most of these waters. Stay on the bank but cast with confidence – fish lie close to the shore.

LUNGAWATER   3/235525

Permission: Shetland Anglers Association, A. J. Miller, 3 Gladstone Terrace, Lerwick.
Tel: Lerwick (0595) 3729

Lungawater is a large roadside loch which forms part of the public water supply. The trout average 10 oz. and, from time to time, fish of up to 2 lb. are caught. As with most of the Shetland waters, anglers are advised to fish from the shore and avoid wading. Lungawater fishes well in a good wind – of which there is no lack in Shetland. To the south-west of Lungawater, but approached from Walls via the track to the radio station, lie three excellent little lochs known as the Sma Lochs. Do not miss them.

THE WEST SIDE LOCHS   3/240540

Permission: Shetland Anglers Association, A. J. Miller, 3 Gladstone Terrace, Lerwick.
Tel: Lerwick (0595) 3729

Follow the A971 north westwards from Lerwick until you run out of road. Within the immediate vicinity are nearly 200 lochs all with good stocks of ½–¾ lb. trout. This angler's paradise is available to the visitor through the association and it would be impossible to do justice to the variety and beauty of this lovely area. All the fishing is from the bank and the best flies to use include Invicta, Black Zulu, Soldier Palmer and Loch Ordy.

LOCH OF GIRLSTA
3/435520

Permission: Shetland Anglers Association, A. J. Miller, 3 Gladstone Terrace, Lerwick.
Tel: Lerwick (0595) 3729

Shetland Anglers Association have boats available for hire to visitors. Contact J. M. Johnston, Geirhilda, Girlsta.
Tel: Gott (059584) 444

Loch of Girlsta is adjacent to the A970 10 miles north of Lerwick and contains brown trout and char. Fishing is from the bank only and the best places to fish are the shallow bays and rocky points, particularly from the south-east shore near the island. Girlsta has a long record of producing heavy fish, the finest being a trout of 12½ lb. Trout of up to 6 lb. are often caught and 1981 saw a fish of 6 lb. 6 oz. caught on Loch Ordie. However, Girlsta is dour and a basket of 2–3 fish would be doing well. Average weight is 1 lb. and the loch is easily accessible. Stop and try your luck/skill, which ever you put most faith in.

LOCH OF BENSTON
3/462535

Permission: Shetland Anglers Association, A. J. Miller, 3 Gladstone Terrace, Lerwick.
Tel: Lerwick (0595) 3729

Benston is stocked by the Association and contains very good trout indeed. Ten miles north of Lerwick turn right after Loch of Girlsta and follow the sign to Benston. The average weight is 2 lb. and a good day might bring you a basket of 2 fish. Each season trout of 3 lb. are caught and the best fishing area is along the shore line near the church. Flies to try include Loch Ordy, Soldier Palmer and Black Pennell. The early months of the season are best since the loch becomes weedy during the summer. An excellent loch and well worth visiting.

LOCH OF SPIGGIE
4/373166

Permission: Shetland Anglers Association, A. J. Miller, 3 Gladstone Terrace, Lerwick.
Tel: Lerwick (0595) 3729

Shetland Anglers Association have boats available for hire to visitors. Contact W. H. Burgess, Lochview, Scousburgh.
Tel: Sumburgh (0950) 60542

Spiggie is one of the largest lochs on Shetland and can be waded from shore to shore at the north end where the best bank fishing is a favourite spot called the 'Deep', but it can only be reached with chest waders. From the boat the east and west banks are the most productive areas and the trout average ¾–1 lb. in weight. An average basket should consist of 5–6 trout and fish of up to 6 lb. are caught on Spiggie, so be prepared. Sea trout run into the loch from August onwards. Spiggie is set in a gentle landscape of rolling hills and farmland and is a RSPB conservation area. Boats are available but outboard motors are not allowed. A beautiful loch and highly recommended.

LOCH OF GRIESTA
4/408438

Permission: Shetland Anglers Association, A. J. Miller, 3 Gladstone Terrace, Lerwick.
Tel: Lerwick (0595) 3729

This is an excellent limestone loch near the B9074 to the north of Scalloway. The trout are fierce fighters and average ¾ lb. with several heavier fish taken each season. Permission also includes the right to fish the series of lochs south of Griesta in the area of the Hill of Burwick and these waters contain trout in the ½–¾ lb. range. There are seven lochs including tiny Loch of Houlland and much larger Loch of Ustaness and from time to time they produce fish of up to 2 lb. Spend the day and enjoy yourself among the hills. Use standard loch fly patterns and good walking shoes.

LOCH OF TINGWALL
4/414425
LOCH OF ASTA
4/413415

Permission: Shetland Anglers Association, A. J. Miller, 3 Gladstone Terrace, Lerwick.
Tel: Lerwick (0595) 3729

Shetland Anglers Association have boats available for hire to visitors. Contact J. Irvine, South Setter, Tingwall.
Tel: Gott (059584) 209

The Loch of Tingwall is the most popular loch on Mainland Shetland and lies to the west of Lerwick. Follow the A970 for 4 miles and turn left at Tingwall crossroads. The B9074 gives easy access for bank fishing on Tingwall and Asta from the west shore, and boats may also be available to the visitor. Tingwall is stocked by the Association and the trout average ¾–1 lb. A good day can produce baskets of up to 10 fish, your most probable catch will be 3–4. The shallow bays at the southern end fish well and a good drift is down the east shore. Bank fishing is best in the vicinity of the island, from either bank. Loch Asta also contains brown trout

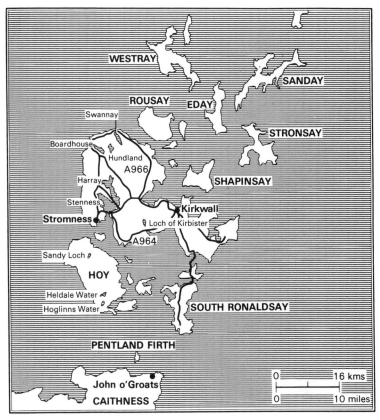

Map 3 *Orkney*

of excellent quality which fight well and give great sport. The east
bank of Asta is best for bank fishing. These are both limestone
lochs with good natural feeding and trout grow fast. Use standard
loch fly patterns. Very lovely lochs and good fishing.

LOCH BOARDHOUSE   6/270260
Permission: Not required

I shall always have a soft spot for lovely Loch Boardhouse since it
was there that I introduced my eldest son, then aged 5, to the art
of fly fishing. Boardhouse is a shallow loch and fishes well over its
total area. In the centre of the southern end it is weedy and this
area fishes very well. Baskets of 9–12 fish were caught by the
weeds regularly during the 1981 season and sample catches ranged

from zero to baskets of 20 fish. The average weight of trout is ¾ lb. but each season trout of up to 4 lb. are caught. Boardhouse fishes best from the boat and these are available from the Merkister Hotel and the water pumping station on the west side of the loch. Bank fishing can be good but in many places the water is deep close to the edge so wading is difficult. Standard loch pattern flies all work well but try the local fly, the Ke-He. I would consider myself to be improperly dressed without one on the cast.

LOCH HARRAY   6/300140
Permission: Not required

Loch Harray is the most popular of the Orkney lochs and the most frequently fished. It is a large loch being 6 miles long by 1½

2   *A good wave – on Loch Harray.*

miles wide. The trout average ¾ lb. in weight but many fish of between 2 and 5 lb. are caught each season. The heaviest fish to be caught on the loch was a trout of 17½ lb. in 1964 and a fine basket of 11 fish taken in 1968 weighed 18¼ lb. Harray still gives first-class sport and the fishing is managed and controlled by the Orkney Trout Fishing Association who stock the loch. The trout are pink-fleshed and fight hard and a reasonable day should bring you a basket of 6 fish. Flies to use include all the standard loch fly patterns including Black Pennell, Soldier Palmer, Wickham's Fancy, Invicta and butcher – and the local Ke-He. When fishing from the boat most anglers keep the bottom in sight and carefully fish the shallows. Pay particular attention to the many bays – I suspect you would anyway – and if it is too windy to use the boat fish from the bank. Bank fishing on Harray is excellent particularly during March and April. Fish the burn mouths at Ballarat on the east bank and Bankhead at the north end. Halfway up the west shore there are a number of rocky islands and bays all of which are good fishing areas. Below the Ring of Brogar is also a favourite spot and on the east shore the Holm Bay area deserves your close attention. One word of warning when using the boat and outboard motor. The loch is full of sudden shallows and outcrops so drive carefully. Boats are available from the Merkister Hotel. A sample basket caught during the 1981 season accounted for 7 trout weighing 6¼ lb. Go thou and do likewise.

LOCH OF HUNDLAND   6/295260
Permission: Not required

This is a small peaty loch lying between Swannay and Boardhouse and has the reputation for being dour. It is stocked by the Association and the best areas to fish are at the southern end where the Burn of Hillside enters the loch. Boats are available from L. Hourston at Muckle Quoy Farm and the Merkister Hotel. The average weight is ¾ lb. but trout of 2½ lb. and more have been taken. A good day would account for 4–6 fish and the standard loch fly patterns work well. Bank fishing can be good but wading requires great care due to the rather soft margins in many areas.

LOCH OF STENNESS   6/280130
Permission: Not required

Dominated by the backdrop of the mountains on the Island of

Hoy and overlooked by the famous standing stones and Ring of Brognar, Stenness is a dramatic loch to fish. The largest trout ever caught in the Orkneys was taken from Stenness and weighed a mighty 29½ lb. It used to be the most popular loch on the islands but Harray now claims this distinction. The trout average ½–¾ lb. and some good baskets are taken each season, but the loch is mostly fished these days for sea trout which enter at the Bridge of Waithe. Fish the northern end in the vicinity of Ness and down the north-east shore. Boats are available from the Merkister Hotel.

LOCH OF SWANNAY   6/310280
Permission: Not required

Swannay is my favourite Orkney loch and lies in the northern part of Mainland. In spite of Costa Hill and Vinquin to the east, Swannay can be very windy indeed. It is a shallow loch so high winds churn up the bottom and make life generally difficult, but the quality of the trout more than makes up for such minor hazzards. The best areas to fish are southwards from Dale on the west shore but the north end can also produce excellent results. Swannay holds the largest fish of all the Orkney lochs and trout of between 2 and 5 lb. are frequently taken. The early months of the season are best and even during a blizzard trout will rise. I caught two perfectly matched 1½ lb. fish from the bank during a snow-storm in April 1979. Yes, I know, sheer madness, but you know what it is like and the fish were in superb condition. A sample basket from Swannay during the 1981 season was 2 fish weighing 4 lb. 2 oz. and the best ever catch was in the late 1950s when a basket of 42 fish weighed in at 69 lb. 10 oz. Standard loch fly patterns will do though in 1981 the Poacher seemed to do most of the damage. Always mount a Black Pennell or Black Zulu. Boats on Swannay can be arranged through W. Sabiston at Ludenhill and E. Sabiston at Dale and the Merkister Hotel. Make sure to fish Swannay if you visit Orkney, it could be your 'day to remember' and is well worth a visit.

LOCH OF KIRBISTER   6/370080
Permission: Not required but ask local farmers for permission for access.

Kirbister lies five miles west of Kirkwall along the A964 and is the ideal beginners' loch. Fish are of good quality and average ½–¾ lb. There are no boats but good wading is available north from Breck along the west shore.

LOCHS OF HOY

SANDY LOCH	7/219030
HELDALE WATER	7/255923
HOGLINNS WATER	7/250914

Permission: Not required

Although the quality of the fishing on these lochs may not be of the same standard as the principal Orkney Mainland waters, their magnificent setting is more than adequate compensation; and, unlike the main lochs, you will probably have them to yourself all day.

There are ferries from Kirkwall to Lyness at the south of Hoy and from Stromness to Linkness at the north end of the island. Sandy Loch is the most easily accessible and is but a short walk westwards from the road. The loch lies on the line of the footpath out to the village of Rackwick and the famous stack The Old Man of Hoy. Hoglinns and Heldale are close to each other and make a super venue for a memorable day out. Park at Heldale (284913) and follow the track westwards up the Burn of Heldale. Brown trout in the Hoy lochs are reputed to be dour but worth catching – fish of up to 5 lb. have been taken. Use standard pattern flies and crossed fingers – you never know your luck.

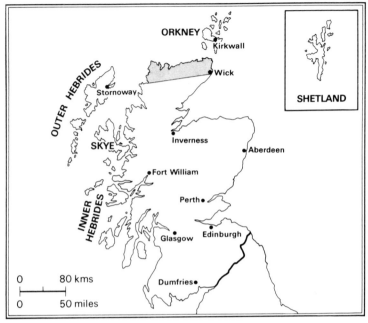

Map 4 *Caithness and North Sutherland*

2 Caithness and North Sutherland

A map of the north of Scotland is a Mona Lisa to trout fishermen. From east to west the canvas is filled with lochs and lochans. Mountains and moorlands cover the landscape and deciding where to start is as agonising a decision for the angler as ever confronted small boys in sweet-filled shops. Everywhere you look exciting waters beckon, round each corner sparkles a new surprise. To guide you through this fisherman's paradise I have outlined some of the more accessible lochs and divided the area into compact sections. Centre yourself on any of these and you will be assured of a memorable fishing holiday. Caithness has the more easily approachable lochs whilst for Scourie you may need compass and map. The limestone lochs of Durness should not be missed nor the lovely hill lochs of Strath Halladale. You could spend a lifetime wandering in the hills and never manage to fish all the waters available. This is the land of eagle, otter and wild cat. Red deer will hesitatingly mark your progress over the moor and divers will haughtily observe your efforts on the loch. The area has some of the finest trout fishing in all of Scotland. Get there if you can and experience all that is best in angling.

LOCH WATTEN   11/230560
Permission:
Harpers Fly Fishing Services, Drill Hall, Thurso.
Tel: Thurso (0847) 63179;
The Loch Watten Hotel, Watten.
Tel: Watten (095582) 232;
D. Gunn, Watten Lodge, Watten.
Tel: Watten (095582) 217;
J. A. Barnetson, Lynegar, Watten.
Tel: Watten (095582) 205

Forss House Hotel, Forss, by Thurso.
Tel: Forss (084786) 201;
Sinclair Swanson, Banks Lodge, Watten.
Tel: Watten (095582) 208;
Pentland Sports Emporium, 14 Olrig St., Thurso
Tel: (0847) 62473

Loch Watten lies 10 miles from Wick on the road to Thurso. It is

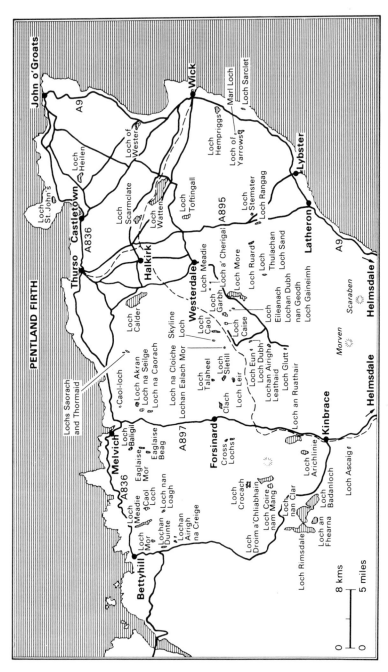

Map 5 *Caithness, Strath Halladale and Strath Naver*

a shallow loch, over 3 miles long and contains excellent trout. The average weight is 1¼ lb. but fish of 2–3 lb. are taken each season. In September 1984 the writer had a fish of 3 lb. 2 oz. near the Old Hall Boat House and in 1985 a visitor had a trout of 4 lb. 8 oz. at West Watten. However, expert Wick angler Sandy Meiklejohn had the best fish of recent years: a 9 lb. salmon! An average basket should account for between 4–6 trout and fish rise and are caught all over the loch. Fishing from the boat is best although bank fishing can be very rewarding, particularly in the late evening when big fish move closer in. Favoured drifts in the boat are down the middle of the loch, from Sandy Bay on the north shore over to the boat house at Old Hall and in Shearer's pool which is the top end of the loch. Best flies for Watten include all the standard favourites but I should start off with Ke-He, March Brown and Silver Butcher. The trout are pink-fleshed and fight like the devil and everything about the loch pleases. Highly recommended for a visit. Book a boat well in advance and look out for some first class sport.

LOCH SCARMCLATE   12/200595

Permission: Harpers Fly Fishing Services, The Drill Hall, Sinclair Street, Thurso.
Tel: Thurso (0847) 63179;
Forss House Hotel, Forss, by Thurso.
Tel: Forss (084786) 201

Also known locally as Stemster Loch but not to be confused with the Achavanich Stemster Loch mentioned later. Scarmclate is joined to Loch Watten by a canal and acts as a nursery for its big brother. Access is from the A882 Wick–Thurso road at 180585. Cross the railway line – carefully – and drive down to the loch. The quality of Scarmclate trout is excellent and, although they are not as large as Loch Watten fish, they fight every bit as well. This is a shallow loch so if you risk using an outboard engine make sure that you take along plenty of spare sheer pins. Best fishing area is the east side of the loch, particularly in the vicinity of the outlet burn, but fish can be caught everywhere. A special treat for the angler who is also an ornithologist and botanist – as most of us are – since Scarmclate is haven for many species of birds and flowers. Look, don't touch, for this is a Site of Special Scientific Interest. Place a visit to Scarmclate high on your list.

LOCH SAORACH   11/015605
LOCH THORMAID   11/010604
Permission: Mrs Atkinson, c/o The Bradford & Bingley Building Society, Sinclair Street, Thurso.
Tel: Thurso (0847) 63291

A forestry track leaves the minor road from Shebster at 027612 giving easy access to both lochs. They are largely an unknown quantity since few folk have fished them. Ann and I had a day there two years ago and caught more fish in Thormaid than Saorach – fish of about 6–8 oz.

Nevertheless, I suspect that there are much larger fish lurking in the depths and the new owners are putting a boat on the lochs in 1987 to help you try.

LOCH TOFTINGALL   12/190520
Permission: Mrs Atkinson, c/o The Bradford & Bingley Building Society, Sinclair Street, Thurso.
Tel: Thurso (0847) 63291. Open to the public on Wednesday and Thursday only.

Toftingall is a shallow loch extending to 130 acres. Access is from the B870 Watten–Mybster road and there is a good track down to the lochside. A bag limit of 10 fish per rod is operated and limit catches are caught frequently. Trout average ¾ lb. in weight although, from time to time, larger fish are caught. Toftingall becomes unfishable in high winds due to the bottom being churned up and the water discoloured.

LOCH CALDER   11/070600
Permission: D. G. Mackay, Achaguie, Scotscalder, Halkirk.
Tel: Halkirk (084783) 650;
Forss House Hotel, Forss, by Thurso.
Tel: Forss (084786) 201
Pentland Sports, Harpers, Tackle Shop – see Loch Watten

Calder is the largest and deepest of the Caithness lochs. It is the main water supply for the town of Thurso and the loch is over 100 ft deep at the north-east end. It holds a multitude of small trout and some char. There are also a few very large fish indeed. The heaviest trout to come off Calder in recent years was a fish of 7 lb. and each year sees a few trout of 3 lb. landed. Bank fishing requires extreme caution, especially when fishing the western shore. The margins are soft and the water deepens suddenly in several places. Boat fishing is best and D. G. MacKay has good boats available for visitors at the southern end of the loch. The best areas to fish are the shallow inlet off the south-western corner and down the west bank. With the correct wind blowing flies off the heather, this bank can produce great sport. Standard loch fly patterns all work well and on its day Calder is great fun and worth a visit.

LOCH ST JOHN'S   12/225720

Permission: The Northern Sands Hotel, Dunnet, Caithness.
Tel: Barrock (084785) 270;
Forss House Hotel, Forss, by Thurso.
Tel: Forss (084786) 201

Loch St John's is one of the best known lochs in Scotland and owes its fame to the size and quality of its trout. It is not a loch for beginners, but to the experienced angler it represents a superb challenge with the possibility of a 4 lb. trout as the prize. The loch is well managed and organised and there is a good access road and sheltered mooring bay. The Loch St John's Angling Association stock the loch with fish reared in their own hatchery in order to preserve the quality of trout. Boat fishing is best and the most favoured drifts are from the harbour over to the mouth of the spawning burn. Bank fishing can be good and is best from the south shore. During the first or second week in June there is mayfly hatch and this is the best time to fish St John's. Dry fly does well during this period and at all other times standard pattern loch flies work well. St John's is the most northerly trout water on the mainland and a must for the angler visiting Caithness.

LOCH HEILEN   11/255685

Permission: H. Pottinger, Greenland Mains, Castletown.
Tel: Castletown (084782) 210;
Forss House Hotel, Forss, by Thurso.
Tel: Forss (084786) 201;
Harpers Fly Fishing Services, The Drill Hall, Sinclair Street, Thurso.
Tel: Thurso (0847) 63179

It is said that Loch St John's was stocked originally with fish from Loch Heilen and the quality of the trout on both lochs is the same – beautifully formed fish with bright pink flesh. Describing them is a lot easier than catching them and Heilen is a dour loch to fish.

The water level has recently been reduced and weed growth makes fishing difficult. There are two boats available for use by visitors and bank fishing can be just as productive with easy, safe wading. The trout are few and far between but the largest I have ever seen was an eight pounder taken from the loch during 1981.

Several excellent fish were taken during June 1986; Forss House Hotel guests had 6 fish weighing 19 lb. and the heaviest, which weighed 4 lb., was caught by yours truly when he wasn't looking. Other anglers, who were looking all the time, had several superb fish of 2 lb., 2 lb. 8 oz. and 3 lb. Don't be disappointed if you have a blank day, it's worth a try and a very lovely loch to fish. Standard loch fly patterns and 'stalking' could bring you one for the glass case.

LOCH RUARD   11/140430

Permission: Mrs Atkinson, c/o The Bradford & Bingley Building Society, Sinclair Street, Thurso.
Tel: Thurso (0847) 63291

Loch Ruard lies to the west of the A895 north of Latheron. It is an easy walk out but after heavy rain it is wiser to leave the car at the main road since turning can be difficult at the end of the track. From this track follow the path which winds round the burn and head for the patch of green grass amidst the heather in the middle distance. At the farm buildings walk up the right hand side of the burn until you reach the loch. Do not try the other side. It is covered by deep heather and very hard walking indeed. Ruard has a good boathouse and serviceable boat and, being a small loch, the angler quickly gets the feel of it. The best fishing area is down the bank across from the boathouse and the trout are pink-fleshed and average ¾ lb. in weight. They fight very well and an average basket should produce 10–12 trout. This is a very lovely loch where the angler may well see an otter and nearly always a pair of black throated divers will be keeping a watchful eye on you. Best results come from the boat but bank fishing can be good. If it is too windy to launch the boat do try the bank. I have caught trout from the shore casting into the teeth of some very high winds with the waves splashing the margins — and feet. Standard loch fly patterns work well though I would suggest a cast with Black Pennell, Grouse and Claret, and Alexandra to start off with. Not available after 12 August so fish Ruard early in the season.

LOCH STEMSTER   11/188423

Permission: Mrs Atkinson, c/o The Bradford & Bingley Building Society, Sinclair Street, Thurso.
Tel: Thurso (0847) 63291

Stemster is a small circular loch to the north of Latheron and adjacent to the A895. There is a good boat and Stemster fishes well throughout the season. It is also possible to fish no matter how strong the wind since there is always a sheltered bank. The fish are pink-fleshed and average ½–¾ lb. with many trout of 1½–2 lb. being taken each season. An average basket would con-sist of up to 6 fish though this loch will rarely send you away empty-handed. Bank fishing is best and at the south-east end two promontories extend out a fair distance into the loch. This is an excellent spot for bank fishing provided you take care not to stray too far left or right. Soldier Palmer, Invicta, Black Pennell and Ke-He all do well. A magnificent ring of standing stones overlook the loch and Stemster is easily accessible making it an ideal loch for a day with the family. Not available after 12 August.

LOCH RANGAG   12/178415

Permission: Mrs Atkinson, c/o The Bradford & Bingley Building Society, Sinclair Street, Thurso.
Tel: Thurso (0847) 63291

Rangag is the first loch that most visitors to Caithness see. It lies alongside the A895 Latheron–Thurso road and has a conspicuous mound close to the east shore. This is the site of the castle of a Caithness 'robber baron', Grey Steel, who thrived in the fifteenth century. All that thrives here now are the brown trout of which there is a large population of ½-lb. fish. Easy access and easy fishing, a good learners' loch.

LOCHAN AIRIGH LEATHAID   11/990390

Permission: Ulbster Arms Hotel, Halkirk.
Tel: Halkirk (084783) 206

This is a group of three classic hill lochs to the west of Dalganachan on the Loch Dubh Estate. Approach via the rough estate road from Westerdale. The walk up to the lochs is hard going but the distance involved is not far and the effort well worth while. The fishing is from the bank and wading is safe and comfortable. The two larger lochs hold trout averaging 1 lb and the smallest loch holds some real monsters with fish of 4 lb. and more. Getting them out is something else and Airigh Leathaid is not for beginners. It will send you away empty-handed more often than not, but the challenge and beauty of the area will lure you back again and again. Use Butchers, Ke-He, Soldier Palmer and Black Pennell to start with.

LOCH OF YARROWS   12/310440
Permission: Thrumster Garage, Thrumster, Wick.
Tel: Thrumster (095585) 252

Yarrows is a very pleasant loch a few miles to the south of Wick. It is the water supply for the town and quite deep. There are three boats available for visitors and the loch is full of small trout. Baskets of 20 and more are common and Yarrows is an excellent loch for the newcomer to fly fishing. Bank fishing is not really practicable since the sides are steep and the water deep near the shores, so book a boat well in advance. Fish rise and are caught all round the loch and most standard pattern loch flies will tempt them.

MARL LOCH   12/302441
Permission: Thrumster Garage, Thrumster, Wick.
Tel: Thrumster (095582) 252

This loch wasn't there when *The Trout Lochs of Scotland* was first published but certainly deserves to be included now. Marl Loch is close to Yarrows and has been re-established by closing a sluice at the north-west corner. Marl is shallow, weedy and difficult to fish. Make the effort because there are really excellent fish in the loch. They average ¾ lb. and are top-quality, wild brown trout.

LOCH SARCLET   12/344428
Permission: Thrumster Garage, Thrumster, Wick.
Tel: Thrumster (095585) 252

Sarclet lies south of Wick, close to the cliffs of Gearty Head. Indeed, the sound of the waves beating on the rock can be clearly heard. Sadly, the sound of rising trout is less often audible for the Sarclet fish are shy, careful beasts. They are, however, some of the finest quality brown trout in Scotland and average ¾–1 lb. To encourage you, let me say that the largest fish caught, so far, weighed over 6 lb. and most seasons fish of up to 3 lb. are taken.

LOCH HEMPRIGGS
12/343470

Permission: Thrumster Garage, Thrumster, Wick.
Tel: Thrumster (095585) 252

Hempriggs lies adjacent to the A9 3 miles south of Wick. It is a
windy loch and fishing is all from the bank. Trout average ½ lb.
with larger fish being taken from time to time. The shore nearest
to the road is the best fishing area but wading requires caution
because of boulders under the surface. Standard loch fly patterns
work well.

LOCH OF WESTER
12/325592

Permission: A. Dunnet, Auchorn Farm, Lyth.
Tel: Keiss (095583) 208

Loch of Wester lies to the north of Wick on the road to John
o'Groats. It is joined to the sea by the Burn of Wester and during
August and September sea trout and salmon enter the loch. The
trout are small averaging three to the pound and a ¾ lb. fish
would be large for this loch. Good baskets can be had and the loch
is a popular venue due to its ease of access. Three boats are available and bank fishing is also allowed.

GARBH LOCH
11/037465

Permission: Mrs Atkinson, c/o The Bradford & Bingley Building
Society, Sinclair Street, Thurso.
Tel: Thurso (0847) 63291

This superb loch lies to the east of the railway a short distance
from Altnabreac Station. Access is via a good forestry road which
takes you to within 150 yards of the south end of the loch. Drive
slowly, however, for it is easy to miss the starting point. Garbh is
a small loch and the average weight of trout is ½–¾ lb. with the
occasional larger trout of up to 3½ lb. They fight well and are
pink-fleshed and I have found that fish rise all over the loch with
no one area being better than another. The same applies to boat
and bank fishing, indeed bank fishing is slightly more productive.
An average day will bring you a basket of 8–10 fish and a good
day will account for many more. A sample basket from the 1981
season included 18 trout weighing 12 lb. Best flies on Garbh are
Ke-He, Black Pennell and Invicta. A lovely loch, easy to get to
and worth visiting.

CAOL LOCH   11/025485

Permission: Mrs Atkinson, c/o The Bradford & Bingley Building Society, Sinclair Street, Thurso.

Tel: Thurso (0847) 63291

Caol lies to the west of the railway near Altnabreac Station and is approached by the same forestry road as for Garbh. The loch is at the end of a good peat track and about 15 minutes walk from the parking place. There is a boathouse and an excellent boat and this loch is one of the most delightful in Caithness. It is a high loch and from it one has a panoramic view of rolling moorlands and the Caithness mountains, Morvern and the Scarabens line the southern horizon. The trout in Caol are beautifully shaped, pink-fleshed and great fighters. They average ¾ lb. but most visits produce a few larger fish of between 1–2 lb. Bank fishing is every bit as good as boat fishing and wading is safe and easy all round the loch. The bay at the top end of the loch is the most popular area though I have caught trout in most parts of the loch. Flies to use are Black Pennell, Soldier Palmer, Invicta, March Brown, Ke-He and Butchers.

SKYLINE LOCH   12/010480

Permission: Mrs Atkinson, c/o The Bradford & Bingley Building Society, Sinclair Street, Thurso.

Tel: Thurso (0847) 63291

An expert's loch, dour, frustrating and yet, on its day, one of the most exciting lochs in Caithness. Follow the forestry road out past Garbh and Caise to the railway line. Turn left and drive past Altnabreac Station. The forestry road crosses the railway a few hundred yards further on and, within half a mile, there is a spur to the right. Skyline lies at the end of this branch road.

The average weight of Skyline trout is 2 lb. but you will have more blank days than heavy baskets. I note from my fishing log that, to have the best chance, you must be in action early since few fish are caught after noon. Fish lie close to the shore so my advice is to stay on the bank and stalk them. Our best day produced four lovely trout weighing 10 lb. Three of them were caught by my better half, who is a much more patient stalker than I am.

LOCH CAISE   12/026466

Permission: Mrs Atkinson, c/o The Bradford & Bingley Building Society, Sinclair Street, Thurso.

Tel: Thurso (0847) 63291

Caise is by the side of the new forestry road out from Loch More.

This is an excellent beginners' loch and the ideal place to introduce young folk to the gentle art of fly-fishing. It is also a good spot for a picnic and, because of easy access, suitable for all ages and all degrees of fitness.

LOCH A'CHERIGAL   12/100489
Permission: Ulbster Arms Hotel, Halkirk.
Tel: Halkirk (084783) 206

Park near Strathmore Lodge on the Thurso river and follow the signpost westwards. Within ten minutes you will arrive at Cherigal, 'the dusky loch'. It can provide really excellent sport but also has many dour days. Best basket recently contained 12 fish weighing 12 lb. and the most productive fishing area is round the headland to the right of the boat mooring place. The west side of the loch is unsuitable for bank fishing due to soft margins and weeds and best results come from the boat.

LOCH MEADIE   12/090480
Permission: Ulbster Arms Hotel, Halkirk.
Tel: Halkirk (084783) 206

Meadie is a delightful roadside loch, full of hard-fighting little trout. Another first-class beginners' loch where both boat and bank fishing brings good results. My son Blair and I had 14 nice fish in one windy drift down the west shore a few years ago and, regardless of wind direction, fishing is usually possible from either bank.

LOCH EILEANACH   12/070475
LOCHAN DUBH NAN GEODH   12/060477
LOCH GAINEIMH   12/050470
Permission: Ulbster Arms Hotel, Halkirk.
Tel: Halkirk (084783) 206

These three lochs lie close to the new forestry road from Loch More and regularly produce good baskets of good quality wild brown trout which average ½–¾ lb. However, like most of the lochs round Altnabreac, there are some really big fish lurking in the depths. Eddie MacArthy, the Thurso Fishery Manager, had a trout of 4 lb. 12 oz. from nan Geodh in June 1986, so treat every rise with caution and respect.

LOCH GLUTT   11/993375
Permission: Ulbster Arms Hotel, Halkirk.
Tel: Halkirk (084783) 206

Another experts' loch, Glutt can drive the ordinary angler (me)
mad with frustration. The water is very clear and few fish rise.
But they are there, are very large and fish of up to 4½ lb. will not
raise too many eyebrows. It is just getting them out that is the
problem. Glutt lies deep in the Caithness hills and moors, at the
end of a long, rough estate road which should be approached with
care and caution. Fish or not, Glutt is one of the special places –
lonely, remote and lovely. Have a look for yourself.

LOCH EUN   11/893426
Permission: The Ulbster Arms Hotel, Halkirk.
Tel: Halkirk (084783) 206

Eun is perhaps the best of the Ulbster Arms Hotel waters; it is
certainly one of the most remote and beautiful. Follow the road
on the south side of the railway at Altnabreac and take the track to
Cnoc Seasaimh. Eun is half a mile further on. The estate has
stocked this small loch in recent years and during 1986 there were
reports of a basket of 19 fish, each weighing over 1 lb. and the
best being close on 2 lb. Hasten slowly along the pot-holed road,
but get there if you can – well worth the trouble.

LOCH DUBH   12/011441
Permission: The Ulbster Arms Hotel, Halkirk.
Tel: Halkirk (084783) 206

You pass little Loch Dubh on the way to Eun. Lochdubh Lodge
towers over the water, a gaunt, empty monument to grander
times. Trout average ½ lb. but larger fish of up to 3 lb. have been
taken in years gone by.

LOCH THULACHAN   12/106414
LOCH SAND   12/098410
Permission: The Ulbster Arms Hotel, Halkirk.
Tel: Halkirk (084783) 206

Follow the road from Westerdale out to Loch More. There is a
locked gate here and, in order to reduce the length of your walk,
make sure that you obtain a key for it when you make your
booking. Drive on and park the car at 084443. From here a good

track leads south-eastwards into the hills, past the ruined cottage of Balavreed, on to the first loch, which is Thulachan. A few hundred yards west of the end of the loch is Sand.

Trout in these lochs average ½ lb. but they are great fun to catch and, personally, I am sure that there are much larger fish, particularly in Loch Sand. This is one of the most delightful fishing venues in Caithness and a great place for wildlife. Over the years we have seen wild cat, otter, arctic skua, peregrine falcon, greenshank and divers. A wonderful place to fish.

LOCH SLETILL   11/958470
Permission: Forsinard Hotel, Forsinard, Sutherland.
Tel: Halladale (06417) 221

Loch Sletill is one of the best lochs in the north and lies to the east of the A897 Helmsdale–Melvich road. Access to Loch Sletill is by a new forestry road which takes you to within a few minutes walk of the loch. Sletill is remote, beautiful and full of excellent trout. The average weight is 1 lb. and baskets of 10–15 fish are common. The heaviest fish caught during the 1981 season was a trout of 3½ lb. and each season produces trout of over 2 lb. There are two boats on the loch and fish rise and take all over. Bank fishing is first class and wading safe and comfortable so if it is too windy to

3   *Well hooked and about 1 lb. 12 oz.*

use the boat don't worry, you will catch as many from the shore. The north shore probably fishes best and fishing from the bank near the promontory nearly always brings results. If the wind is blowing on to this shore persist in trying to cast across the wind – you will find the trout rise like rockets from the depths to snatch the fly just before it leaves the water. There is a large rock in the middle of the north-west bay. Fish round this and drift down the south shore. Best flies include Ke-He, Black Pennell, Soldier Palmer, Invicta, Grouse and Claret, March Brown, Greenwell's and Butchers. Top quality fishing amidst lovely surroundings.

LOCH LEIR   11/955458
Permission: Forsinard Hotel, Forsinard, Sutherland.
Tel: Halladale (06417) 221

Loch Leir lies to the south of Sletill and is a similar distance from the A897 Helmsdale–Melvich road. A new forestry track takes you, by car, nearly all the way to the loch, so access is easy. Loch Leir is a small hill loch full of well-shaped, hard-fighting trout. Their strength is remarkable and I know of no other loch where the fish fight so well. The average weight is ¾ lb. and baskets of 20–30 fish are often caught. An average day should bring you 10–12 fish. A good boat is available and bank fishing is just as productive. Same flies as for Sletill and other loch patterns. A great loch and worth the walk out.

LOCH TALAHEEL   11/955489
Permission: Forsinard Hotel, Forsinard, Sutherland.
Tel: Halladale (06417) 221

Follow the new forestry road to Sletill and walk on from there. The loch is a 20-minute 'plodge' northwards over the moor. The average weight of the Talaheel fish is ½–¾ lb. but larger fish are taken from time to time and the 1981 season produced a fish of 1½ lb. They are of excellent quality and rise well all over this small loch. An average basket should produce 8–10 fish but on a good day much larger baskets can be had. Standard loch fly patterns work well and Talaheel is a delightful loch to fish.

LOCHAN EALACH MOR   11/967480
LOCH NA CLOICHE   11/975475
Permission: Forsinard Hotel, Forsinard, Sutherland.
Tel: Halladale (06417) 221

Previously inaccessible to all but the most determined and fittest, these remote lochs can now be reached in relative comfort from the new forestry road that scars the moor from Strath Halladale in Sutherland to Loch More in Caithness. Expect to catch large numbers of bright little trout – ideal beginners' lochs and very pleasant to fish.

LOCHAN NAN CLACH GEALA   11/935495

Permission: Mrs J. Baird, Forsinard House, Forsinard, Strath Halladale.
Tel: Halladale (06417) 220.

Start again from Forsinard Farm on the A897 Helmsdale–Melvich road but instead of following the Sletill track walk straight on. Clach is only a short walk from the gate leading on to the hill. There are two lochs both of which contain good trout and there is a boat on the larger water. Clach is very exposed and can be windy so a sea anchor is very useful if you have one. If not, then fish from the bank with fullest confidence since as many fish come from bank fishing as from the boat. The average weight of trout in Clach is 1¾ lb. and fish of 2–3 lb. are taken each season. One superb basket from Clach, taken a few years ago, accounted for 10 fish weighing 21½ lb. But they do not give themselves up easily so do not be too disappointed if you have a blank day. If you like a challenge, however, head for Clach and take along Black Pennell, Invicta, Grouse and Claret and Worm Fly. These patterns catch most of the fish.

THE CROSS LOCHS   10/870465

Permission: Forsinard Hotel, Forsinard, Sutherland.
Tel: Halladale (06417) 221

These lochs lie to the west of the Forsinard Hotel in Strath Halladale and involve a walk of about 2 miles into the hills. There are five main lochs and they can be the most infuriating waters in the north. There are times when you would swear that there wasn't a single fish in them, but don't be fooled. There are, and big ones at that. Hardly a season passes without some trout of 3–5 lb. being taken and during the 1979 season a fish of 8½ lb. was caught. The first loch is very clear with a marl bottom and requires skill and cunning to tempt the fish. The others are peaty and dour. All are exciting and you must be ready all the time for that grab. Don't walk out expecting to return with a lot of fish, but if you do catch one it most probably will be a good one. Flies to try include all the standard loch patterns, but the Blue Zulu seems to do rather better than most.

LOCH CROCACH   10/805437

Permission: Forsinard Hotel, Forsinard, Sutherland.
Tel: Halladale (06417) 221

This remote loch lies 5½ miles to the west of Forsinard Hotel in Strath Halladale. A track starts off from the roadside at Forsinard Lodge on the A897 Helmsdale–Melvich road and leads you into the hills for the first 3 miles. From there on you are on your own. Crocach is a most lovely place and the loch is situated close to the two Ben Griams. It is full of ½ lb. trout and is only fished infrequently. At times two or three seasons will pass without a visit and yet it is one of the most attractive of the Strath Halladale waters. Standard pattern flies, strong lungs and a good day are all that are required to enjoy this beautiful loch.

LOCH NA CAORACH   10/913584

Permission: Melvich Hotel, Melvich, Sutherland.
Tel: Melvich (06413) 206

Caorach is at the Melvich end of the A897 Strath Halladale road and lies in the hills to the east of the road. There is a grassy car park close to the River Halladale a few miles down the Strath from Melvich. Head for the fence running over the shoulder of the hill and follow this up to the loch. The loch contains brown trout and both boat and bank fishing are available. The trout average ¾ lb. and fight well. Fish over 1½ lb. are taken frequently and the best area to fish is in the southern bay and off the headland on the south-east shore. Another excellent area is in the vicinity of the feeder burn on the east shore. Black Pennell, Grouse and Claret, and Butcher should produce a basket of 3–4 fish. Expect several more on a good day.

LOCH NA SEILGE   11/920585

Permission: Melvich Hotel, Melvich, Sutherland.
Tel: Melvich (06413) 206

Follow the same route as for Caorach. When you reach the boat mooring bay on Caorach, bear left, round the loch and follow the line of the inlet burn. There is a track, alongside the remains of an old fence, and this leads to Seilge (pronounced Shallag).

Seilge is one of the most productive lochs in Strath Halladale. Fish are caught all over the loch but perhaps the most productive areas are the east shore and in the vicinity of the little island – a super lunch spot. Trout average ¾ lb. with the odd fish of over 2 lb. being taken each season. Boat fishing is best although good sport may also be had from the bank.

LOCH AKRAN   11/925605

Permission: Melvich Hotel, Melvich, Sutherland.
Tel: Melvich (06413) 206

Park the car at the same place as for Caorach but instead of
walking up to the fence, head off left and follow the line of the
pylons. This will bring you safely to the loch. Akran is a small
loch, beautifully situated and full of small fish which give superb
sport. They average ½ lb. and rise freely – really – to the fly.
Excellent baskets are taken each season and both boat and bank
fish well. The best drift is down the south shore. At the end of
this drift turn into the lovely southern bay. The headland is a
great spot to do some damage and in adverse winds this area
should be carefully fished from the bank. Use standard loch fly
patterns. A super loch for beginners and experts alike and well
worth a visit.

CAOL-LOCH   11/923615

Permission: Melvich Hotel, Melvich, Sutherland.
Tel: Melvich (06413) 206

Take the same route as for Akran but continue round the east
shore of the loch and follow the pylons, keeping them on your
right. A short walk brings you to Caol-loch. Like Akran, Caol is
full of ½-lb. trout with the chance of the odd larger trout of up to
2 lb. The south shore, by the promontory and tiny island, is the
most productive area to fish.

LOCH NA H-EAGLAISE MOR   10/862600
LOCH NA H-EAGLAISE BEAG   10/855590

Permission: Melvich Hotel, Melvich, Sutherland.
Tel: Melvich (06413) 206

Take the peat track to the west of the Melvich Hotel and park at
the end. The walk from this point is about 1½ miles over the
moor and it can be difficult particularly after heavy rain. Eaglaise
Mor is the first loch and contains a good stock of trout which
average ½–¾ lb. These fish are of excellent quality, pink-fleshed
and fighting fit. Larger trout are regularly caught and fish of over
2 lb. are taken each season. The best fishing area is down the east
shore and the top bay. Keep fairly close to the shore and fish
down to the large rock. Bank fishing does not seem to be as productive on Mor and best results come from the boat. An average
basket should consist of 6–8 fish but much larger catches are
common. Eaglaise Beag lies half a mile to the south of Mor and

contains larger fish. Trout of 2–3 lb. are often caught although the loch holds a sizeable stock of good ½ lb. trout as well. Beag is a small loch and easily fished. Off the west shore are two large patches of weed and it is in this area that most of the larger fish lie. Several feeder burns enter on the west bank and they also can offer good sport. Bank fishing is good on Beag and if the wind is too strong don't hesitate to have a go at them from the shore. Wading is easy and the water quite deep close in. Best flies for both lochs include all the standard pattern loch flies, but I should start with Ke-He, March Brown and Alexandra.

LOCH AN RUATHAIR   17/865370
Permission: Factor, Langwell Estate Office, Berridale, Caithness.
Tel: Berridale (05935) 237

Loch an Ruathair lies adjacent to the A897 midway between Helmsdale and Melvich in Strath Halladale. It is a windswept loch of one mile long by three-quarters wide and has an average depth of 10–12 feet. The Langwell Estate has a cottage for rent at Greamachary and this is well situated for fishing Ruathair and other nearby lochs. This loch is full of good ½–¾ lb. trout and can give really excellent sport. Baskets of 15–20 fish are frequently taken and the trout rise well to all the standard pattern loch flies. The most productive area on Ruathair is at the northern end of the loch where the feeder burns enter.

LOCH ARICHLINIE   17/847350
Permission: Factor, Langwell Estate Office, Berridale, Caithness.
Tel: Berridale (05935) 237

Arichlinie lies to the south-west of Ruathair close to the A897 Strath Halladale road and is a shallow loch with an average depth of 4–5 feet. The average weight of trout is ½ lb. and a 1 lb. trout would be considered a monster for this loch. Nevertheless, from time to time Arichlinie surprises everyone by producing a trout of 2 lb. or more and it is a pleasant loch to fish. There is a good boathouse and boat and bank fishing are both allowed. The best areas to fish are in the vicinity of the Alt Airighdhamh burn and baskets of 20–30 trout are taken regularly. Park at Auchentoul Farm and follow the track westwards from there. Standard pattern flies will do fine.

LOCH COIRE NAM MANG   10/800405

Permission: Polson MacKenzie, Badanloch, Kinbrace, Sutherland.
Belgrave Arms Hotel, Helmsdale, Sutherland.
Tel: Helmsdale (04312) 242;
The Gravault Hotel, Kinbrace, Helmsdale, Sutherland.
Tel: Kinbrace (04313) 224

This small, shallow loch lies 1½ miles from the B871 Kinbrace–
Bettyhill road near the Garvault Hotel. Both boat and bank
fishing are allowed although best results come from the boat. The
track out is well marked and Coire Nam Mang is a circular loch
half a mile in diameter and contains brown trout and some char.
The average depth is 12 feet and its deepest, 33 feet. The quality
of the trout is excellent and the fish average ¾ lb. in weight.
Baskets of 10 fish are not unusual and the loch produces several
trout of 4–5 lb. each season. Three small feeder burns enter in the
south-east corner of the loch and this is a favourite fishing area.
Standard loch pattern flies work well. A remote, beautiful loch
with first-class trout.

LOCH DRUIM A CHLIABHAIN   10/810410

Permission: Polson MacKenzie, Badanloch, Kinbrace, Sutherland.
Belgrave Arms Hotel, Helmsdale, Sutherland.
Tel: Helmsdale (04312) 242;
The Gravault Hotel, Kinbrace, Helmsdale, Sutherland.
Tel: Kinbrace (04313) 224

This loch is joined by a short stream to Coire nam Mang and is 2
miles from the B871 Kinbrace–Bettyhill road near the Garvault
Hotel. The loch is over 1½ miles long by half a mile wide and
both boat and bank fishing are available. The loch has a reputation
for holding some large trout and the average weight is ¾ lb. The
fish are pink-fleshed and rise well to the fly with baskets of 15
trout being caught regularly. Standard loch fly patterns all
produce good results and the west shore of the north bay is a
good place to start. Superb scenery with the Ben Griams to the
east and Beinn a'Mhadaidh to the west.

LOCH BADANLOCH   17/770340

Permission: Polson MacKenzie, Badanloch, Kinbrace, Sutherland.
Belgrave Arms Hotel, Helmsdale, Sutherland.
Tel: Helmsdale (04312) 242;
The Gravault Hotel, Kinbrace, Helmsdale, Sutherland.
Tel: Kinbrace (04313) 224

Badanloch is to the south of the B871 Kinbrace–Bettyhill road and is one of three interlinked lochs which cover an area 4½ miles long by one mile wide. Badanloch fishes best from the boat and the most productive area is in the 'narrows' between the island of Rubha Mor and the shore. The average weight of trout is ½ lb. and baskets of 20 fish are often taken. The loch also contains some much larger trout and fish of 5–6½ lb. are caught each year. Most of these larger fish come to the dap and this method is much favoured on Badanloch. The loch has an average depth of 17 feet and the water level is subject to variation during the season. This does not seem to upset the trout too much. Boats are moored at the eastern end of the loch.

LOCH NAN CLAR   16/755355
Permission: Polson MacKenzie, Badanloch, Kinbrace, Sutherland.
Belgrave Arms Hotel, Helmsdale, Sutherland.
Tel: Helmsdale (04312) 242;
The Gravault Hotel, Kinbrace, Helmsdale, Sutherland.
Tel: Kinbrace (04313) 224

Loch nan Clar is a continuation of Badanloch and the best area to fish is where the loch narrows before joining Loch Rimsdale. It is not unusual to encounter salmon at this point and many an angler has been taken unawares by an 8 lb. salmon grabbing at a trout fly. Be ready and watchful. Trout on Loch nan Clar average ½ lb. and baskets of 20 or more fish are frequently taken. Each year sees a few 5–6 lb. fish landed and, again, the dap accounts for most of them. With the boats being moored at the Badanloch end it's a long row up to the loch. However, it is possible to hire an outboard motor should you not have one. Take great care on these lochs with the outboard, as there are sudden shallows. The average depth is 12 feet but at the narrows the bottom is only 4 feet away. Use standard loch fly patterns.

LOCH RIMSDALE   16/740355
Permission: Polson MacKenzie, Badanloch, Kinbrace, Sutherland.
Belgrave Arms Hotel, Helmsdale, Sutherland.
Tel: Helmsdale (04312) 242;
The Gravault Hotel, Kinbrace, Helmsdale, Sutherland.
Tel: Kinbrace (04313) 224

Loch Rimsdale is the last of the Badanloch waters and contains brown trout char and the occasional salmon. Rimsdale lies more north/south than its neighbours and is 3 miles long by three-quarters of a mile wide. The boats are moored at the north-east corner where there is easy access from the B871 Kinbrace–

Bettyhill road. Rimsdale is a shallow loch with an average depth of 12 feet and dapping and standard loch fly patterns bring good results. Baskets of 20 trout are frequent and Rimsdale also produces its fair share of 5–7 lb. trout. The Badanloch Lochs are most attractive and worthy of your close attention.

LOCH AN FHEARNA   16/750335
Permission: Polson MacKenzie, Badanloch, Kinbrace, Sutherland.
Belgrave Arms Hotel, Helmsdale, Sutherland.
Tel: Helmsdale (04312) 242;
The Gravault Hotel, Kinbrace, Helmsdale, Sutherland.
Tel: Kinbrace (04313) 224

This small loch lies to the south of the Badanloch Lochs and is about half a mile across. Approach from Badanloch Lodge on the road that runs along the south shore of Badanloch and Loch nan Clar. Fhearna is a shallow loch with an average depth of 14 feet and the trout are small but fight well. They average ½ lb. but fight like 1 lb. fish. There are larger trout as well with fish of up to 5 lb. often being taken. Most standard loch patterns will bring results and fish rise all over the loch. Again dapping is a favourite method and there is generally enough wind to make it worth while. Bank fishing is not so productive as fishing from the boat.

LOCH ASCAIG   17/850255
Permission: The Estate Factor, Borrobol Estate, Strath of Kildonan, Helmsdale, Sutherland.
Tel: Kinbrace (04313) 252

A few miles north of Suisgill Lodge in Strath of Kildonan, turn left down an estate road which crosses the Helmsdale river. The keeper's house is to the right of the lodge. From here a good track leads westwards into the hills to Loch Ascaig. Although the fish are not monsters, Ascaig trout are great fun to catch – and there are a lot of them waiting, eager to grab your flies as soon as they touch the water. Great sport for novice and old hand alike amidst superb scenery.

LOCH MEADIE   10/753600
Permission: Bettyhill Hotel, Bettyhill, Sutherland.
Tel: Bettyhill (06412) 202

Meadie is a long, narrow loch 1½ miles long by 250 yards wide. It is easily accessible and a good track leaves the A836 east of

Bettyhill. Both boat and bank fishing are available but best results come from the boat. Meadie is an exciting loch to fish and even in windy conditions the angler will find a sheltered corner amongst the many bays. May and June are the best months on Meadie and all the standard loch fly patterns work well. The south end of the loch is the best area to fish.

LOCH MOR   10/720609
Permission: Bettyhill Hotel, Bettyhill, Sutherland.
Tel: Bettyhill (06412) 202

Loch Mor is small and lies a few hundred yards to the south of the Bettyhill Hotel. It contains excellent trout with an average weight of ¾ lb., but heavier fish of over 2 lb. are sometimes caught. Standard loch fly patterns will do.

LOCHAN DUINTE   10/717584
Permission: Bettyhill Hotel, Bettyhill, Sutherland.
Tel: Bettyhill (06412) 202

This small loch lies close to the minor road which runs south of Bettyhill. Instead of crossing the River Naver go straight on and the loch is on your left about one mile down the road. This is a charming little loch and fish rise all over. Both boat and bank fishing are available and due to the high crags to the east Duinte can be sheltered when high winds make other waters difficult. Standard loch fly patterns work well.

CAOL LOCH   10/763597
Permission: Bettyhill Hotel, Bettyhill, Sutherland.
Tel: Bettyhill (06412) 202

Caol Loch lies to the east of Loch Meadie in the shadow of Creag Meadie. This is a remote and lovely little loch about 700 yards long by 80 yards wide. It contains good brown trout which rise well to standard loch fly patterns all round the loch. The most productive area, however, is at the south end of the loch and great sport can be had with excellent baskets of trout being caught.

LOCH NAN LAOGH   10/770570
Permission: Bettyhill Hotel, Bettyhill, Sutherland.
Tel: Bettyhill (06412) 202

Loch nan Laogh means 'loch of the deer calf' and this water is the furthest out of the Bettyhill Hotel fishings. It involves a walk of about 3 miles and you approach from the A836 and take the route

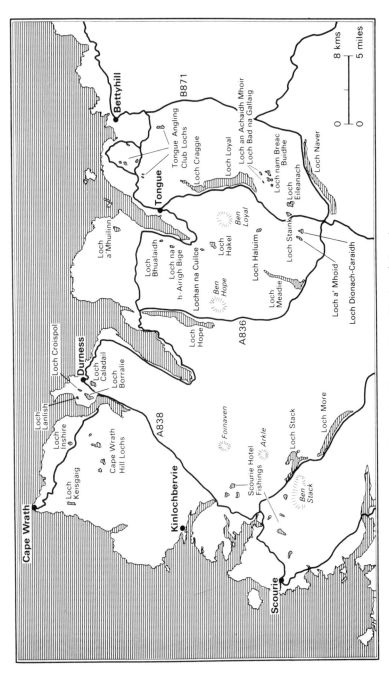

Map 6 *Tongue, Cape Wrath and Scourie*

south past Loch Meadie. This is as remote and distant a loch as you will find in the north, peaceful and quiet set amidst really grand scenery. Trout average ½–¾ lb. and rise well to the old standard loch fly patterns. A delightful loch and well worth the walk out.

LOCHAN AIRIGH NA CREIGE   10/730582
Permission: Bettyhill Hotel, Bettyhill, Sutherland.
Tel: Bettyhill (06412) 202

There are two lochs here joined by a short feeder burn and both offer excellent sport in lovely surroundings. The name means 'loch of the little rocky shealing' and they are a short walk from the minor road going south from the bridge over the Naver, near the Bettyhill Hotel. Standard loch fly patterns will suffice.

LOCH MEADIE   16/495400
Permission: Altnaharra Hotel, Altnaharra, by Lairg, Sutherland.
Tel: Altnaharra (054981) 222

Loch Meadie is a long, narrow loch and lies adjacent to the minor road from Altnaharra to Loch Hope. Both boat and bank fishing are available and the loch contains a good stock of brown trout. The most productive area on Meadie is the south end amongst the bays and promontories and also around the many islands. There are dramatic views of Ben Hope (927m) and on a good day dramatic baskets of excellent trout. Use standard loch fly patterns.

LOCH STAINK   10/580406
Permission: Altnaharra Hotel, Altnaharra, by Lairg, Sutherland.
Tel: Altnaharra (054981) 222

Loch Staink lies to the east of the A836 Altnaharra–Tongue road and is easily accessible. Both boat and bank fishing are available and the best flies to use are Black Pennell and those of that ilk. Grand scenery predominates with Ben Loyal (764m) to the north. Fish rise all over this small loch and good baskets are taken frequently.

LOCH NAM BREAC BUIDHE   10/617434
Permission: Altnaharra Hotel, Altnaharra, by Lairg, Sutherland.
Tel: Altnaharra (054981) 222

This loch lies 6 miles north of Altnaharra on the A836 to Tongue. It is to the east of the road amidst the low hills south of Loch

Loyal. Both boat and bank fishing are available and visitors should leave the car at Inchkinloch and walk out from there. Breac Buidhe is heart shaped and about 200 yards across. There is a small island of the east shore and this is a good area to try. Standard loch fly patterns work well and the walk is not difficult, so do make the effort since this is a lovely loch with first-class trout.

LOCH EILEANACH   10/593405

Permission: Altnaharra Hotel, Altnaharra, by Lairg, Sutherland.
Tel: Altnaharra (054981) 222

This lovely loch is 3 miles north of Altnaharra on the A836 road to Tongue and is an easy 30 minute walk to the east of the road. Park by Loch Staink and follow the shore round the top of the loch. Halfway down the far side strike off east. Loch Eileanach is separated into two distinct sections by a narrow channel. The northern section contains five small islands and fishing round them is good. A boat is available but bank fishing can be just as rewarding. Standard loch fly patterns.

LOCH AN ACHAIDH MHOIR   10/620424
LOCH BAD NA GALLAIG   10/630428

Permission: Altnaharra Hotel, Altnaharra, by Lairg, Sutherland.
Tel: Altnaharra (054981) 222

This is a series of five lochs and lochans interlinked by feeder burns and emptying into Loch Loyal. Fishing is from the bank only and the average weight of trout is in the ½–¾ lb. range. A

4   *Loch Eileanach from the slopes of Ben Stack.*

very pleasant place to spend the day and each of these lochs will give good sport. Great fishing – away from it all. Use standard loch fly patterns and strong shoes. There's a 2 mile walk involved but it's worth it.

LOCH DIONACH-CARAIDH   10/559402
Permission: Altnaharra Hotel, Altnaharra, by Lairg, Sutherland.
Tel: Altnaharra (054981) 222

Park just before the forest to the left of the A836 and near to Loch Staink. Dionach-Caraidh is approximately one mile west from the road. Bank fishing only on this small water.

LOCH A'MHOID   10/568410
Permission: Altnaharra Hotel, Altnaharra, by Lairg, Sutherland.
Tel: Altnaharra (054981) 222

Loch a'Mhoid lies in the middle of a new forest and access is via a locked gate and forest track. Mhoid is also known as the Plantation Loch and holds excellent fish. The water is very shallow and, in windy conditions, fishing is difficult – as is controlling the boat. But it is worth the effort since anything under 1 lb. must be returned to the water.

LOCH HALUIM   10/561455
Permission: Altnaharra Hotel, Altnaharra, by Lairg, Sutherland.
Tel: Altnaharra (054981) 222

The most productive loch in the area: also the longest walk involving an hour's hard slog over the southern slopes of Ben Loyal. Haluim is a maze of points and corners and close by are a number of other lochs and lochans all of which offer excellent sport. Anglers must be accompanied by a gillie.

LOCH CRAGGIE   10/615515
Permission: Tongue Hotel, Tongue, Sutherland.
Tel: Tongue (084755) 206
Altnaharra Hotel – see Loch Meadie

Loch Craggie is separated from Loch Loyal by a narrow strip of land and lies to the south of Tongue. Craggie is 1¼ miles long by about one-third of a mile across. It is more sheltered than Loyal and often fishes very well whilst larger Loyal is unfishable due to high winds. Best results come from the boat and the trout average ½–¾ lb. although there are much larger fish but they are difficult to tempt. The best areas to fish on Craggie are at the southern end where the loch is shallower. A good drift is down the west shore and into the large bay. Boats are moored at the foot of a little track from the main road through a small wood of birch and alder. Watch out for the iron gate at the road, it's very easy to miss. A lovely loch and very pleasant to fish. Standard loch fly patterns will do fine.

LOCH LOYAL   10/620480
Permission: Ben Loyal Hotel, Tongue, Sutherland.
Tel: Tongue (084755) 216;
Tongue Hotel, Tongue, Sutherland.
Tel: Tongue (084755) 206;
Altnaharra Hotel, Altnaharra, by Lairg, Sutherland.
Tel: Altnaharra (054981) 225

Loch Loyal lies to the south of Tongue and is one of the most beautiful lochs in the area. It is 4½ miles long by up to one mile wide and easily accessible from the A836 which runs alongside the western shore. An outboard motor is very useful on Loyal since conditions can be stormy at times, and it helps to cover the eastern shore more easily. The trout average ½–¾ lb. in weight and good baskets are often taken. A reasonable day should bring you 6–8 fish and catches of 15–20 trout are frequent. Loch Loyal is over 200 feet deep and most trout are caught close to the shore and in the shallow bays. The large southern bay, from the mouth of the feeder burn from Loch na Gallaig down to where the stream from Loch Coulside enters, is an excellent area. Much larger fish lie here and trout of over 2 lb. are caught. On 7 May 1985 an excellent trout weighing 4 lb. 15 oz. was taken on a size 12 Grouse and Claret by one of the Ben Loyal Hotel boats. The island-dotted eastern bay can also provide excellent sport. A good drift on Loyal is from just north of Lettermore over the shallow bay where Allt Torr an Tairbh burn comes down from the lower slopes of Ben Loyal. If the wind is right, try dapping on Loch Loyal otherwise it's on with the Black Pennells, Butchers and Greenwells. Good fishing in lovely surroundings with the chance of a really big one.

LOCH NAVER   16/610360

Permission: Altnaharra Hotel, Altnaharra, by Lairg, Sutherland.
Tel: Altnaharra (054981) 222

Loch Naver is some 6 miles long by about half a mile wide and is
mostly fished for its salmon and sea trout. However, there are
good brown trout in this deep loch and good sport can often be
had with them when the larger cousins are being unco-operative.
The loch is easily accessible from the B873 which runs along the
north shore. It is possible to hire an outboard motor
from Altnaharra Fishings and this makes life much easier. Trout
fishing is best during May and June, but this is really a
salmon loch.

LOCH A'MHUILINN   10/568609

Permission:
Ben Loyal Hotel, Tongue, Sutherland.
Tel: Tongue (084755) 216;
Tongue Hotel, Tongue, Sutherland.
Tel: Tongue (084755) 206

This loch is over the Kyle causeway and to the west of the
Achinver–Lubinvullin road. The loch holds brown trout which
average ½–¾ lb. and it is a short walk from the road. Leave the
car near Melness House and follow the track out from there.
There is a large island where the loch narrows in the south and
this is a favoured fishing area. Also try the bay to the west of the
island and where the feeder burn enters. Use standard loch fly
patterns.

LOCH BHUALAIDH   10/537563
LOCH NA H-AIRIGH BIGE   10/550550

Permission:
Ben Loyal Hotel, Tongue, Sutherland.
Tel: Tongue (084755) 216;
Tongue Hotel, Tongue, Sutherland.
Tel: Tongue (084755) 206

Turn south of the Kyle causeway and follow the minor road for
about 1½ miles. Park where the road almost touches the sea and
you will see a track to your right. The walk out is about 1½ miles
and the track takes you past Loch Fhionnaich on the way.
Bhualaidh is worth the walk and contains hard-fighting trout
of excellent quality. It is a small loch and easy to fish. Standard

loch fly patterns all produce results. Loch na h-Airigh Bige is further down this same minor road. A quick scramble up the hill and you could be fishing within 15 minutes of leaving the car. Both these lochs are most attractive and delightful places to fish.

LOCHAN HAKEL 10/570530
Permission:
Ben Loyal Hotel, Tongue, Sutherland.
Tel: Tongue (084755) 216;
Tongue Hotel, Tongue, Sutherland.
Tel: Tongue (084755) 206

Both boat and bank fishing are available on Loch Hakel and this loch is one of the most attractive in the area. It is one-third of a mile long by a few hundred yards wide and is the sort of loch the visitor very quickly falls in love with. The views of Ben Loyal are spectacular and the surrounding countryside a constant delight. The brown trout fight well, average ½–¾ lb. and rise to the standard loch fly patterns. Hakel is easily accessible from the minor road south of Tongue which runs round the Kyle. Well worth a visit.

LOCHAN NA CUILCE 10/585535
Permission: Ben Loyal Hotel, Tongue, Sutherland.
Tel: Tongue (084755) 216

Known locally as the Lily Loch, the Tongue and District Angling Club have a boat which may be available for use by visitors. Cuilce is four miles south of the village, on the right of the road out to Hakel.

LOCH MODSARIE 10/649616
Permission: Ben Loyal Hotel, Tongue, Sutherland.
Tel: Tongue (084755) 216

Loch Modsarie is 700 yards long by 150 yards wide and lies to the east of the road out to Skerray from the A836. The loch is under the control of the Tongue and District Angling Club and contains brown trout with an average weight of ½–¾ lb. An easily access-ible loch in a delightful setting. Standard pattern loch flies work well.

LOCH A'CHAORUINN   10/667600
LOCH SKERRAY   10/663600
Permission: Ben Loyal Hotel, Tongue, Sutherland.
Tel: Tongue (084755) 216

These lochs are managed by the Tongue and District Angling Club and contain brown trout with an average weight of ½–¾ lb. They are best approached via the minor road out to Skerray from Borgie Bridge on the A836. Skerray holds the best fish and the area of the island is a favourite fishing spot. There are pleasant bays and points and the trout rise to the usual standard pattern loch flies.

LOCH AN TIGH-CHOIMHID   10/663608
Permission: Ben Loyal Hotel, Tongue, Sutherland.
Tel: Tongue (084755) 216

This little loch is near the Skerray ring road from the A836 and is best approached from the Modsarie side. Walk out past Loch Modsarie and Loch nam Burag, Tigh-Choimhid is to the south-east. Another Tongue and District Angling Club water holding good fish which rise well to standard loch fly patterns.

LOCH DUBH BEUL NA FAIRE   10/648593
Permission: Ben Loyal Hotel, Tongue, Sutherland.
Tel: Tongue (084755) 216

This small loch lies close to the A836 at its highest point between Tongue and Borgie. Easily accessible and controlled by the Tongue and District Angling Club. Brown trout of ½–¾ lb. rise to standard pattern loch flies. A bit public but a pleasant loch for a few casts when passing.

LOCH NAM BREAC BUIDGE   10/650567
Permission: Ben Loyal Hotel, Tongue, Sutherland.
Tel: Tongue (084755) 216

Approach from A836 past Borgie Forest. There is a track south-wards and the walk is about one mile. The loch is a quarter of a mile long by that same distance wide and fishing is managed by the Tongue and District Angling Club. This is an excellent loch containing good trout and the most favoured fishing area is amongst the bays and headlands in the south-east corner and around the island in the north-west bay. Use standard loch fly patterns.

LOCH HOPE   9/460540

Permission: Altnaharra Fishings, Altnaharra, by Lairg, Sutherland.
Tel: Lairg (054981) 225

Loch Hope is one of the most beautiful lochs in all Scotland and lies between Tongue and Durness south of the A838. It contains trout but the main interest to anglers is the sea trout fishing and most visitors concentrate on them. Have a look, it's a lovely loch in superb surroundings.

THE CAPE WRATH HOTEL FISHINGS   9/381662

Permission: Altnaharra Hotel, Altnaharra, by Lairg, Sutherland.
Tel: Altnaharra (054981) 222;
Ben Loyal Hotel, Tongue, Sutherland.
Tel: Tongue (085755) 222

The Cape Wrath Hotel offers to guests and visitors some of the best trout fishing in Scotland. The hotel and lochs are in an area of great natural beauty and this is Scotland at its finest; a remote wonderland of hills, mountains, rushing streams and secret lochs. Every aspect of game fishing is offered from salmon and sea trout in the River Dionard to the mighty trout of the limestone lochs and the superb hard-fighting, wild brown trout of the lochs on the Cape Wrath peninsula. I highly recommend the Cape Wrath Hotel fishings and whilst nothing is certain in fishing I would like to quote from a letter I received concerning a visit made during the 1981 season. This will explain very clearly what makes the Cape Wrath Hotel fishings so highly praised. 'My best fish were 4 lb. 10 oz. from Loch Caladail, 3 lb. 9 oz. from Borralie and 2 lb. 10 oz. from Lanlish. I had lots of trout of 1½ lb. from Caladail. I also had three days salmon fishing on the River Dionard and had a total of 4 salmon and 3 sea trout. I am going again in late July and early August of next year.' I'm not surprised either.

LOCH CROISPOL   9/390680

Permission: Cape Wrath Hotel, Keoldale, Lairg, Sutherland.
Tel: Durness (097181) 274

Croispol lies to the west of Balnakeil Craft Village, is limestone, perfect and contains beautifully marked trout. Both boat and bank

5 *The ones that didn't get away.*

fishing are allowed but, apart from the west shore, the rest of the bank is private. All trout under ¾ lb. must be returned to the water and the average weight is just over 1 lb. The best trout taken during the 1981 season weighed 6½ lb. If there is a good wind then use the standard loch fly patterns but otherwise dry fly and nymphing will produce the best results. There is one deep hole which should be avoided but apart from that fish rise and are taken all round the loch particularly round the edge of the weed beds. Croispol trout fight hard and leap like sea trout. A carefully presented dry fly on a warm summer evening should do the trick – just make sure you are using strong enough tackle.

LOCH CALADAIL 9/397667

Permission: Cape Wrath Hotel, Keoldale, Lairg, Sutherland.
Tel: Durness (097181) 274

This limestone loch is to the east of the A838. Both boat and bank fishing are available but the hotel bank fishing is restricted to the west side of the loch. All fish under 1 lb. must be returned to the water and an average basket should produce 3 trout. Caladail trout are beautifully golden with bright pink flesh. Avoid the deep water at the northern end, the rest of the loch fishes well since there are good weed beds even in the middle. A basket taken during 1981 on the dry fly during August consisted of 6 fish weighing 14 lb. and trout of 4–6 lb. are common. Most anglers fish with a six-pound breaking strain cast. Use the dap in a strong wind or standard loch fly patterns. Watch out for sunken dry stone dykes – and very large trout.

LOCH LANLISH 9/385684

Permission: Cape Wrath Hotel, Keoldale, Lairg, Sutherland.
Tel: Durness (097181) 274

This small limestone loch lies to the north of the Cape Wrath Hotel and holds the largest fish. They are also the most difficult to get out. All fish under 2 lb. must be returned so that gives you some idea of the size of the rest. These trout are of excellent quality both physically and mentally and do not give themselves up easily. However, with that in mind you should not leave Cape Wrath without having a go at least once. Fishing is from the bank only and dry fly can work well as could the standard loch fly patterns, or nymphing, or sedges – just keep trying. To encourage you I may say that the best trout during 1981 was a fish of 6 lb. In the 'thirties and 'forties trout of over 10 lb. were common but a sample basket taken during 1981 is still pretty respectable; 3 trout weighing 12½ lb. This is a loch for the experienced angler so don't be too upset if you return fishless, but approach the subject with great hope and confidence – you might just be lucky.

LOCH BORRALIE   9/384670
Permission: Cape Wrath Hotel, Keoldale, Lairg, Sutherland
Tel: Durness (097181) 274

This is the largest of the limestone lochs and the water is as clear as crystal. Consequently poor casting will scare everything within miles. A good wind helps and the finer the tackle the better the chance you have of catching one of the beautiful Borralie trout. All fish under 1 lb. must be returned and the average weight here is 1½–1¾ lb. These trout are perfectly shaped, spotted, and of a Loch Leven strain and Borralie also contains excellent char. Some of these char weigh over 1 lb. and the best time to have a go at them is on a warm summer evening. Depending upon the strength of the wind try dapping or the standard loch fly patterns. Otherwise use the dry fly, Olives, Stone Flys, Sedges and Nymphs. The most productive area to fish is where the loch begins to deepen, about 6 to 10 feet from the shore. Another excellent area is in the shallow triangle south of the island off the east shore. Four fish from this loch will weigh about 6–7 lb. and the best trout last season (1981) was a fish of 5 lb. There are much larger trout in Borralie and fish of up to 10 lb. can be confidently expected.

LOCH INSHORE   9/330696
Permission: Cape Wrath Hotel, Keoldale, Lairg, Sutherland.
Tel: Durness (097181) 274

A small loch to the north of the only road on the Cape Wrath peninsula. Take the ferry from Keoldale and thence either by foot or minibus. Standard loch fly patterns work well and it is unlikely that you will be disturbed by anything other than the sound of rising trout. Remote and beautiful and a basket of up to 30 trout weighing possibly 12–14 lb.

LOCH BAD AN FHEUR-LOCH   9/338672
LOCH AIRIGH NA BEINNE   9/325663
Permission: Cape Wrath Hotel, Keoldale, Lairg, Sutherland.
Tel: Durness (097181) 274

Cross the Kyle and follow up the Daill River. Bad an Fheur is first and contains brown trout which average three to the pound.

There is the possibility of a salmon or sea trout in August depending on how much rain there has been. Beinne is the same with regards to fish and both these lochs are delightfully remote and infrequently fished. Standard loch fly patterns will suffice and your day out should produce a good basket of fine trout.

LOCH NA GAINMHICH   9/306658
LOCH NA GLAIC TARSUINN   9/298662
LOCH NA GLAMHAICHD   9/290668
Permission: Cape Wrath Hotel, Keoldale, Lairg, Sutherland.
Tel: Durness (097181) 274

These three lochs lie to the south of the Cape Wrath road and involve a walk of about 3 miles. This is wonderful scenery, provided that the weather is kind and all the lochs contain hard-fighting, small brown trout. Fishing is from the bank and large baskets of trout can be had. Standard loch fly patterns work well and none of these lochs are overfished. A whole season can pass without a visit and the beauty of the scenery and peace of the area will more than reward you for your effort.

LOCH KEISGAIG   9/267680
Permission: Cape Wrath Hotel, Keoldale, Lairg, Sutherland.
Tel: Durness (097181) 274

This is the best loch on Cape Wrath and it lies 6 miles south of the lighthouse. Cross the Kyle and take the minibus out towards the lighthouse. Get off the bus where the Kearvaig River passes under the road and strike out south. Make sure that you are properly equipped and that people know where you are going. Loch Keisgaig is approximately 700 yards long by about 250 yards wide. It holds a large stock of $\frac{1}{2}$–$\frac{3}{4}$ lb. trout but also some nice fish of between $1\frac{1}{2}$–$2\frac{1}{2}$ lb. As you can imagine it is not over-fished and the walk out is well worth while. Standard loch fly patterns will be all you will need. Perfect, remote and beautiful.

THE SCOURIE HOTEL FISHINGS   9/156448
Permission: The Scourie Hotel, Scourie, Sutherland.
Tel: Scourie (0971) 2396

It is impossible to describe properly and do justice to all the fishing available to guests and visitors to the Scourie Hotel. There are over 200 lochs available, all containing brown trout which vary in size from bright $\frac{1}{2}$ lb. fish to monsters of 5 lb. and more.

The hotel reserves the fishing for guests but visitors are always found a loch and Ian Hay of the Scourie Hotel is a keen angler himself and always ready to help. Scourie Hotel operates a fishing rota which makes sure that during the course of their visit guests have the opportunity to fish the water of their choice and no loch is bookable in advance. This is one of the best fishing hotels in Scotland with a very friendly and welcoming atmosphere.

PARSONS LOCH   9/187422

Permission: Scourie Hotel, Scourie, Sutherland.
Tel: Scourie (0971) 2396

Parsons Loch lies in the hills to the east of Scourie and is one of the ten lochs which make up a 'beat' at the Scourie Hotel. The trout in Parsons are small, ½ lb. but from time to time larger fish are caught and in the other lochs on the beat are excellent trout with fish of 2 lb. plus being taken each season. Walk out to Parsons Loch from the shepherd's hut on the A894 at Geisgeil near Loch Bad nam Mult. All the fishing is from the bank and wading is not really required since the loch is deep close to the shore. Black Pennell, Grouse and Claret, Invicta, and other standard patterns work well.

LOCH EILEAN NA CRAOIBHE MOIRE   9/209435

Permission: Scourie Hotel, Scourie, Sutherland.
Tel: Scourie (0971) 2396

Hutchinson's Loch, as it is commonly known and quicker said, lies to the south of Scourie between Gorm Chnoc and Creaga'Chlar Locha. Leave the car at the west end of Loch a'Bhag Ghainmhich and follow the burn up and round Loch a'Mhuirt. Hutchinson's Loch is about half a mile further south. The trout here fight very well indeed and there are 16 other lochs on this beat all with good fish and never enough time to fish them all. Such is life at Scourie. The loch shelves quickly so wading isn't necessary and all the old favourite flies work well.

LOCH NAN UIDH   9/195415

Permission: Scourie Hotel, Scourie, Sutherland.
Tel: Scourie (0971) 2396

This is a long straggle of lochs lying to the east of the A894 a few miles south of Scourie. Walk out from the same starting point as for Parson's Loch at the shepherd's hut. Apart from the two miles or so of main loch, there are several smaller lochs and lochans which have excellent trout. One of them, on the hill to the north of Uidh, has really large trout with fish of 5–6 lb. lurking in the depths. The scenery is magnificent. Foinaven (908m), Arkle (757m) and Ben Stack (721m) are never out of sight for long and neither are the fish. Loch nan Uidh has lots of ½–¾ lb. trout and several fish of 2 lb. and more. There is a good boat available and the eastern end of the loch fishes best, particularly round the island in the bay where the boat is moored. Bank fishing produces just as good results and all the standard loch fly patterns will attract fish. To the south of Uidh lie two of the most perfect trout lochs in all of Scotland, beautiful, peaceful and remote. If there are trout lochs in the hereafter, then they will most probably look like them. Fine fishing in grand surroundings.

LOCH AN TIGH SHELG   9/297486
Permission: Scourie Hotel, Scourie, Sutherland.
Tel: Scourie (0971) 2396

Beat 6 on the Scourie Hotel waters. Start at Loch Stack Lodge and follow the path out round Arkle towards Foinaven. The distance is about 5 miles but the track is easy. At the end, you will find a series of lochs, all containing good wild brown trout. The principal water, Tigh Shelg, produces fish in the order of ¾ lb. upwards and in 1985 our party took home 9 good trout. All bank fishing. Also fish the inlet stream; this can give great sport, particularly after heavy rain.

GORM LOCH   9/215446
Permission: Scourie Hotel, Scourie, Sutherland.
Tel: Scourie (0971) 2396

Park at 183450. Follow the gully up onto the moor and head south-west. You should take a compass since it is very easy to become lost in these hills. The first large water you pass, on your left, is Loch a'Mhuirt – The Murder Loch – which contains large numbers of small trout. Gorm Loch is divided neatly into two sections and there is a boat moored at 211444. Finding the channel through to the island-clad north section is not so easy as it looks; nor is finding your way back – so do make sure you mark well the narrow channel. Great sport on the main loch and in the surrounding smaller lochs and lochans.

LOCH EILEANACH   9/244426
Permission: Scourie Hotel, Scourie, Sutherland.
Tel: Scourie (0971) 2396

There is a stone building by the side of the A838 at 265438, just
before Loch Stack. Park here and look for the stalkers' path up
Ben Stack. Follow it – after a while you will be unaware of the
deep thumping in your chest and just feel numb. The little loch to
your right, on the way up the hill, is Loch na Seilge, with its
single island – lots of small fish here. March on and after about 45
minutes you will see the straggle of Eileanach sparkling silver at
the bottom of the track. Excellent fish of up to 3 lb. are regularly
taken from this delightful series of lochs. Make the effort – it's
well worth while.

LOCH CROCACH   15/197395
Permission: Scourie Hotel, Scourie, Sutherland.
Tel: Scourie (0971) 2396

Follow the A894 south from Scourie to Kylesku and at 184384
look out for the old road, on your left. Crocach is a short, stiff
walk up the hill to the north. Again, as with all the Scourie
fishings, you would be well advised to go with map and compass
at the ready: it is very easy to get lost – I know, I have done it
myself, in spite of the fact that I am familiar with most of the
waters. There is a boat at the end of the walk and a loch which
contains fish of up to 4 lb. and more. If the main loch proves
dour, have a cast in some of the smaller lochs surrounding it –
you might get a very pleasant surprise.

DUARTMORE   15/205370
Permission: Scourie Hotel, Scourie, Sutherland.
Tel: Scourie (0971) 2396

Duartmore has improved greatly over recent years, largely due to
the food escaping from the fish farm. Trout are excellent, averaging ¾ lb., and there is a good boat available for guests. Easy
access makes this loch a good place to rest from the daily hikes
out to the other Scourie waters.

LOCH STACK   9/300425
LOCH MORE   15/330372
Permission: The Westminster Estate, Estate Office, Achfary, Lairg.
Tel: Lochmore (097184) 221

Although these lochs contain good brown trout, they are most famous for their salmon and sea trout fishing. They lie 31 miles north of Lairg alongside the A838 and all fishing is from boats. Bank fishing is not allowed. Bookings are only taken the day before fishing is required and anglers should contact the estate office the evening before to see if a boat is available. On Stack all anglers must use the services of a gillie from the estate and detailed information concerning the best place to fish will be provided by them. Excellent salmon and sea trout but suggest you try further north for brown trout.

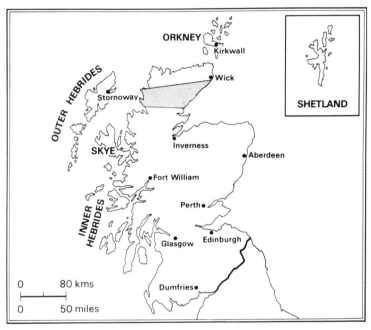

Map 7 *Sutherland*

3 Sutherland

Many of the large lochs described in this section contain **ferrox** and Loch Assynt and Loch Shin produce trout of up to 9 lb. each season. All the lochs will provide good sport in attractive surroundings. Do be careful of high winds though. A sudden storm on Loch Shin can bear a marked resemblance to a rough crossing of the Pentland Firth and you must be able to cope. The same applies when walking in the hills. Always make sure that someone knows where you are going and when you expect to return – far better safe than sorry. The Assynt Angling Club controls most of the lochs in the Lochinver area and many of them are stocked regularly by the club. The club also produces an excellent brochure which is a must for anyone visiting the area for the first time. Assynt and the Inchnadamph National Nature Reserve are among the most attractive and interesting areas in the north and contain a wealth of prehistoric remains, underground passages and important and rare flora with alpine plants growing strongly amidst the limestone outcrops. This is a lovely area which will please and impress you, and send you home refreshed – with a full basket of fine trout.

LOCH CUL FRAIOCH   15/025330
Permission: Tourist Information Office, Lochinver, Sutherland.
Tel: Lochinver (05714) 330

This is a wild, beautiful loch near the cliffs on the Point of Stoer. The name means 'the loch behind the heath' and Cul Fraioch is about a mile long by 700 yards wide. The loch has a reputation for being dour but it is stocked and the trout average ¾ lb. A basket of four fish would be considered good but on a good day much better baskets are taken. Boats are available for the visitor and bank fishing is also allowed though it is not as productive as fishing from the boat. Use standard loch fly patterns.

LOCHAN SGEIREACH   15/040290
Permission: Tourist Information Office, Lochinver, Sutherland.
Tel: Lochinver (05714) 330

Lochan Sgeireach lies to the north of the village of Stoer adjacent to the B869. It is easily accessible and about 350 yards long by 100

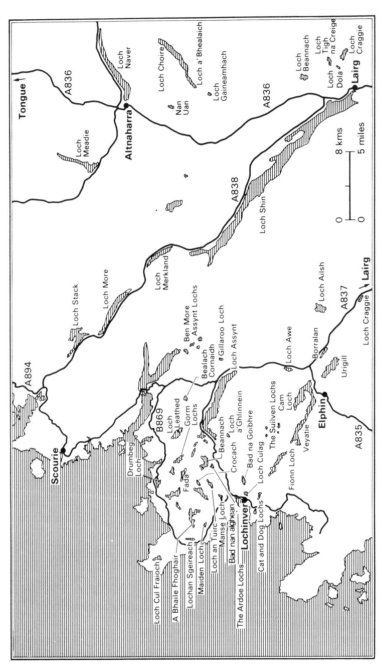

Map 8 *Lochinver, Assynt and Lairg*

yards wide. Fishing is from the bank only and wading requires care. Fishing is managed by the Assynt Angling Club and the trout average ½ lb. Good baskets are taken and the roadside position of the loch makes it popular with visitors.

THE MAIDEN LOCH 15/050268
Permission: Tourist Information Office, Lochinver, Sutherland.
Tel: Lochinver (05714) 330

The Maiden Loch lies adjacent to the B869 near Clachtoll. It is one of a series of small trout-filled lochs which extend from the Bay of Stoer to Drumbeg. Bank fishing only here, and the average weight of fish is ½–¾ lb. The Maiden Loch is joined by a short stream to Loch na Airighe Bige and this is also worth fishing, particularly round the island. Use standard pattern loch flies.

LOCH LEATHED A' BHAILE FHOGHAIR
15/055280
Permission: Tourist Information Office, Lochinver, Sutherland.
Tel: Lochinver (05714) 330

This is a good trout loch lying to the east of the B869 near Clachtoll. The loch is 800 yards long by 100 yards wide and both boat and bank fishing are allowed. The Assynt Angling Club controls the fishing and has stocked the loch in the past. The trout average ¾ lb. and fish of up to 4 lb. have been caught as well and an average day should bring you about 6 fish. A basket taken during 1981 contained 4 trout weighing 3 lb. Standard loch fly patterns work well. This loch is also known as Lexy's loch and the name means 'the loch of the echoes'. Easily accessible and well worth a visit.

LOCH AN ARBHAIR 15/079189
Permission: Tourist Information Office, Lochinver, Sutherland.
Tel: Lochinver (05714) 330

Also known as the Cat Loch, this small loch is easily accessible and lies close to the road south of Inverkirkcaig. Fishing is managed by the Assynt Angling club which stocks the loch regularly. Trout rise well all over the loch and both boat and bank fishing are available. Standard pattern loch flies in 12–14 dressings work well and during the 1981 season they caught 57 trout weighing 41¼ lb. during one week. Excellent fishing in very pleasant surroundings.

LOCH A'CHOIN   15/083186

Permission: Tourist Information Office, Lochinver, Sutherland.
Tel: Lochinver (05714) 330

Loch a'Choin lies next to Loch an Arbhair and is also known as
the Dog Loch. South of Inverkirkcaig, it is easily accessible and
contains trout which average ½ lb. The Assynt Angling Club
which manages the loch has tried rainbow trout in the Dog Loch,
but without much success. Bank and boat fishing are available and
an average basket would hold about 5 fish weighing 3½ lb. Small,
standard pattern loch flies and the Dunkeld seem to do very well.
Very pleasant surroundings.

LOCH CULAG   15/098217

Permission: The Culag Hotel, Lochinver, Sutherland.
Tel: Lochinver (05714) 209

Loch Culag lies to the south of Lochinver and holds salmon, sea
trout and brown trout. Fishing is controlled by the Culag Hotel
and guests have priority. This is a very shallow loch with an
average depth of only 3½ feet and fishes best in a strong wind.
Fishing from the boat only, which is locked to the Hydro Board
pole. Brown trout are small and the loch is of more interest to
salmon anglers.

THE MANSE LOCH   15/095248

Permission: Tourist Information Office, Lochinver, Sutherland.
Tel: Lochinver (05714) 330

The Manse Loch is a small loch to the north of Lochinver and is
part of the Loch Roe system. The excellent Assynt Angling Club
manages the fishing and during the past few years has stocked the
Loch Roe system with over 120,000 sea trout fry. Sea trout
fishing on the Manse Loch is best during August and the fish
average 1½ lb. The brown trout in the loch average ½–¾ lb. and
have a reputation for being hard to catch. A normal basket should
bring you 3–4 fish and trout of 1¾ lb. have been caught. Use
standard loch fly patterns.

LOCH BAD NA GOIBHRE   15/107227

Permission: The Culag Hotel, Lochinver, Sutherland.
Tel: Lochinver (05714) 209

This is a small, shallow loch to the east of Lochinver and it holds
very good trout indeed. Bank fishing only and the trout are pink-
fleshed and fighting fit. This is an easily accessible loch and hotel
guests have priority. Standard loch fly patterns.

LOCH CROCACH   15/105275
Permission: Culag Hotel, Lochinver, Sutherland.
Tel: Lochinver (05714) 209

Hotel guests have priority and visitors should call at the hotel to
request permission to fish. This is a very lovely loch and a good
track leads out to it from the B869 north of Lochinver, at Rhicarn.
Crocach is a shallow loch with an average depth of 15 feet and is
1½ miles long by a half a mile wide at its widest point. Both boat
and bank fishing are available and the loch has a multitude of
small islands which makes for interesting and exciting fishing.
The average weight is ¾–1 lb. and all the standard loch fly
patterns produce results. Baskets of up to 30 fish are often taken
on Crocach and this loch is also an important nesting area for
birds. A very lovely loch indeed and worth fishing.

LOCH AN TUIRC   15/115260
Permission: Tourist Information Office, Lochinver, Sutherland.
Tel: Lochinver (05714) 330

Loch an Tuirc lies at the head of the Loch Roe system and is
joined to the Manse Loch by Allt Loch an Tuirc Burn. Bank
fishing is not allowed and Loch an Tuirc is a scattered loch of
narrow bays and sheltered corners. It is in a delightful setting and
contains good trout which average ¾ lb. A recent basket contained 22 trout weighing 14 lb. and fish rise well to all the
standard loch fly patterns.

LOCH BAD NAN ALGHEAN   15/133256
Permission: Tourist Information Office, Lochinver, Sutherland.
Tel: Lochinver (05714) 330

This is a small triangular shaped loch and it lies to the north of the
A837 near Little Assynt. Fishing is managed by the Assynt
Angling Club and at present is from the bank only. The average
size of the trout is ½–¾ lb. and baskets of 8–12 fish are common.
Larger trout used to be taken from the loch but these days they
seem to be staying out of sight and out of trouble. The loch
is about 700 yards by 500 and fish rise all round the shore.
Easily accessible and pleasant to fish. Use standard loch pattern
flies.

LOCH BEANNACH 15/140265

Permission: Tourist Information Office, Lochinver, Sutherland.
Tel: Lochinver (05714) 330

This is a shallow, island-dotted loch to the north of the A873 at
Little Assynt. It is 1¾ miles long by some 600 yards wide and at
its deepest, 40 feet. It is joined to Loch Bad nan Alghean and
fishing is managed by the Assynt Angling Club. The club has two
boats on the loch and there is also a Culag Hotel boat. The
average weight of trout is ½–¾ lb. and baskets of 10–20 fish are
often caught. A sample of what this lovely loch can produce is a
basket caught during 1981 of 12 trout weighing 7½ lb. This is a
rocky loch so take care when wading or using the boat. Standard
loch pattern flies work well and fish rise and are caught all over
the loch. A perfect spot for a picnic with the family since
Beannach is not too far to walk.

LOCH A'GHLINNEIN 15/170234

Permission; Tourist Information Office, Lochinver, Sutherland.
Tel: Lochinver (05741) 330

Loch a'Ghlinnein lies to the south of the A837 and is approached
from Little Assynt and the western end of Loch Assynt. Cross the
bridge over the River Inver and follow the track to the right for a
few hundred yards. Then turn left up the Allt an Tiaghaich burn
and this will lead you to the loch. It is a circular loch and fishing is
from the bank only. The north-east corner is the best fishing area
but a lot depends upon the direction of the wind. Best results
come in a good wind and the trout are of excellent quality, pink-
fleshed and averaging ¾ lb. Standard loch fly patterns will do.

THE ARDOE LOCHS

LOCH INEIG	15/080243
LOCHAN AN TAIRBH	15/085240
LOCH DUBH	15/074240
LOCH NA GAINEAMHAICH	15/076233
LOCH CAMUS NA FRITHEARACHD	15/069233
LOCH BRAIGH A'BHAILE	15/066237
LOCH THORMAID	15/066235

Permission: Tourist Information Office, Lochinver, Sutherland.
Tel: Lochinver (05741) 330

All these lochs are looked after by the Assynt Angling Club who
also make them available to visitors. The Club ploughs back all

the money received from the sale of permits into loch improvement works in order to make better fishing for both resident and visitor alike and they deserve every angler's fullest support in their selfless work. The lochs lie to the north west of Lochinver and may be approached either from the B869 or along the track that wends out onto the moor from Baddidarach on the north shore of sea Loch Inver. Expect to catch trout in the order of ½–¾ lb. in most waters and all fishing is from the bank.

LOCH ASSYNT   15/200250

Permission: Inchnadamph Hotel, Assynt, Lochinver, Sutherland.
Tel: Assynt (05712) 202;
Culag Hotel, Lochinver, Sutherland.
Tel: Lochinver (05714) 209

Loch Assynt lies adjacent to the A837 between Lochinver and Ledmore Junction. It is 6 miles long and, at its broadest point, one mile wide. The loch covers an area of 2,000 acres and to the north of the island of Eilean Assynt it drops to nearly 300 feet in depth.

6   *Ardvreck Castle, Loch Assynt.*

Best results on Assynt come from the boat and whilst bank fishing is allowed it can be dangerous due to the depth of water close to the shore. Assynt is prone to sudden gales and an outboard motor makes life a lot easier. But beware of underwater obstructions or you might lose the propeller. Loch Assynt contains salmon, sea trout and brown trout. About 50 salmon were taken during the latter part of the 1981 season and fish tend to stay in the loch all summer. Trout average ½–¾ lb. and a reasonable large ferox and 1981 saw a 9 lb. trout caught. Each year since then, Assynt has continued to produce some whoppers: 1984, 3 fish weighing 20 lb. 8 oz.; 1985, 2 trout over 7 lb.; and by June 1986 (the time of writing) another 2 fish of over 8 lb. had been caught. There are also fish of 3–4 lb. and they are occasionally taken on the fly. The best fishing areas on Assynt are in the shallow water close to the shore. Eilean Assynt bay and round the island is a favourite spot and a long drift down the north shore from Rubh an Doire Chuilinn should produce results. The southern end of the loch is also very good as are the two bays on either side of the ruins of Ardvreck Castle. Montrose was imprisoned in this gaunt, grim castle before being taken to Edinburgh and execution in 1560. The Assynt area is very beautiful and offers the visitor an unmatched host of interesting things to see and do. There are underground caves and passages, prehistoric remains, superb wild flowers and incredible scenery. All this and fishing too. What angler could ask for more?

LOCH BEALACH CORNAIDH   15/209282
Permission: Inchnadamph Hotel, Assynt, Lochinver, Sutherland.
*Tel:*Assynt (05712) 202

As far as possible choose a good day since the walk out to Bealach Cornaidh is quite long and the countryside wild and windswept. This loch lies on the upper slopes of the east face of Quinag (808m), and is a delightful loch to fish. The trout are not very large, averaging three to the pound but the setting is majestic and there is always the chance of a larger fish – if you can tempt them to rise. Approach from the A894 Skiag Bridge–Unapool road. Two miles north of Skiag Bridge you will see a clearly defined track on your left. Follow this track for 1¼ miles and where it ends go straight on and follow the Allt na Bradhan burn up to the loch. An exciting loch in superb surroundings and well worth a visit.

LOCH AWE   15/245154
Permission: Inchnadamph Hotel, Assynt, Lochinver, Sutherland.
Tel: Assynt (05712) 202

Unlike its namesake further south the Sutherland Loch Awe is
small and shallow. It lies close to the A837 between Inchnadamph
and Ledmor Junction and is ¾ mile long by 500 yards wide. The
occasional salmon makes its way up the River Loanan depending
on water conditions and the loch holds good trout. The average
depth of Loch Awe is only 5 feet so it tends to become a bit
weedy during the season, but the weeds provide good cover for
the fish. The best areas to fish are round the several islands and
baskets of 4–6 fish would be considered reasonable. Use standard
loch fly patterns.

LOCH A'CHOIRE DHUIBH
LOCH A'CHOIRE DHERIG   15/252272
LOCH BEALACH A'BHUIRICH   15/262280
LOCH A'CHOIRE GHUIRM   15/262268
Permission: Inchnadamph Hotel, Assynt, Lochinver, Sutherland.
Tel: Assynt (05712) 202

These lochs lie in the high corries and gullies of the Ben More
Assynt range. They are not too difficult to get to but make sure
you are properly attired and that people know where you are
heading. Start off from Loch na Gainmich on the Skiag Bridge–
Unapool road. Follow the rough track round the north end of the
loch up into the hills. Loch a'Choire Dhuibh holds small fish but
the other three are considered to be among the best in the area.
There are excellent trout here and of course the setting is perfect.
As an added bonus – if the fish are not rising – walk on to the
spectacular Eas Coul waterfall. After heavy rain this is a
thunderous splash of silver cascading 600 feet down the face of
Leitir Dhubh. The translation of Eas Coul is 'maiden's tresses'. In
its downward plunge the waterfall splits into several strands
against the rock face and from a distance gives the impression of
strands of hair. Don't underestimate the walk/climb, but get there
if you can. Standard pattern loch flies will do.

LOCH MAOL A'CHOIRE   15/276194
Permission: Inchnadamph Hotel, Assynt, Lochinver, Sutherland.
Tel: Assynt (05712) 202

This loch is better known as the Gillaroo Loch because of the
similarity of the trout it used to hold to the famous Irish fish of

that name. It's a long time since any were caught in Sutherland, however, and the loch has now been stocked with brown trout. The trout average ¾ lb. and the southern end where the feeder burn enters is a good fishing area. This is a small, shallow loch beautifully situated on the slopes of Ben More Assynt (998m) and there is a good track up which starts off just behind the Inchnadamph Hotel. Standard loch fly patterns will do fine.

LOCH DRUMBEG   15/117326
Permission: Drumbeg Hotel, Assynt, by Lairg, Sutherland.
Tel: Drumbeg (05713) 236

Loch Drumbeg is a scattered loch full of bays and points with several tree-covered islands. It is easily accessible and lies adjacent to the B869 to the west of the village. The loch contains brown trout with an average weight of ½–¾ lb but fish of up to 1½ lb. are taken regularly and trout of over 2 lb. are sometimes caught. An average day should produce a basket of 6 trout and catches of 8–10 fish are frequent. A sample basket from the 1981 season had 8 fish weighing 5½ lb. with the heaviest trout weighing 1½ lb. Both boat and bank fishing are allowed but best results come from the boat. The loch is divided into two sections by a channel known as the 'narrows'. The eastern shore of the west bay is the best place to fish whilst in the main section of the loch the best sport is to be found round the islands and in the vicinity of the feeder burn which enters in the south bay. Best flies include Claret Dun, Greenwell's Glory, Black Pennell, Blue and Black Butcher. Hotel guests have priority.

LOCH SKERRACH   15/119308
Permission: Drumbeg Hotel, Assynt, by Lairg, Sutherland.
Tel: Drumbeg (05713) 236

This small loch is adjacent to the peat track that leads southwards from the Drumbeg Hotel. Fishing is from the bank only and the average weight of the Skerrach trout is ¾–1 lb. A basket of 3 fish should weigh about 2½ lb. and trout of up to 1½ lb. are sometimes caught. Loch Skerrach fishes well all over but the best areas are along the western bank and in the south-east corner. Use Nymphs, Blae and Black, Invicta and Red Sedge. June and July are the best months to fish this lovely little loch. But be warned, the midges think so too. Hotel guests have priority.

LOCHAN FADA
LOCH AN TOLLA BHAID
LOCH NA LOINNE

15/113304
15/117295
15/126293

Permission: Drumbeg Hotel, Assynt, by Lairg, Sutherland.
Tel: Drumbeg (05713) 236

These three lochs lie to the south of Drumbeg and are an easy walk from the west end of Loch Drumbeg. There is a good peat track for the first 2 miles. Where it ends, walk westwards to Loch Fada. Fish down the loch to where the burn runs out at the southern end. Follow this burn and within half a mile it will bring you to Tolla Bhaid and thence eastwards to Na Loinne. The trout in these lochs are bright little fish averaging three to the pound and baskets of 20 or more fish are common. However, they are a delight to fish, remote and peaceful and a wonderful place to spend a day. Fishing is from the bank and trout rise to all the standard pattern loch flies. Rowan and birch clad shore lines, bays and points and solitude. Well worthwhile.

GORM LOCH MOR
GORM LOCH BEAG

15/142298
15/143288

Permission: Drumbeg Hotel, Assynt, by Lairg, Sutherland.
Tel: Drumbeg (05713) 236

These lochs lie to the south of Drumbeg and are approached from Nedd on the B869. Follow the surfaced track southwards for half a mile to the crofts. A grass track leads on from here. After a quarter of a mile strike south-east over the ridge near Loch a'Bhraighe. The boat on Mor is moored at the top end of the loch (139304). The trout on Gorm Loch Mor average three to the pound but fight very hard indeed. Six to eight trout will weigh up to 2½ lb. and the best flies to use are Invicta, Greenwell's Glory, Black Pennell, and Mallard and Claret. Fishing is best from the boat, and round the two islands in the main section of the loch can be a very productive area to fish. The southern bay, where the burn runs in from Loch Odhar, can also be very good. The best way of getting to Gorm Loch Beag is to take the boat down Mor to the southern end and walk over the shoulder of Gorm Chnoc. Beag is deeper and more dour than Mor and the trout average ½–¾ lb. Three fish will weigh 2–2¾ lb. and there are fish of 1½ lb. which may be tempted from time to time. A boat is available here as well and the best places to fish are round the rocky bays along the eastern shore. Best flies on Beag are Invicta, Silver Butcher, Red Sedge, and Blue and Black Zulu. Hotel guests have priority.

LOCH BORRALAN   15/260110

Permission: Inchnadamph Hotel, Assynt, Lochinver, Sutherland.
Tel: Assynt (05712) 202;
Culag Hotel, Lochinver, Sutherland.
Tel: Lochinver (05714) 209

Loch Borralan is adjacent to the A837 near Ledmore Junction and
is a shallow weedy loch, one mile long by quarter of a mile wide.
It holds char, some large ferrox and ½–¾ lb. brown trout. A
basket of 10 fish would weigh 6 lb. and trout rise and are caught
all over the loch. Two boats are available. Borralan has a mayfly
hatch in mid June/early July and during this period the loch is
alive with feeding fish. Bank fishing can be quite productive but
best results come from the boat. All the standard loch fly patterns
bring results and the surrounding scenery is perfect with Cul Mor
(849m), Suilven (731m) and Canisp (846m) dominating the
western horizon.

LOCH URIGILL   15/240100

Permission: Inchnadamph Hotel, Assynt, Lochinver, Sutherland.
Tel: Assynt (05712) 202;
Culag Hotel, Lochinver, Sutherland.
Tel: Lochinver (05714) 209

Urigill lies to the south of Borralan and although considerably
larger suffers from a prolific growth of weed, which makes
fishing difficult as the season progresses. The best time to fish
Urigill is during the mayfly hatch in June and July when baskets
of 30–40 trout are often taken. The average weight on this loch is
½ lb. but there are ferrox and they are caught by trolling. Fish of
1–1½ lb. are taken from time to time, most often at the back end
when fish move up the feeder burns to spawn. All the standard
loch fly patterns work well and the best areas to fish are round the
islands in the south-west corner and in the vicinity of the feeder
burns along the eastern shore. The loch is best approached by
rowing over Borralan from the hotel and following the track to
the boats. These are moored in the small bay halfway down the
north bank and adjacent to the small island. Excellent results can
be had bank fishing on Urigill and wading is reasonably
comfortable.

7   *Three Assynt monsters weighing a total of 20 lb. 8 oz.*

CAM LOCH   15/210140
Permission: Altnacealgach Hotel, Elphin, by Lairg, Sutherland.
Tel: Elphin (085484) 231

Cam is a large, beautiful loch fed by crystal clear streamlets that
tumble into the loch from the slopes of Suilven and Canisp. The
southern end of the loch is adjacent to the A835 at Elphin and the
loch is 3 miles long by three-quarters of a mile wide. Boats are
moored directly below the little cemetery near Elphin where there
is adequate parking space also. The first bay on Cam is often
sheltered when the rest of the loch is very wild and good sport can
be had round Eilean na Gartaig. The bay at the east end can also
be productive as are the bays on either side of the narrows along
the west shore. Keep close to the shore when fishing Cam. This is
a very deep loch and the water shelves very quickly only yards
from the edge. Be very cautious before you step out of the boat.
Apart from *ferox*, Cam holds a good stock of ½–¾ lb. trout and
a basket of 10–12 fish should reward your day's efforts. The
mayfly hatch, if it comes, in June and July is the best time on Cam
and this is a very lovely loch to fish. Use standard loch fly
patterns, they all work well.

LOCH VEYATIE   15/190130
Permission:
Culag Hotel, Lochinver, Sutherland.
Tel: Lochinver (05714) 209;
Altnacealgach Hotel, Elphin, by Lairg, Sutherland.
Tel: Elphin (085484) 231

Loch Veyatie has a more sombre feel about it than neighbouring
Cam. Cul Mor (849m) towers over the water casting long
shadows and Suilven (731m) dominates the northern skyline.
Veyatie is a deep loch being 126 feet in the north end and, as with
Cam, visitors should be very cautious when landing from the
boat. The eastern end of the loch offers the best sport and the
shallows should be fished carefully. However, there are dozens of
bays and corners where fish can be caught and towards the end of
the loch, lying at right angles to it, is Loch a'Mhadail separated by
a narrow rock bar from the main loch. This loch can also produce
excellent sport and at times becomes joined to Veyatie. There are
no roads, tracks or footpaths in this wilderness of hills and lochs
and the surrounding scenery is as wild and untamed as any in
Scotland – as can be the weather. Try and take along an outboard
since a sudden storm could present difficulties on this 4 mile long
loch. Veyatie fishes best in a south-west or west wind and the
trout average ½–¾ lb. Ferrox are there as well but rarely rise to
the fly. Baskets of 20–40 fish come from Veyatie regularly and the
mayfly hatch during June and July and that is the time to be there.
Approach from Elphin. There is a good road down to the eastern
end of the loch where a fish farm has been established, and the key
for the gate may be obtained from the Culag Hotel. All the
standard loch fly patterns will catch fish.

FIONN LOCH   15/130176
Permission: The Culag Hotel. Lochinver, Sutherland.
Tel: Lochinver (05714) 209

This is the best loch in the area and lies in the valley formed by
Cul Mor to the south and Suilven to the north. Fionn is best
approached from Inverkirkaig to the south of Lochinver. Just
south of the village leave the car and follow the track through the
trees. It soon opens out and for 2½ miles follows the river up past
the Falls of Kirkaig. It is not a difficult walk and the views of
Suilven and Cul Mor are magnificent. Fionn is 2½ miles long by
about 500 yards wide. It holds first-class trout, the average weight
being ¾ lb. and in the deeper water, *ferox*. Baskets of 20–30 fish
are often taken and a good cast to start with might consist of Blue

Zulu, Invicta and Bloody Butcher. The loch has many delightful bays and headlands and trout are caught all over the loch. The western end is perhaps the most favoured and a number of feeder burns enter here. Fionn is beautiful – if the fish are not rising there could be few lovlier places upon which not to catch trout. Highly recommended.

THE SUILVEN LOCHS
LOCH DRUIM SUARDALAIN   15/115217
Permission: The Culag Hotel, Lochinver, Sutherland.
Tel: Lochinver (05714) 209

Suardalain lies to the south of Glencanisp Lodge and offers salmon, sea trout and good brown trout fishing. Trout are small, but fight well and baskets of up to 30 fish are common. Fishes best in a good wind.

LOCH SUILEAG   15/152218
Permission: Culag Hotel, Lochinver, Sutherland.
Tel: Lochinver (05714) 209

An hour's walk from the car park on the Glencanisp road brings you to this lovely hill loch with its tree-clad island. A boat is available for Culag Hotel guests and the fish have the reputation of being some of the hardest fighting trout in Assynt.

LOCH NA BARRACK   15/157188
Permission: Culag Hotel, Lochinver, Sutherland.
Tel: Lochinver (05714) 209

Na Barrack is the largest of the cluster of lochs that crowd below the grey heights of Caisteal Liath (the Grey Castle), highest point of Suilven (731m). All these lochs contain typical highland trout – and some very large fish as well. You will have a memorable day finding out for yourself where the big fish lie.

LOCH A'CHREISG   15/220155
LOCHAN FADA   15/206167
LOCH NA GAINIMH   15/175185
Permission: Culag Hotel, Lochinver, Sutherland.
Tel: Lochinver (05714) 209

Spend a whole day fishing the above lochs. Set out from the east end of Loch Cam, near Elphin at 229121, and follow the stalker's track along the shores of the loch. As the path climbs towards Canisp (846m) you will see a'Chreisg to your right. This is the perfect beginner's loch, full of bright little trout. Go back to the path and follow it westwards to Fada and Gainimh. If you have someone special you wish to introduce to hill walking and trout fishing, then there are few finer places to start.

LOCH CRAGGIE   15/325055
Permission: The Oykel Bridge Hotel, Rosehall, by Lairg, Sutherland.
Tel: Rosehall (054984) 218

This is a small, trout-filled loch adjacent to the A837 set in a small forest and joined to the River Oykel by a short stream. The average weight of fish is ½–¾ lb. and the best fishing area is in the vicinity of the two feeder burns. Craggie also has some rainbow trout and from time to time sea trout are caught. Standard loch fly patterns work well and this is an easily accessible and pleasantly situated loch. Be careful, it's deeper than it looks and drops to 40 feet in places.

LOCH AILSH   15/315110
Permission: The Oykel Bridge Hotel, Rosehall, by Lairg, Sutherland.
Tel: Rosehall (054984) 218

Loch Ailsh lies to the north of the A837 near Rosehall and is easily accessible via a good estate road. The hotel boats are moored at the south end of the loch and Benmore Lodge boats at the north end. Permission to fish may also be obtained by applying at the Lodge. Both boat and bank fishing are allowed on Loch Ailsh and outboard motors may also be used. The loch has a good stock of ¾ lb. brown trout and larger fish of 1½ lb. and over are often caught. The most productive fishing areas are round the islands and down the east bank. The north and south ends of the loch, where the River Oykel enters and leaves are also good fishing areas. Salmon and sea trout are occasionally caught in Loch Ailsh but that depends on the water level in the river Oykel. Best flies include Black Pennell, Soldier Palmer, Zulu and Butcher. The small island is a nesting site and during the early months of the season anglers must take care not to disturb the birds. Look by all means – if you have my sort of luck that's exactly when a monster trout will have a go. Ailsh is a first-class loch and well worth a visit.

LOCH SHIN   16/500160

Permission: Lairg Angling Club, J. M. Ross, Post Office, Lairg, Sutherland.
Tel: Lairg (0549) 2010

Loch Shin is 18 miles long by about one mile wide and is one of the largest lochs in Scotland. It gives the visitor to Sutherland his first real glimpse of the massive grandeur of the area and this vast water has a somewhat grim attractiveness of its own. Shin is a hydro-electric loch, water from the River Cassley being diverted into it via the power station below Maovally on the north-west shore. Shin is very deep and drops to over 200 feet in places. Fishing is for salmon, trout and char and both boat and bank fishing are allowed. An outboard motor is almost essential and these can be hired from the Lairg Angling Club. The A838 runs the full length of the east shore and makes access for bank fishing easy and indeed excellent baskets are taken from the shore. The average weight of trout is ½–¾ lb. and a reasonable day should produce a basket of 10–12 fish. Larger baskets are common and Shin has its fair share of *ferox* as well and trout of up to 12 lb. have been caught. The Lairg Angling Club 1981 competition was won with a basket of 26 trout weighing 12 lb. 5 oz. and the runner up had 19 fish weighing 9 lb. 1 oz. Best flies on Loch Shin include Black Pennell, Woodcock and Mixed, Silver Butcher, Peter Ross, Black Zulu, Invicta and Loch Ordie. Favourite fishing areas are round the bay opposite Fiag River on the north-east shore, Gull Island and in the shallower water at the north end of the loch near the power station.

LOCH CRAGGIE   16/625075

Permission: Sutherland Arms Hotel, Lairg, Sutherland.
Tel: Lairg (0549) 2016

This excellent loch lies to the north of Lairg and there is a good track to the boathouse. The fishing is let with holiday chalets and so it is advisable to inquire well in advance. Craggie is the best loch in the area and the fish average 1 lb. and are full of fight. A limit of 15 fish per day is placed on catches and is often reached. Fish of 3–4 lb. are frequently caught. There is one boat and bank fishing is not allowed. Fish rise and are caught all over the loch but the most favoured areas are in the south-west bay near the boathouse and along the south shore. Worm Fly, Greenwell's Glory, Black Zulu, Peter Ross and Soldier Palmer do particularly well.

LOCH DOLA   16/607080
LOCH TIGH NA CREIGE   16/615093
Permission: Sutherland Hotel, Lairg, Sutherland.
Tel: Lairg (0549) 2016

These two lochs lie to the west of Craggie and the fish they contain, though smaller, are more ready to rise to the fly. During one memorable hour in May 1986 I was catching ½–¾ lb. trout almost with every cast on Dola. There is a boat available but I think bank fishing is every bit as productive, particularly along the north shore by the ruins of the old boathouse.

Tigh na Creige is at the end of a good peat track, north of Dola. Great sport with bright little trout and the odd 'monster' of 2 lb. Again, the north shoreline seems to be the best area, particularly where a burn enters from Cnoc Neill. Standard pattern flies.

LOCH BEANNACH   16/599125
Permission: Sutherland Arms Hotel, Lairg, Sutherland.
Tel: Lairg (0549) 2291

Beannach lies to the east of the A836 and is sheltered by Dalchork Wood. The loch is three-quarters of a mile long by 700 yards wide and fishing is from the boat only. Trout average ½–¾ lb. and the eastern shore is the most productive area to fish particularly in the vicinity of the two small islands and the bay where the feeder burn enters the loch. Standard loch fly patterns do well.

LOCH MERKLAND   16/393310
Permission: Overscaig Hotel, by Lairg, Sutherland.
Tel: Merkland (054983) 203

Merkland is adjacent to the A838 Lairg–Scourie road and is 3 miles long by a quarter of a mile wide. It is a dramatic loch lying in a basin between the enfolding slopes of Meallan Liath Mor (683m) to the north and Creag nan Suibheag (465m) to the south. Merkland holds large ferrox and good stocks of ½–¾ lb. fish and the most favoured fishing area is in the northern end. This is a deep loch, 80 feet in places, so fish near to the shore. Standard loch fly patterns will do. The Overscaig Hotel also have fishing rights in several hill lochs in the area and these are all worth fishing.

LOCH NAN UAN 16/567292
Permission: Altnaharra Hotel, Altnaharra, Sutherland.
Tel: Altnaharra (054981) 222

A thousand feet up on the slopes of Ben Klibreck nan Uan is a small loch, half a mile long by 300 yards wide. This is a wild lonely country and the loch is approached from Vagastie on the A836 Lairg–Altnaharra road. The walk out is steep, long and rough but the quality of the trout makes it more than worth while. The 1979 season saw a trout of 7¾ lb. caught and 1981 produced a fish of 4½ lb. The average weight is 1 lb. and fish of 3 lb. are often caught. An average basket could include 4–6 fish but you will have to fish hard for them since they don't give themselves up easily. Use standard loch fly patterns. Marvellous scenery and first-class fishing.

LOCH GAINEAMHACH 16/583245
Permission: Crask Inn, Lairg, Sutherland.
Tel: Altnaharra (054981) 241

The walk out takes about 1½ hours but there is a good track to follow and this starts just south of the inn on the A836 Lairg–Altnaharra road. Gaineamhach is 500 yards long by 350 yards wide and lies in a valley formed by Creag Sgoilteach to the west and Meall an Fhuarain to the east. Fishing is from the bank only and the best places are where the two feeder burns enter on the east and south shore. Trout average ¾ lb. in weight and are of excellent quality. An average basket from this delightful loch should consist of 10–15 fish and trout of 1½–2 lb. are taken occasionally. Black Pennell, Invicta and Butchers all do well and this loch is well worth visiting.

LOCH CHOIRE 16/630280
LOCH A'BHEALAICH 16/600270
Permission: Altnaharra Hotel, Altnaharra, Sutherland.
Tel: Altnaharra (054981) 222

These two lochs are separated by a short stream and lie in the Choire Forest between Lochs Naver and Shin. They involve a fair walk but hold good stocks of brown trout averaging ¾ lb. in weight. Choire is the larger being 3 miles long by half a mile wide. Bank fishing is good, particularly where the many feeder

8 *Everything under control.*

burns enter from the slopes of Ben Klibreck. Boats were to become available during the 1982 season. Some large trout are taken and a fish of 7 lb. was landed during the 1981 season and trout of 2–3 lb. are caught regularly. Although these lochs have a reputation for being dour, they can offer excellent sport and are set amidst very lovely surroundings.

LOCH NAM BREAC BEAGA   16/651188

Permission: Sutherland Estates, Estate Office, Golspie, Sutherland. *Tel:* Golspie (04083) 268

This is a small loch in the Ben Armine Forest and lies on a ridge on the slopes of Meallan Liath Mor (461m). Fishing is from the bank only and the loch has a plentiful supply of good ½ lb. trout. There are a few larger fish and from time to time trout of 1½ lb. are caught. This is also known as the Dhli Loch and an average basket should amount to 10–15 fish. Good sport may be had all round the loch but fishing from the north-west bank is easiest

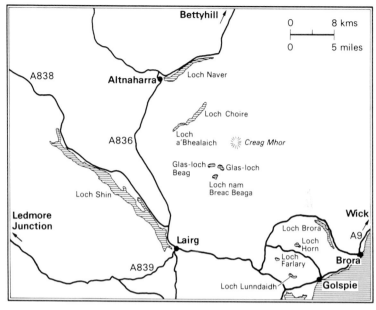

Map 9 *Brora*

from the point of view of wading. Best flies are Soldier Palmer, Zulus, Loch Ordie and Gold Butcher. Approach from Brora by the minor road up the side of the loch and turn onto the estate road at Sciberscross.

GLAS-LOCH BEAG   16/660202
Permission: Sutherland Estates, Estate Office, Golspie, Sutherland. *Tel:* Golspie (04083) 268

Glas-Loch Beag is a small, triangular-shaped loch to the west of Glas Loch and it is shallow and full of small trout. Getting up to the loch may make you catch your breath a bit but baskets of 30–40 trout are not remarkable and may be sufficient reward for your efforts. Fish average three to the pound and there are a few of ¾ lb. and more. Bank fishing only and the west shore-line produces the best results. All the standard loch fly patterns take fish and this delightful little loch is an ideal place to take a newcomer to fishing. Approach from Brora and Sciberscross.

THE GLAS LOCH   16/670195

Permission: Sutherland Estates, Estate Office, Golspie, Sutherland.
Tel: Golspie (04083) 268

The Glas Loch lies on a ridge to the west of Creag Dhubh Dail nan Gillean and reaching it involves a stiff climb. It's worth it though and the average weight of fish is ¾ lb. There is a good boat and bank fishing is also allowed but the rocky nature of the shore makes wading difficult. The best fish to be taken recently was a 3 lb. trout in 1979. The Glas Loch also contains char and a local angler caught three on the same cast during 1979, each fish weighing 12 oz. This lovely loch fishes best early in the season and it is spring fed, with excellent feeding for the fish. The trout are of a high quality and fight well. Standard loch fly patterns all produce results. Approach from Brora by way of Loch Brora and turn on to the estate road at Sciberscross.

LOCH FARLARY   17/772050

Permission: Lindsay and Co., Main Street, Golspie, Sutherland.
Tel: Golspie (04083) 212

Loch Farlary is an easily accessible roadside loch managed by the Golspie Angling Club. It lies 5 miles up Dunrobin Glen and is a shallow loch with both boat and bank fishing allowed. The trout average ½–¾ lb. and rise well to all the standard pattern loch flies. A good loch for the newcomer to fly fishing and very pleasant to fish.

LOCH LUNNDAIDH   17/785006

Permission: Lindsay and Co., Main Street, Golspie, Sutherland.
Tel: Golspie (04083) 212

Fishing is controlled by the Golspie Angling Club and getting to this pleasant loch involves a walk of about 40 minutes. There is a good track and so the walk is not difficult. Lunndaidh is three-quarters of a mile long by 350 yards wide and lies between Beinn Lunndaidh (446m) to the north and Aberscross Hill (257m) to the south. The trout average ¾ lb. and fish of up to 2 lb. are also taken. The Peter Ross does very well on this loch and baskets of up to 4 fish may be expected. The loch is stocked by the angling club and the far end, where the loch narrows, is considered to be the best fishing area.

LOCH HORN 17/796060

Permission: Lindsay and Co., Main Street, Golspie, Sutherland.
Tel: Golspie (04083) 212

This is a beautiful loch lying at an altitude of 1,000 ft. The walk up takes about half an hour. Follow the minor road just past the church as you leave Golspie northwards and park at the roadside at the Bridge of Horn. There is a track to the north. The trout on Loch Horn average ¾ lb. and fight hard. One boat is available and the angling club stock the loch. Fishing is best round the margins and bank fishing, especially in the evenings can be very productive indeed. There are large fish in Loch Horn but they tend to stay there, being very hard to catch. Standard loch fly patterns will do.

LOCH BRORA 17/850080

Permission: Rob Wilson, Fountain Square, Brora, Sutherland.
Tel: Brora (04082) 373

Loch Brora lies 3 miles to the west of the town and is best known for its salmon and sea trout fishing. The loch does hold trout but they tend to be small and the average weight is in the order of three to the pound. However, from time to time larger fish are taken and trout of up to 5 lb. have come from the loch. The best trout fishing is in the southern end, in the first of the three basins that comprise the loch. Fishing is from the boat only and standard loch fly patterns work well. A very lovely loch and worth visiting – but mostly for the salmon and sea trout.

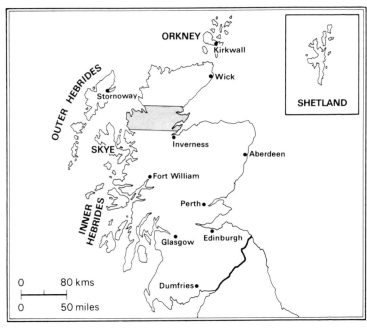

Map 10   *Ross and Cromarty*

4 Ross and Cromarty

Of all the lochs in Scotland, I think that Sionascaig, near Ullapool, is one of the finest. It is remote, beautiful and lovely, and surrounded by some of the finest scenery in the world. It also contains excellent trout and nearby are many other lochs and lochans all of which offer great sport. This area is Scotland and the highlands at their finest and no words of mine could ever do proper justice to its majestic grandeur. In spite of many efforts, I have yet to take a photograph which really captures the true magnificence of the region and so I suppose all I can advise you to do is to go and see for yourself. You will not be disappointed, I promise you, either with the scenery or the trout fishing. From Ullapool to Shieldaig and Golspie to Strathpeffer, there are trout lochs to suit all tastes and all degrees of physical fitness. You may choose a roadside reservoir or walk miles into the hills and there is now a small commercial rainbow fishery as well. Ross and Cromarty is well worth a visit and an excellent centre for a fishing holiday.

THE DAM LOCHS

LOCH BEINN DEIRG	15/155000–20/153000
LOCH NA MAOILE	15/160000–20/157998
LOCH BAD NA H-ACHLAISE	20/158995
LOCH DUBH	20/150985

Permission: Frigate Shop, Argyle Street, Ullapool, Ross-shire.
Tel: Ullapool (0854) 2488

These lochs cover an area of nearly one square mile and lie to the north of Ullapool. There is good access to them via a hydro board road which branches off the A835 one mile south of Strathkanaird. The water level in the lochs is subject to fluctuations but this does not seem to affect the fishing adversely. Boats are available and good catches are taken from the bank, particularly from the south-eastern shore of Loch Dubh where several feeder burns enter the loch. The Dam Lochs are stocked from time to time and hold brown and rainbow trout. Loch Beinn Deirg holds the largest fish and the average weight is in the region of 1½ lb. It is a dour loch though and you should not expect the fish to come leaping into the boat with their hands up. Loch Dubh

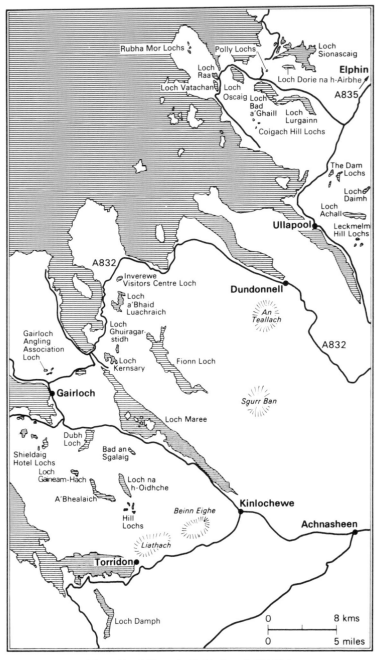

Map 11 *Ullapool, Gairloch and Shieldaig*

trout average 1 lb. and na Maoile and Bad na h-Achlaise average ½–¾ lb. An average basket should bring you 6 fish weighing 4–6 lb. – on a good day, but trout of over 3 lb. are also caught. Best flies to use are Black Pennell, Greenwell's, Grouse and Claret, and Butchers.

LOCH ACHALL   20/175950
Permission: Frigate Shop, Argyle Street, Ullapool, Ross-shire.
Tel: Ullapool (0854) 2488

Loch Achall is to the east of Ullapool on the Ridorroch Estate and there is a good road out to the loch. Boats are available but bank fishing is not allowed. The loch is stocked occasionally and there are sometimes salmon and sea trout. Trout are small, averaging ½ lb. but large baskets are taken and 20–30 fish would not be an exceptional catch. The best fishing areas are in the bays close to the shore and a good drift is along the south shore where several feeder burns enter the loch from Beinn Eilideach. A sample basket from last season held 20 trout weighing 9 lb. Teal and Green, Invicta, Black Pennell and Butchers produce the best results. A very pleasant loch for a day out in the hills.

LECKMELM ESTATE HILL LOCHS
LOCH COIRE NA BA BUIDHE   20/200918
LOCHANAN FIODHA   20/192925
LOCHANAN A'MHUILINN   20/195918
LOCH AN ACHA   20/198915
Permission: Leckmelm Holiday Enterprises, Leckmelm, Ullapool, Ross-shire.
Tel: Ullapool (0854) 2488

These hill lochs are to the east of Leckmelm on the A835 Ullapool—Loch Broom road. They are stocked from time to time and all contain brown trout with an average weight of ¾ lb. The odd larger fish is sometimes taken and trout of 2–2½ lb are not infrequent whilst the largest trout taken recently weighed 4 lb. Access is via an estate road either on foot or by land rover and apart from the named lochs there are 16 other beautiful lochs which may be fished as well. All bank fishing and good baskets of well-shaped excellent trout to be had. Lovely surroundings and great place to go.

LOCH DAIMH   20/275944

Permission: Highland Coastal Estates, Coulmore, Kessock, by Inverness.
Tel: Kessock (046373) 212

Loch Daimh is a remote, delightful loch to the east of Ullapool on the Rhidorroch Estate. It lies in a steep-sided valley with Cnoc Damh (591m) to the north and Mullach a'Chadha Bhuidhe (442m) to the south. The fishing is let with the Rhidorroch Lodge and is reserved for guests. Trout average ¾ lb. and excellent baskets are taken frequently on all the standard loch fly patterns. Good fishing in superb scenery.

LOCH LURGAINN   15/110090

Permission: Royal Hotel, Ullapool, Ross-shire.
Tel: Ullapool (0854) 2181

Loch Lurgainn lies adjacent to the minor road out to the Summer Isles and is 4 miles long by half a mile wide. Ragged hills rise from the shoreline with the Coigach Mountains dominating the horizon. Lurgainn contains trout which average ½–¾ lb. but each season usually brings a few much larger fish and the loch also holds ferox. An excellent trout of 5 lb. 12 oz. was landed by the Royal Hotel barman in June 1986. The western section of the loch, with its sheltered bays and islands, is the best fishing area and all the standard loch fly patterns will produce results. An average basket should contain 6–8 trout.

LOCH BAD A'GHAILL   15/080100

Permission: Inverpolly Estate Office, Inverpolly, Ullapool, Ross-shire.
Tel: Lochinver (05714) 252

Loch Bad a'Ghaill is 2 miles long by half a mile wide and is adjacent to the Summer Isles road out from the A835 at Drumrunie. This is a loch with a dour reputation but it holds brown trout, salmon and sea trout. The majority of the trout are in the order of ½ lb. but some very large trout have been taken from Bad a'Ghaill over the years. Both boat and bank fishing is allowed and the loch is easily accessible and in magnificent surroundings. Standard loch fly patterns.

LOCH OSCAIG   15/042123

Permission: Summer Isles Hotel, Achiltibuie, Ullapool, Ross-shire.
Tel: Achiltibuie (085482) 282

Oscaig is the last in the chain of lochs that lie between Inverpolly and Coigach. From Oscaig, the system drains through the rocky River Garvie to the sea in Garvie Bay. Loch Oscaig is best known as a sea-trout fishery although some good brown trout are taken as well, particularly along the wooded south-west shore.

LOCH RAA   15/017120
LOCH VATACHAN   15/017110
Permission: Summer Isles Hotel, Achiltibuie, Ullapool, Ross-shire.
Tel: Achiltibuie (085482) 282

Delightfully situated, both these lochs hold the occasional salmon and sea trout but the main sport is brown trout. They average ¾–1 lb. in weight and good baskets are taken especially in May and June. The lochs are easily accessible and there are boats available for visitors. Standard loch fly patterns work well and hotel guests have first call on fishings.

COIGACH HILL LOCHS
LOCHAN SGEIREACH   15/048097
LOCHAN LEACACH   15/055095
LOCHAN FADA   15/055093
LOCHAN EALLACH   15/063094
Permission: Summer Isles Hotel, Achiltibuie, Ullapool, Ross-shire.
Tel: Achiltibuie (085482) 282

The Coigach Hill Lochs are all about an hour's walk from the Summer Isles Hotel. You will not catch any record-breaking fish but you will have great sport with typical Highland wild brown trout – and there are few more dramatic places to catch them.

RUBHA MOR LOCHS
LOCH A'MHEALLAIN   15/992110
LOCH CAMAS AN FHEIDH   15/994118
LOCH NA CREIGE DUIBHE   15/006117
LOCH NA BEISTE   15/005125
LOCH TOTAIG   15/980160
LOCH AIRIGH BLAIR   15/986170
Permission: Mrs T. G. Longstaff, Badentarbat Lodge, Achiltibuie, Ullapool, Ross-shire.
Tel: Achiltibuie (085482) 225

This remote corner of Ross-shire offers all that is best for a complete family holiday: excellent game fishing, superb hill walks and climbs, marvellous empty, shining white sands, glorious bird and plant life. The lochs detailed above will all provide good sport with 6–8 oz. trout, but there are a few very large trout lurking in some of the lochs, so be warned. My own favourites are the more remote waters not because they are any better, but because they are yours for the day to share only with curlew and lark – not another human being for miles.

POLLY LOCHS

LOCH CALL AN UIDHEAN   15/092146
LOCH BUINE MOIRE   15/097155
Permission: Inverpolly Estate Office, Inverpolly, Ullapool, Ross-shire.
Tel: Lochinver (05714) 252

These lochs lie to the north of Polly Farm and fishing is mostly from the bank. Occasionally boats may be available but good catches are taken from the bank and the lochs are safe to fish from the shore. The average weight of trout is ¾ lb. and a good day should produce 4–6 fish. During the 1981 season a trout of 5½ lb. was caught and there are some really large fish in these pleasant lochs, with several 3 lb. trout being taken each year. Best flies to use are Black Pennell, Blue Zulu and Hairy Mary. The Inverpolly Estate also have available to the visiting angler a number of hill lochs where baskets of 20–40 fish are often caught. But be alert since some of these small hill waters hold very large fish and generally catch you unaware and leave you cursing.

LOCH SIONASCAIG   15/120140
Permission:
Inverpolly Estate Office, Inverpolly, Ullapool, Ross-shire.
Tel: Lochinver (05714) 252
Royal Hotel, Ullapool, Ross-shire.
Tel: Ullapool (0854) 2181

Sionascaig lies at the heart of the Inverpolly National Nature Reserve to the north-east of Ullapool and must be one of the most dramatically beautiful lochs in all of Scotland. It is a large scatter of shimmering water, studded with little islands and a shore line that meanders in and out over 16 miles of bays and headlands in a vista of mountain, moorland and water. There are two adjacent lochs, Lochan Gainmheich and Lochan Doire Dhuibh, joined to Sionascaig by a short stream and these too are splendidly lovely. The boats are moored in Boat Bay, grid reference 098152, a short

9 *Lovely Loch Sionascaig from Boat Bay.*

stroll from the road. Walk out amidst the beauty of Stack Polly, Cul Beag, Cul Mor and Suilven, and if you are discovering this area for the first time you will be overwhelmed by the sheer size of the landscape. Sionascaig is a deep loch and near the largest island, Eilean Mor, the water drops to nearly 200 feet. Fishing is best, therefore, round the margins and in the shallow water. Except for the ferrox and you will have to troll deep and long to attract them. Trout average ½–¾ lb. and good baskets are often taken, particularly during the early months of the season. Fish of 5½ lb. and 7½ lb. were caught last year and all the standard loch fly patterns will produce results. To make your passage round the loch easier, hire an outboard from the estate office. Sionascaig seems to have everything; trout of up to 17 lb., numerous 5–10 lb. fish and baskets of 20–30 ½–¾ pounders. Yes, you will have blank days as well, but this is a loch that you must fish, you will not be disappointed.

LOCH DORIE NA H-AIRBHE 15/105127

Permission: Inverpolly Estate Office, Inverpolly, Ullapool, Ross-shire.
Tel: Lochinver (05714) 252

There is no easy way in. Getting to na h-Airbhe involves a stiff

walk from all directions. Park at 082136 and head east towards
the peak of Stac Polly. An alternative approach is by boat, via
Sionascaig; come ashore at 102131 and walk up the hill, south-
west. Whichever way you choose, once there this fine loch will
more than repay you for your efforts. We found the most
productive area to be the south-east shoreline, particularly along
the wooded east end. Trout average ¾ lb. and there are much
larger fish as well.

THE FAIRY LOCH   19/810712
Permission: Shieldaig Lodge Hotel, Badachro, Gairloch,
Ross-shire.
Tel: Badachro (044583) 250

The Fairy Loch is a mile walk from the hotel and guests have
priority. There is one boat available and bank fishing is also
allowed. This loch holds excellent trout and fish of up to 3½ lb.
are caught. A sample catch from the 1981 season recorded two
fish weighing 6 lb. 6 oz. and the best flies to use are Soldier
Palmer and Grouse and Green. This is a small loch dotted with
islands and fishing is best round them. Bank fishing is good from
the points and headlands but you will count the fish on the fingers
of one hand rather than both. Excellent trout, though, if you do
tempt them.

SPECTACLES   19/817705
Permission: Shieldaig Lodge Hotel, Badachro, Gairloch,
Ross-shire.
Tel: Badachro (044583) 250

This is the highest up of the Fairy Lochs and fish average ¾ lb. It
is bank fishing only and an average basket will account for up to
10 fish. Standard loch fly patterns produce results and the loch is
an easy walk from the hotel. Guests have priority.

THE AEROPLANE LOCH   19/808711
Permission: Shieldaig Lodge Hotel, Badachro, Gairloch,
Ross-shire.
Tel: Badachro (044583) 250

If the midges are not too bad this is an ideal spot for some after
dinner casting and good baskets are taken. Trout average ½ lb.
and 15–20 fish are frequently caught. Best flies include Kingfisher,
Butcher, Red Tag, Peter Ross and Wickham's Fancy. A good loch
to restore one's confidence if things get a bit hard on the Fairy
Loch.

THE DIAMOND LOCH   19/810702
Permission: Shieldaig Lodge Hotel, Badachro, Gairloch,
Ross-shire.
Tel: Badachro (044583) 250
This is a small loch about 500 yards by 200 yards and the average
weight of trout is ¾ lb. It is a short walk from the hotel and
fishing is from the bank only. Catches of double figures are not
uncommon and the trout rise to all the standard patterns of loch
flies. The south-east bank in the vicinity of the small island is a
favourite spot though fish are caught all round the shore.

LOCH BAD NA H-ACHLAISE   19/770737
Permission: Shieldaig Lodge Hotel, Badachro, Gairloch,
Ross-shire.
Tel: Badachro (044583) 250
This is a beautiful roadside loch to the west of the hotel along the
B8056 to Redpoint. It fishes best early in the season and both boat
and bank fishing are available. The loch is in two sections and the
best area is in the western section of the northern bay, towards
Port Henderson. Two feeder burns enter the southern section of
the loch from Meall Bad a'Chrotha and this is also a good area to
try. Flies to use include Silver Butcher, Blue Charm, Peter Ross
and Dunkeld. This loch is sometimes very calm and dry fly can
bring good results under these conditions. Excellent trout
averaging ¾ lb., and a delightful loch to fish.

LOCHAN SGEIREACH   19/810708
Permission: Shieldaig Lodge Hotel, Badachro, Gairloch,
Ross-shire.
Tel: Badachro (044583) 250
This is a small loch in the group known as the Fairy Lochs and is a
short walk from the hotel. Trout average ¾ lb. and rise well to all
the standard pattern loch flies. Fishing is from the bank only and
good baskets are taken regularly.

LOCH BAD A'CHROTHA   19/786728
Permission: Shieldaig Lodge Hotel, Badachro, Gairloch,
Ross-shire.
Tel: Badachro (044583) 250
This is an extension of the River Badachro and the loch is known
as Badachro loch locally. The main interest here is salmon and sea
trout, the trout only average three to the pound. Have a day off
from the hill lochs, the trout will still be there tomorrow.

LOCH BRAIGH HORRISDALE   19/797705
Permission: Shieldaig Lodge Hotel, Badachro, Gairloch,
Ross-shire.
Tel: Badachro (044583) 250

This loch is on the same track as the route to the Fairy Lochs, to
the south of the hotel. It lies adjacent to the track and is full of
bright little fish with suicidal tendancies. This is the ideal loch for
newcomers to fly fishing and perfect for a picnic with the family.
There are two boats on the loch and wading is safe all round
although it is 50 feet deep in the middle. Baskets of 20 fish are
often taken and 50 would not really raise an eyebrow in the hotel.
Best flies are Peter Ross, Blue Zulu, Silver Butcher and Invicta.
Sandy beaches, peace and quiet, free rising trout and a pleasant
day out.

LOCH NA H-OIDHCHE   19/890650
Permission: Shieldaig Lodge Hotel, Badachro, Gairloch,
Ross-shire.
Tel: Badachro (044583) 250

This loch is a distance of 5 miles from the hotel and the track
starts from the A832 and the eastern end of Loch Bad an Sgalaig.
Na h-Oidhche is 1,250 feet above sea level and surrounded by
magnificent scenery. It is 1½ miles long by half a mile wide and
has a well-deserved reputation for being dour. It holds good
trout, though, and the average weight is 1 lb. with several 2 lb.
fish being taken each season. A good day can produce 8–10 trout
and one basket caught during 1981 produced 22 fish weighing
17½ lb. Best flies are Black Pennell, Black Zulu, Greenwell's Glory,
and Grouse and Claret. This can be a wild place to fish and at the
head of the loch there is a hut which can give welcome shelter.
However, the loch fishes well in a good wind and dapping can be
very effective. Loch na h-Oidhche is over 100 feet deep and the
shallower water at the north and south ends are the best fishing
areas. An exciting water in majestic scenery.

LOCH A'BHEALAICH   19/870640
Permission: Shieldaig Lodge Hotel, Badachro, Gairloch,
Ross-shire.
Tel: Badachro (044583) 250

This is the largest loch in the Shieldaig Forest and it lies to the
west of Baosbheinn (875m) 8 miles south of the hotel. The loch is
1¾ miles long by half a mile wide and both boat and bank fishing

are available. Although over 100 feet deep in places, at the western end the loch shallows to a mere 2 or 3 feet and the shallows are the best fishing areas. Pay particular attention to where the many feeder burns enter the loch and also try the depths for *ferox*. The average weight is ¾ lb. and the best fish taken during 1981 was a trout of 2¾ lb. Use lures such as Sweeny Todd and Ace of Spades and standard loch fly patterns, all can produce good results. In spite of the considerable walk involved, this is a very attractive loch to fish – the surroundings could not be grander.

LOCH GAINEAMHACH   19/834670
Permission: Shieldaig Lodge Hotel, Badachro, Gairloch,
Ross-shire.
Tel: Badachro (044583) 250

Loch Gaineamhach is a 6 mile walk south of the hotel and lies to the left of the track up the Abhainn Braigh Burn. This is a shallow loch over half a mile long by a quarter of a mile wide and fishing is from the bank only. Wading is easy and the best fishing areas are along the west bank and north shore. Large baskets of small fish are caught here and the average weight is ½ lb. Great sport, and the flies to attract them with are Invicta, Woodcock and Hare, and Greenwells. A very pleasant loch to fish amidst lovely surroundings.

LOCH FADA   19/922627
Permission: Shieldaig Lodge Hotel, Badachro, Gairloch,
Ross-shire.
Tel: Badachro (044583) 250

Loch Fada lies at the head of Strath Lungard and is a 9 mile walk from the hotel. This is a small loch full of ½ lb. fish and is best approached from the track that starts by Loch Bad an Sgalaig on the A832. It is a long walk but the scenery is spectacular and there are several other small lochs nearby which are also worth fishing. To the south of Fada there is Lochan Carn na Feola (920618) and Loch a'Chaorainn (928621). They also hold large stocks of good little trout as do Loch na Cabhaig (892625) and Gorm Loch Fada at the head of h-Oidhche. You are surrounded here by some of the most dramatic countryside in the north with Beinn an Eoin (855m), Liathach (1054m) and Beinn Eighe (972m) towering over the lochs. A wonderful, remote and lonely place to fish and worth every step of the journey out. All the standard patterns of loch flies will catch fish. You will catch your breath at the beauty and peace all around.

LOCH CLAIR 19/773717
LOCHAN NAM BREAC ODHAR 19/767720
LOCH AIRIGH UILLEIM 19/755720

Permission: Shieldaig Lodge Hotel, Badachro, Gairloch, Ross-shire.
Tel: Badachro (044583) 250

These lochs lie to the west of Shieldaig and are approached by a track which leaves the B8056 where the Badachro River crosses under the road. Clair is a shallow loch and there is a boat on it. Bank fishing is also allowed and this loch fishes best in a strong wind. The shoreline is irregular and there are many good bays and points from which to fish. The best areas are to the southern end of the loch and along the east shore. Trout average ½–¾ lb. and you should catch up to 10 fish. A sample basket taken during the 1981 season had 33 trout weighing 18½ lb. so great sport can be expected. Best flies are Wickham's Fancy, Grouse and Green, and Blae and Black. Follow the track on from Loch Clair and you will come to the other two named lochs. The fish are a bit smaller but just as ready to come to the fly and a day's fishing in this area is splendid fun.

LOCH A'BHAID-LUACHRAICH 19/890860

Permission: Inverewe Visitors Centre, Poolewe, Ross-shire.
Tel: Poolewe (044586) 229

This loch lies to the south of the A832 near Drumchork and is 1½ miles long by one mile wide. Spurs from Carn Bad na h-Achlaise and Maol na Bruaich almost divide the loch in two and the approach is from Drumchork via a good track. Only bank fishing is available. There are good bays and points all round the loch and the southern, shallower bay is the best fishing area. Trout average ½–¾ lb. and rise well to the standard loch pattern flies.

LOCH GHUIRAGARSTIDH 19/890810

Permission: Inverewe Visitors Centre, Poolewe, Ross-shire.
Tel: Poolewe (044586) 229

This loch drains out into Loch Kernsary and is approached from Poolewe via Kernsary by a rough track and a 60 minute walk. It is a small shallow loch about three-quarters of a mile long by 350 yards wide. The loch contains good brown trout and the most productive areas are in the vicinity of the small islands. Standard loch fly patterns work well.

LOCH KERNSARY   19/880804

Permission: Inverewe Visitors Centre, Poolewe, Ross-shire.
Tel: Poolewe (044586) 229

Fishing on Kernsary is managed by the National Trust for
Scotland and the loch is a ragged, beautiful water of 1½ miles in
length by half a mile wide. This is a deep loch, nearly 100 feet
towards the eastern end and it contains good trout and is stocked
by the National Trust. Sea trout sometimes wander up from Loch
Maree and there are dozens of good fishing points all round the
shore. A lovely loch and well worth a visit.

FIONN LOCH   19/950785

Permission: Creg Mor Hotel, Gairloch, Ross-shire.
Tel: Gairloch (0445) 2068

Fionn lies to the north of Loch Maree and is one of the most
lovely lochs in the north. It is immortalised for anglers by a
passage in Osgood MacKenzie's book, *A Hundred Years in the
Highlands*. It relates the story of a basket of trout taken from the
loch by trolling which weighed in at 87 lb. 12 oz. Difficult to
match today, but nevertheless big trout are still caught on Fionn
and fish of 4–5 lb. are frequently caught. Fionn is 5 miles long by
1½ miles wide and is an endless delight of small bays and
charming points. A narrow causeway separates Fionn from the
Dubh Loch at the eastern end and along the south shore a short
stream leads into Lochan Beannach Mor. Both these adjacent
lochs are also worth fishing. This is magnificent country and the
loch is surrounded by superb peaks: Slioch (980m), Meall
Mheinnidh (720m), and Beinn Airigh Charr (791m) dominate the
south shore whilst Beinn a'Caisgein Mor (857m), Ruadh Stac Mor
(918m) and Mullach Coire Mhic Fhearchair (1019m) crowd in to
the north and east. Well worth fishing and highly recommended.
Standard pattern loch flies do fine.

LOCH MAREE   19/920730

Permission: Lochmaree Hotel, Lochmaree, by Achnasheen,
Ross-shire.
Tel: Lochmaree (044589) 200

This most famous of all sea trout lochs must be mentioned, but it
is not for brown trout that anglers make the pilgrimage north.
Therefore, although the loch holds excellent brown trout they are
caught by accident rather than by design. The hotel will give you

permission to fish for trout if you so desire, but you would be well advised to look elsewhere for better sport. For sea trout, however, there is nowhere else to match the loch and the fishing is first class.

LOCH BAD AN SGALAIG   19/850710
LOCH DUBH   19/845700

Permission: The Wild Cat Stores, Gairloch, Ross-shire.
Tel: Gairloch (0445) 2242

These two lochs lie to the south of the A832 Gairloch–Kinlochewe road and have been joined into one by the construction of a dam. They cover an area of 2 miles by half a mile and are easily accessible from the road. The fishing is managed by the Gairloch Angling Club and both boat and bank fishing are allowed. The trout average ¾–1 lb. and standard loch pattern flies work well. Larger fish are caught often and the club stock the loch.

LOCHAN NAM BREAC   19/815783
LOCH FEUR   19/809781
LOCH COIRE NA H-AIRIGH   19/805784

Permission: Wild Cat Stores, Gairloch, Ross-shire.
Tel: Gairloch (0445) 2242

These small hill lochs are managed by the Gairloch Angling Club and contain good trout which rise well to standard pattern loch

10   *Loch Bad an Sgalaig with Baosbheinn in the background.*

flies. They are to the north of the A832 and a short walk from the road. Fish average about ½–¾ lb. and fight well. Superb surroundings.

LOCH NA BA CAOILE 19/872827

Permission: Inverewe Visitors Centre, Poolewe, Ross-shire.
Tel: Poolewe (044586) 229

This is a little loch by the A832 Poolewe–Drumchork road and it is 350 yards long by 50 yards wide. The name means 'the lean cow' and fishing is from the bank only. The loch is stocked and the trout average ¾ lb. Bank fishing only and size 14 standard pattern loch flies will do fine. Easily accessible and ideal for a few hours casting.

LOCHNANDAILTHEAN 19/877830

Permission: Inverewe Visitors Centre, Poolewe, Ross-shire.
Tel: Poolewe (044586) 229

The National Trust manage this pleasant roadside loch. It is shallow, averaging only 10 feet deep and drains out to the sea at Loch Thurnaig, so in spate conditions there is the chance of salmon and sea trout. A boat is available and trout average ¾ lb. This loch is stocked and good baskets are often taken to standard loch fly patterns.

LOCH DAMPH 24/862510

Permission: Loch Torridon Hotel, Torridon, Ross-shire.
Tel: Torridon (044587) 242

The principal Torridon Hotel water, this long, narrow loch is most famous as a salmon and sea-trout loch with fish entering the system via the River Balgy. But good brown trout are caught as well, particularly at the south end of the loch where the Abhainn Dearg burn enters.

LOCH NAN EUN 33/952266
LOCH BHUIC MHOR 33/923260
LOCH BEINN A'MHEADHOIN 33/923286

Permission: The Factor, Inverinate Estate, Dornie, by Kyle, Ross-shire.
Mrs E. Huggett, Bundalloch, Dornie, by Kyle, Ross-shire.

These small lochs lie in the hills to the north of the A87 Shiel Bridge–Kyle of Lochalsh road, and involve a good walk to reach

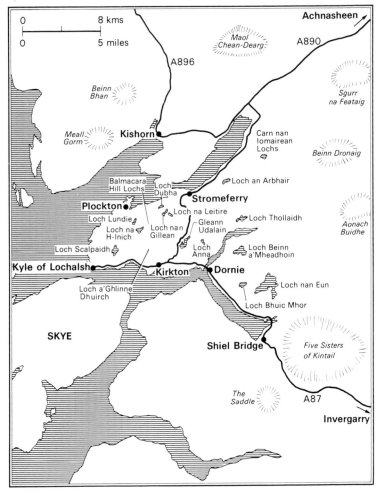

Map 12   *Ross-shire*

them. The trout are small but great fighters and good baskets will be taken using standard loch fly patterns. The greatest attraction is the marvellous scenery. The hills and mountains of the Inverinate and Kintail Forests dominate the horizon and the Five Sisters line the southern sky. This is a truly magnificent place to fish. Get permission, fasten your boots and have a memorable day.

LOCH SCALPAIDH	33/780288
LOCH LUNDIE	24/807317
LOCH NA H-INICH	24/812308

Permission: Not required

These lochs are to the north of Kyle of Lochalsh and easily accessible. Trout on Scalpaidh average three to the pound and good baskets are taken on most of the standard pattern loch flies. Loch Lundie was stocked some years ago with rainbow and brook trout but both Lundie and na h-Inich have a reputation for being dour. There are good trout on na h-Inich, as well as pike, and fish of 2½–3½ lb. are sometimes caught.

LOCH NAN GILLEAN	24/840325
LOCH NA LEITIRE	24/844322
LOCH DUBHA	24/832328

Permission: Not required

This group of small lochs lies to the south-east of Plockton and may be approached via a good track which leaves the minor 'ring road' round Loch Lundie. The first part of the walk is fairly steep but the effort involved is well worth while since the scenery is grand and the trout fishing excellent. The lochs are known locally as the Craggs. Loch Dubha holds the largest fish and a trout of 5 lb. was taken recently. Baskets of 4–5 fish are frequently caught and the fish average between ¾-1¼ lb. Best fly on this loch is a Kingfisher Butcher so make sure you have one in the box before you set off. Best time to fish is late May, early June.

BALMACARA HILL LOCHS

LOCH NAM BREAC MORA	24/838308
LOCH NA DOIRE MOIRE	24/827304
LOCH NA SMEORAICH	24/844304
LOCH A'GHLINNE DHUIRCH	33/837299

Permission: Not required

You will puff and pant a bit getting there, but these are excellent little trout lochs and should be visited. Fishing is all from the bank and they are known locally as the Balmacara Hill lochs. Trout average ¾ lb. and fish of 2 lb. and more are not infrequently caught. Flies to use are Butchers, Greenwell's Glory, Blue Zulu and Peter Ross.

GLEANN UDALAIN   33/853290
Permission: Not required

This is a small reservoir to the east of the A890 Stromeferry–Kyle road. It suffers from great fluctuations in water level and the trout average three to the pound. However, it is easily accessible and when the water level is right fish of up to ¾–1 lb. are sometimes caught.

LOCH ANNA   33/879292
Permission: Not required

It's a fair walk out to Loch Anna and the water has a reputation for being dour. Nevertheless, it can produce excellent results and trout of up to 2 lb. are caught. All fishing is from the bank and standard pattern lochs flies will do.

LOCH THOLLAIDH   24/896306
Permission: Not required

This is a tiny hill loch to the north of Conchra and trout average ½ lb. in weight. The fish are very pretty being bright and golden. Flies to use should match the trout's colour and patterns such as Kingfisher Butcher, Dunkeld and Silver Invicta work well. Only the left-hand bank is worth fishing.

LOCH AN ARBHAIR   24/883342
Permission: Not required

An easily accessible loch to the east of Stromeferry, Loch Arbhair has a reputation for holding some very large trout indeed. It's getting them out that causes all the trouble and you will have a lot of blank days trying. But trout of up to 10 lb. are caught here which may have something to do with why folks keep trying. Just what flies you use to tempt them I do not know, but keep trying.

CARN NAN IOMAIREAN LOCHS   25/915357
Permission: Not required

These lochs all lie to the south of Attadale on Loch Carron and are hill lochs containing trout which average three to the pound. Really good baskets are taken and the fish rise to the standard pattern loch flies. Lovely countryside and a great place for a day out in the hills.

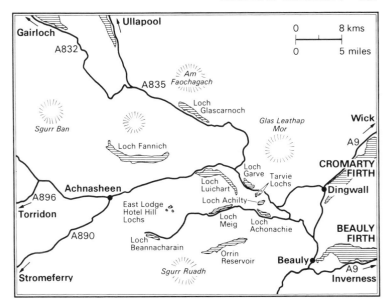

Map 13   *Strathpeffer*

LOCH FANNICH   20/210650
Permission: Strathgarve Lodge Hotel, Garve, Ross-shire.
Tel: Garve (09974) 204

Fannich is a hydro-electric loch 7 miles long by three-quarters of a
mile wide. It is approached from the A832 Dingwall–Gairloch
road just before the power station at the River Grudie. Loch
Fannich is a wild, desolate place but a track runs the length of the
north shore giving good access for bank fishing and this is
productive at the head of the loch where the main feeder burn
enters. This is the shallowest part of the loch and fishes best from
the boat as well. Another good drift is eastwards from the forestry
plantation among the bays and inlets below Torran Ruadh. Trout
average ½–¾ lb. with good baskets taken using Black Pennell,
Grouse and Claret, and Butchers.

LOCH GLASCARNOCH   20/300735
Permission: Aultguish Inn, Aultguish, by Garve, Ross-shire.
Tel: Aultguish (09975) 254

Loch Glascarnoch is a new loch recently formed as part of the
Conon Valley Hydro-Electric Scheme. The loch is 4½ miles long

by one mile wide. Bank fishing only and take great care on the edges. Frequent water level changes make the margins very soft in places. This is a dour loch, wild and windy and trout are difficult to catch. The average weight is ½–¾ lb. but fish of up to 4 lb. have been caught. The A835 Garve–Ullapool road follows the south shore so Glascarnoch is easily accessible, if somewhat public.

LOCH BEANNACHARAIN   25/230515

Permission:
S. W. Tough, MBE, East Lodge Hotel, Strathconon, Ross-shire.
Tel: Strathconon (09977) 222;
M. Burr, The Tackle Shop, Cromartie Buildings, Strathpeffer, Ross-shire.
Tel: Strathpeffer (09972) 561

This loch is known locally as Loch Scardroy and it lies to the south of Achnasheen. Approach from Inver on the A890 or from Marybank on the A832 up the River Meig. Beannacharain is 1¾ miles long by 400 yards wide and a boat is available for anglers. Bank fishing is also allowed. The loch is over 150 feet deep in the middle and the best fishing is to be found in the shallow water round the margins, especially at the western end of the loch. The loch has been stocked in the past and it contains Loch Leven trout and brown trout with an average weight of ½–¾ lb. Fish of up to 4 lb. are sometimes caught and 12–14 fish would constitute a good basket. The average would be 4–5 fish. Very pleasant loch to fish and all standard loch pattern flies produce results.

LOCH BHAD GHAINEAMHAICH   26/325590
LOCH AN ALLTAIN BHEITHE   26/319595
LOCH AN EILEIN   26/305584
LOCH CUL   26/305586

*Permission:*S. W. Tough, MBE, East Lodge Hotel, Strathconon, Ross-shire.
Tel: Strathconon (09977) 222

These fine hill lochs are managed by the East Lodge Hotel and all involve an invigorating walk into the hills. Trout average ½–¾ lb. with the occasional larger fish and they rise to standard pattern loch flies. The East Lodge Hotel lies to the west of loch Meig on the minor road from the A832 at Marybank, and is a first-class fishing centre.

ORRIN RESERVOIR   26/376496
Permission: The Fairburn Estate Office, Muir of Ord, Ross-shire.
Tel: Urray (09973) 273

Orrin Reservoir is 5 miles long by half a mile wide and fishing on
it is strictly controlled by the estate. Access is via an estate road
only. The occasional day may be available to visitors and anglers
should contact the estate office for details. Orrin is a remote and
beautiful water containing good trout and baskets of 6–8 fish may
be expected. Low water conditions during 1984 and 1986 have
made fishing more difficult and fewer trout are caught than in
previous years. Standard pattern loch flies work well. There is no
fishing after 31 August.

LOCH LUICHART   20/340620–26/380593
Permission: Jas Shanks & Sons, Tulloch Street, Dingwall,
Ross-shire.
Tel: Dingwall (0349) 2346

Loch Luichart is a hydro-electric loch and fishing is managed by
the Dingwall Angling Club. It is approached directly off the A832
at Lochluichart Station and is a long, dour loch of 5½ miles by
one mile wide. The average weight of trout is ½–¾ lb. but it is
reputed to hold much larger fish. Perhaps when there are boats on
the loch some of these big ones will be caught. There are miles of
interesting shoreline to explore and all the standard loch fly
patterns work well. A basket of 4 fish would be good for a day,
however.

LOCH MEIG   26/367557
Permission: S. W. Tough, MBE, East Lodge Hotel, Strathconon,
Ross-shire.
Tel: Strathconon (09977) 222
M. Burr, The Tackle Shop, Cromartie Buildings, Strathpeffer,
Ross-shire.
Tel: Strathpeffer (09972) 561

Loch Meig lies to the east of Strathpeffer and is a long, narrow
water 2 miles long by 400 yards wide. It is a very lovely loch and
can offer good sport, particularly early in the season. There are
three boats available on Loch Meig but outboard motors are not
permitted. Bank fishing is also allowed and can be good. The
most productive areas are in the north-west corner where several
feeder burns enter the loch and also in the bay on the south shore
at the widest part of the loch. If the water level is high Loch Meig

11 *Safely 'in'.*

does not fish so well. The average weight of trout is 1 lb. and a reasonable day should produce 3–4 fish. Trout of up to 3 lb. are not infrequently taken, but usually at the end of the season. Loch Meig is stocked and evening fishing is generally best. Use Black Pennell, Peter Ross, Coachman, Kingfisher Butcher, Zulu and Greenwell's Glory. This is a most attractive loch to fish and worth a visit.

LOCH GARVE   20/405600–26/410595
Permission: Strathgarve Lodge Hotel, Garve, Ross-shire.
Tel: Garve (09974) 204

Loch Garve lies adjacent to the A832 and is in a delightful setting having wooded banks from which rise the mighty slopes of Ben Wyvis (1046m). The loch is 1½ miles long by half a mile wide and holds good brown trout with fish of up to 4 lb. being caught. Best results come from the boat but bank fishing is also allowed. Garve contains pike and fish of up to 19 lb. have been taken. The best areas to fish are the north-east bay near the outlet and also the shallower waters at the north end of the loch. The average size of trout is 1 lb. but – be warned – they do not give themselves up easily. Try standard loch fly patterns and crossed fingers.

LOCH AN EICH BHAIN 26/423580
Permission: Murray Douglas, Inchdrean, Tarvie, Ross-shire.
Tel: Tarvie 250

These lochs lie to the north of Contin on the A832 road from
Muir of Ord and are easily accessible. Both boat and bank fishing
are available and the lochs are also known as the Tarvie Lochs.
The main loch, An Eich Bhain has a good natural stock of brown
trout and rainbows were introduced during the 1981 season. The
Tarvie Lochs are being developed into a first-class fishery and
already the average weight of trout is 1 lb. The best fish taken
during 1981 weighed 2½ lb. There are two sessions, 9 am–5 pm
and 6 pm–10 pm. Fish rise and are caught all over the loch but the
vicinity of the small islands and weed beds are the most favoured
spots. The Tarvie Lochs are very pleasant to fish, remote yet easy
to get at, and well worth a visit.

LOCH ACHONACHIE 26/433550
Permission: M. Burr, The Tackle Shop, Cromartie Buildings,
Strathpeffer, Ross-shire.
Tel: Strathpeffer (09972) 561

Loch Achonachie lies adjacent to the minor road from Marybank
on the A832 and contains brown trout, perch, pike and the
occasional salmon. Bank fishing is allowed but the boat produces
better results. This is a very dour loch, but it is easily accessible
and in a lovely setting. From time to time trout of up to 4 lb. are
caught but the average is nearer the ½–¾ lb. mark. A good day
might produce 6 fish – less is far more likely. Try the standard
loch fly patterns and fish the east end of the loch, below
Torrachilty Wood, and in the bay in the south-east corner where
the feeder burn enters by the roadside. An outboard is useful.

LOCH ACHILTY 26/435566
Permission:
Craigdarroch Hotel, Contin, Ross-shire.
Tel: Strathpeffer (09972) 265;
Achilty Hotel, Contin, Ross-shire.
Tel: Strathpeffer (09972) 355

Loch Achilty is a sheltered loch, three-quarters of a mile long by
700 yards wide. It is easily accessible from the A832 and is surrounded by trees. Loch Achilty contains brown trout and has been

stocked in the past. Trout average ½–¾ lb. but fish of over 4 lb. have been taken. Achilty can be a very dour loch and a good basket would be 3–4 fish. However, on its day the sport can be fast and furious – it's just being there on that day that is the difficult bit. Use standard loch fly patterns and fish the shallows – Achilty is over 120 feet deep – it is a pleasant loch to fish.

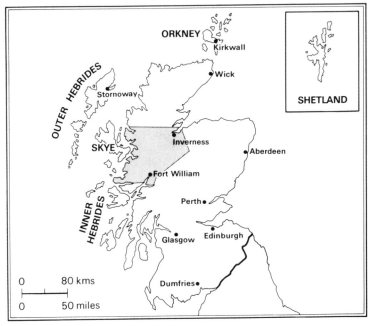

Map 14 *Inverness-shire*

5 Inverness-shire

Inverness-shire covers a vast area and contains hundreds of trout lochs. There are a number of hydro-electric waters, vast, windy and dour, but holding really monster trout up to 20 lb. and dozens of hill lochs such as the Invermoriston waters and the remote waters to the west. You can't travel far in this area without coming across evidence of the 1745 rebellion, and I have often mused upon the thought of what Scotland might have been like today if Prince Charles Edward Stewart had travelled round with a trout rod rather than a ragged army of highlanders. Certainly a lot of heads would have remained more firmly attached to a lot of shoulders and the highlands would have been spared the administrations of Butcher Cumberland. The route taken by Bonnie Prince Charlie after the Battle of Culloden takes you past some of the best trout waters in the area from Ruthven up Glen Garry and over to Loch Quoich. In fact, it would make an excellent path to follow for a present day fishing holiday and give an added sense of excitement to the occasion. My own favourite lochs are the Invermoriston hill lochs and Ruthven and a'Choire to the south of Inverness. Then, of course, there is distant, huge Loch Morar – and never enough time to fish and explore them all. I hope the waters I have described will help you start your journey and see the first trout safely into the net.

DUNDREGGAN LOCH   34/355157
Permission: Glenmoriston Estate Office, Invermoriston, Inverness.
Tel: Glenmoriston (0320) 51202

Dundreggan Loch lies on the upper River Moriston and covers an area half a mile long by some 200 yards wide. It is easily accessible from the A887 which runs along the north shore. This is an excellent loch, pleasant with wooded banks and first-class fish. The estate stocks Dundreggan regularly and the average weight of trout is 1 lb. Best results come from the boat and the estate has two available for visitors. The most favoured fishing area is in the shallower water at the western end of the loch. Another good drift is down the north-west shore. Evening fishing during July and August frequently produces baskets of 15–20 fish and the best trout taken during the 1981 season was a fine fish weighing 7 lb. 4

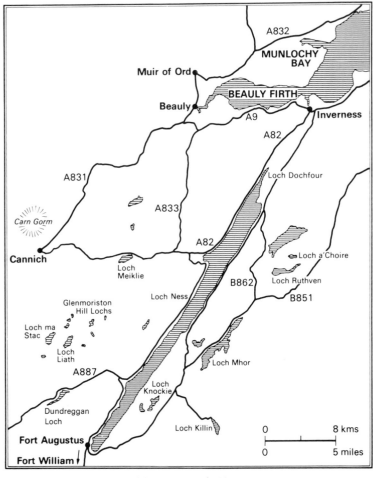

Map 15   *Loch Ness*

oz. and in September 1983 a trout of 7 lb. 2 oz. was taken by Norman Harris – fishing a Green Highlander! Best flies are Black Pennell, Silver Butcher, Black and Blue Zulu, and Grouse and Claret – where are they not? Lovely loch and well worth a visit.

LOCH LIATH   34/335197

Permission: Glenmoriston Estate Office, Invermoriston, Inverness.
Tel: Glenmoriston (0320) 51202

This loch lies to the north of Invermoriston and is 4 miles from

Bhlaraidh on the A887. Access is by an estate road and high wheel based vehicles are recommended – or good boots. Liath contains excellent trout and fishing is from the bank only. The loch is well managed and stocked regularly by the estate and the trout average ¾ lb. Baskets of up to 20 fish are not uncommon and Liath also holds good char. This is a classic hill loch some 1,500 feet above sea level and the surrounding countryside and views are maginficent. Well worth a visit.

LOCH MA STAC   26/340215

Permission: Glenmoriston Estate Office, Invermoriston, Inverness.
Tel: Glenmoriston (0320) 51202

Loch ma Stac is the best trout loch in the area and lies to the north of Invermoriston and the A887. Approach via the estate road from Bhlaraidh in a vehicle with a high wheel base. Loch ma Stac is at an altitude of 1,600 feet and is one mile long by a third of a mile wide. There is a boat on the loch but bank fishing can produce just as good results and the trout average 1 lb. Each year much larger fish are taken and trout of up to 6 lb. have been caught on this fine loch. Loch ma Stac is over 40 feet deep by the east shore and the best fishing area is down the western bank which is fringed with inviting bays and headlands. The area round the islands should also be 'worked over' most carefully. The estate restocked the loch in 1985 and it continues to fish very well indeed. A perfect loch with fine views all round and the Five Sisters of Kintail lining the western horizon. Highly recommended.

THE GLENMORISTON HILL LOCHS   34/422168

Permission: Glenmoriston Estate Office, Invermoriston, Inverness.
Tel: Glenmoriston (0320) 51202

There are more that 20 hill lochs on the estate and all are readily available to members of the public through the estate office. All these lochs contain excellent trout which average from ½ lb. up to real monsters of 6 lb. Most of the lochs involve a fair walk but the angler will be assured of peace and quiet in superb surroundings — and a good basket of fish at the end of the day. The lochs are well managed and regularly stocked and the estate can also arrange good accommodation in well-situated chalets. Not many better places for a few days fishing and highly recommended. Good salmon fishing also on River Moriston and in Loch Ness.

LOCH NESS   SHEETS 24–26
Permission:
Glenmoriston Estate Office, Glenmoriston, Inverness.
Tel: Glenmoriston (0320) 51202;
Foyers Hotel, Foyers, Inverness-shire.
Tel: Gorthleck (04563) 216;
Inchnacardoch Lodge Hotel, Fort Augustus, Inverness-shire.
Tel: Fort Augustus (0320) 6258

Because of its Monster, Loch Ness has become one of the best known lochs in the world, and there is, I am sure, something there. Just what flies to use to tempt it, what breaking strain of nylon or length of rod would be best I don't care to say. Suffice to advise you when fishing on Loch Ness, keep a sharp look out and use plenty of backing – you never can tell! Loch Ness is a most beautiful loch and displays throughout its length every aspect of game fishing. It is easily accessible and often very busy, both along the shores and on the water itself. But there is always some secret, quiet corner to be found and the angler on Loch Ness can be as secluded and remote as he wishes. It is not possible to describe properly all the best fishing areas but I would not be guilty of too great a generalisation if I said that trout can be caught over most of the area. Very large fish are taken off Glenmoriston and there is good bank fishing along the south shore from Dores, before the loch opens out. There are miles of unfrequented bays and corners near Foyers. The trout average ½– ¾ lb. and are well shaped, and in some areas almost golden. Standard pattern flies work fine and Loch Ness is well worth a visit. You may not catch a glimpse of the Monster, but you most certainly will catch a few trout.

LOCH DOCHFOUR   26/605385
Permission: The Factor, The Dochfour Estate, Dochgarroch, Inverness.
Tel: Dochgarroch (046386)218

Loch Dochfour extends from the outflow of Loch Ness to where the weir divides the flow into the canal and the River Ness. The loch contains brown trout and pike and the average size of trout is 1 lb. Fishing is from the bank only and the loch is easily accessible from the A82 which runs along the north shore. It is a rather public place to fish but a very lovely setting. The fish tend to be dour but large trout are caught and standard loch fly patterns should be used.

LOCH RUTHVEN   26/620275

Permission: Estate Office, Brin Estate, Flichty, Inverness-shire.
Tel: Farr (08083) 211;
John Graham & Co., 71 Castle Street, Inverness.
Tel: Inverness (0463) 33178

Loch Ruthven is an excellent loch providing first-class sport in beautiful surroundings. It is 2¼ miles long by half a mile wide with an average depth of 10 feet. This is a well-managed water and the estate stock it regularly. The average weight is 1 lb. and trout of 4–5 lb. are often caught. An average basket should produce 6–8 fish and the best flies to use are Grouse and Claret, Black Pennell, Yellow Invicta and Greenwell's Glory. Bank fishing is not allowed but there are several well equipped boats available. These are moored at the north end of the loch where there are good car parking facilities. Highly recommended to you as a lovely loch to visit and fish. The estate can also arrange accommodation in self-catering cottages which are also of a very high standard.

LOCH A'CHOIRE   26/630293

Permission: Estate Office, Brin Estate, Flichty, Inverness-shire.
Tel: Farr (08083) 211

This is a lovely hill loch to the north of Loch Ruthven on the Brin Estate. Approach from the A9 south of Inverness and take the B851 to Fort Augustus. This is a small loch and it contains brown trout, brook trout and char. The brown trout average ¾ lb. and an average basket should account for 7–8 fish. The best fishing areas are in the north-west bay and at the western end of the loch. Grouse and Claret, Black Pennell and Invicta do well on this loch. Both boat and bank fishing are allowed and the estate can arrange accommodation in first-class cottages nearby. Again, highly recommended for a perfect day's fishing or, if you are lucky, a perfect two weeks' fishing holiday.

LOCH KNOCKIE   34/455135

Permission: Whitebridge Hotel, Stratherrick, Gorthleck, Inverness-shire.
Tel: Gorthleck (04563) 226

This loch lies to the west of the B862 between Whitebridge and Fort Augustus. It is very pleasantly situated and is over 1¼ miles long by 600 yards wide. The most favoured drifts are near to the islands in the north bay and the loch contains brown trout and some char. The trout average ¾ lb. and show a preference for Black Pennells and Zulus. An average basket should net you 4–6 trout but heavier fish of up to 2½ lb. were taken during the 1981 season. Hotel guests have priority. Bank fishing is not allowed.

LOCH KILLIN   35/529105
Permission: The Head Keeper, Garrogie Estate, Gorthleck, Inverness-shire.
Tel: Gorthleck (04563) 284

Loch Killin is to the south-east of Whitebridge and is a dramatic loch lying in a narrow valley with Carn Dubh (726m) to the west and Carn a'Choire Ghlaise (778m) to the east. Fishing is from the bank only. The east bank produces the best results and although the trout only average ½ lb. occasional monsters are taken. This loch is 1,000 feet above sea level and also contains char. Standard loch pattern flies will do, and hotel guests have priority.

LOCH MHOR   35/540197
LOCH BRAN   35/507193
Permission: N. M. S. MacDougall, Foyers Hotel, Foyers, Inverness-shire.
Tel: Gorthleck (04563) 216

Both these lochs lie adjacent to the B862 Inverness–Fort Augustus road in Strath Errick and are most attractive to fish. Loch Mhor used to be two lochs, Loch Farraline and Loch Garth, and these were joined to form a present hydro-electric Loch Mhor. A gravity feed system is used to run turbines at Foyers and this nightly operation does not help the fishing on old Loch Garth. However, it does not seem to affect Loch Farraline and the trout here average ¾ lb. A 4½ lb. trout was caught during 1980 and good baskets can be had to standard pattern loch flies. The lovely bay round Aberchalder and Migovie are favourite areas. Loch Bran is a small forest loch to the north of Loch Mhor with a main section and two large bays. The water is peaty but large fish are often taken and trout of up to 3 lb. have come from Bran. The average is ¾ lb. and Loch Bran is a very pleasant loch to fish.

LOCH MULLARDOCH   25/190305
Permission: Glen Affric Hotel, Cannich, Inverness-shire.
Tel: Cannich (04565) 214

Loch Mullardoch is a remote, beautiful loch 8 miles long by half a mile wide. It is surrounded by magnificent mountains and is in one of the least populated areas of Scotland. Westwards it is roadless to the Atlantic and this is a majestic place to fish. Approach the loch from Cannich village via the A831 road from Lovat Bridge on the A9. Trout average ¾ lb. and a day's fishing should bring you 6–8 fish. There is a track for most of the north shore with many good bays and points where fish lie. Best flies include Black Pennell, Greenwell Glory, Butcher and Alexandra. There are much larger fish in the loch so be prepared for that big one all the time. A superb loch in matchless scenery.

LOCH BEINN A'MHEADHOIN   25/240250
Permission: J. Graham & Co., 71 Castle Street, Inverness.
Tel: Inverness (0463) 33178

This loch is 5 miles long by 700 yards wide and lies at the head of lovely Glen Affric. Mountains rise from the tree-lined shore of the loch and the trout are good fighters, averaging ¾ lb. in weight. A reasonable basket would amount to 8 fish and trout rise well to all the usual patterns. Approach from the A831 from Lovat Bridge. In Cannich go straight on, past the hotel and this road will lead you to the loch.

LOCH OICH   34/320010
Permission:
Miss Ellice, Taigh An Lianach, Aberchalder Farm, Invergarry.
Tel: Invergarry (08093) 287.
The Rod & Gun Shop, 18 High Street, Fort William.
Tel: Fort William (0397) 2656

The Caledonian Canal runs through Loch Oich and the loch is 4 miles long by 900 yards wide. The loch contains salmon and brown trout but the trout are dour and hard to catch. However, they have a good average weight of over 1 lb. and fish of up to 3½ lb. are often taken. Fishing is from the boat only and the best places to fish are in the bays on the north shore. Particularly good is the bay to the west of where the River Garry enters the loch and another good area is in the vicinity of Laggan Lochs. The best time to fish Loch Oich is during the months of June, July and August either in the early morning or at dusk. A basket taken during the 1981 season should encourage you; 6 fish weighing 11 lb. 8 oz. Flies to use are Peter Ross, Alexandra, Black Sedge and Wickham's Fancy. On its day, one of the best lochs in Scotland.

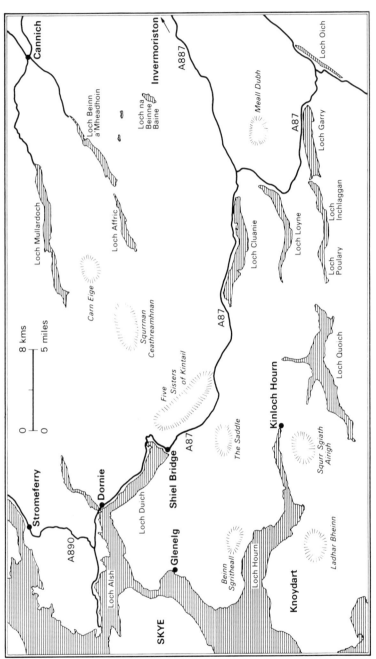

Map 16 *Glen Garry*

12 *Wild country – Loch Cluanie.*

LOCH GARRY   34/230020
INCHLAGGAN   34/180017
LOCH POULARY   34/125014

Permission:
Tomdoun Hotel, Invergarry, Inverness-shire.
Tel: Tomdoun (08092) 218;
Garry Gualach Adventure Centre, Invergarry, Inverness-shire.
Tel: Tomdoun: (08092) 230

Loch Garry and the surrounding lochs are some of the most beautiful in Scotland and cover a vast area of over 8 miles by 1 mile. There are very large fish in these lochs and trout of up to 18 lb. 2 oz. have been caught. This fish was landed in 1956 and at the time was a record for Britain. The 1981 season saw a 9 lb. fish caught and several trout of 4 lb. and heavier are taken during the course of the season. The level of the loch was considerably raised when it became part of the hydro-electric scheme and one of the best areas to fish on Inchlaggan is on the line of the old River Garry. Both boat and bank fishing are available and the lochs are easily accessible. Fishing on Poulary is best from the boat though, since the margins are very shallow and weedy. Glen Garry has a lot to offer the angler and is a pleasant place to spend some time. The Tomdoun Hotel offers all the comforts of a good fishing hotel whereas Garry Gualach on the other side is a holiday activity centre where the accommodation is more simple. Whichever you choose, or indeed if you are passing through, this area will captivate you with its marvellous scenery. All the standard pattern flies work well. During the 1985 season a trout of 16 lb. was caught on Loch Garry and fish of 8, 6 and 5 lb. were also taken.

LOCH QUOICH   33/020020
Permission:
Tomdoun Hotel, Invergarry, Inverness-shire.
Tel: Tomdoun (08092) 218
Lovat Arms Hotel, Fort Augustus, Inverness-shire.
Tel: Fort Augustus (0320) 6206

Loch Quoich, at the head of Glen Garry, is one of the remotest lochs in the north and is a wild, windy and lonely place. It was amidst these ragged wastelands that Prince Charles Edward Stewart hid from the encircling searchers, and it was through these inhospitable hills that he finally escaped to the west. Spare him a thought as you fish this lovely loch. Quoich offers good sport although it can be very dour at times. The loch is easily accessible via the road from Invergarry to the high dam at the eastern end. The average weight of trout is in the ¾ lb. class but Quoich holds the British record with a fish of over 20 lb. Each year produces a few double-figure fish and a number of trout over 4–5 lb. If you have a limited amount of time to spend then an outboard motor is almost essential if you are even to begin to cover this large loch, and Quoich is an endless delight of bays and headlands which must be explored. Better arrange to spend a week on the loch. You might just begin to get the feel of it. Take the standard pattern loch flies and warn them at home to have a glass case ready. Some really large trout were taken during the 1985 season, including two trout of 17 lb. and fish of 16, 15, 14, 13 and 11 lb.

LOCH CLUANIE   33/090115–34/140095
Permission:
Duncan Stoddart, Stalkers Cottage, Cluanie Lodge, Invergarry, Inverness-shire.
Tel: Dalchreichart (0320) 40208;
Cluanie Hotel, Glenmoriston, Inverness-shire.
Tel: Dalchreichart (0320) 40238

Loch Cluanie is to the south of the A87 Invermoriston–Kyle of Lochalsh road and is 7½ miles long by three-quarters of a mile

13   *Evening sunlight on Loch Loyne.*

wide. The loch has a depth of over 200 feet and around it tower
Sgurr nan Conbhairean (1109m) and Beinn Loinne (789m). This is
majestic countryside, wild and lovely. Trout in Cluanie average
1 lb. with much larger fish frequently taken. Both boat and bank
fishing are available. Fishing from the boat is most productive and
outboard motors may be hired. All the standard patterns of loch
flies catch fish and an average day might bring 5 trout. Fish the
shallows where the many feeder burns enter the loch. The vicinity
of the islands can also be good as can Lundie Bay. Outstanding
scenery will make up for perhaps hard fishing, but there is always
the chance of a 7 lb. trout 'bumping' into your flies so watch out
for it.

LOCH LOYNE   34/160050

Permission: Cluanie Hotel, Glenmoriston, Inverness-shire.
Tel: Dalchreichart (0320) 40238

Loch Loyne is 7 miles long by half a mile wide and is a hydro-
electric loch the level having been raised to join two waters into
one. Mountains tower all round this distant water and it is approached from the A87 Invergarry–Kyle of Lochalsh road from the
south or via the A887 Inverness road from the east. This is a

very deep loch and fishing is from the bank only so do be careful. There are good bays to fish along the north shore and the west end of the loch from Glenloyne to the inlet burn is also a good place to try. Loyne holds trout which average ½–¾ lb. with some much larger fish as well, but they are very hard to catch. It also holds some very large pike with fish of up to 30 lb. recorded. For the trout use all the standard pattern loch flies. They work well.

LOCH LOCHY   34/190860–280950
Permission: None required but boats may be hired from Mrs Duck, Poplar Cottage, Bunarkaig.
Tel: Gairlochy (039782) 283

Loch Lochy is 10 miles long by three-quarters of a mile wide and part of the Caledonian Canal system. This is a beautiful loch with wooded shores and the bulk of Ben Nevis dominating the southern view. Loch Lochy holds some very good trout indeed but they are shy creatures and very hard to catch. Persevere, though, since fish of up to 7 lb. can be caught and you may consider the effort worth while. This is an easily accessible loch since the A82 runs next to the southern shore for its full length.

LOCH ARKAIG   33/990915–34/160890
Permission: Rod and Gun Shop, Fort William, Inverness-shire.
Tel: Fort William (0397) 2656

This romantic loch with its association with Bonnie Prince Charlie, sunken treasure and the commandoes of the last war lies 15 miles north of Fort William at the end of the Great Glen. Leave the A82 at Spean Bridge and follow the B8004. This narrow twisting road passes up the Mile Dorcha (The Dark Mile) and eventually ends at Muraggan. Arkaig is surrounded by mountains and is nearly 12 miles long by an average of ½–¾ mile wide. The deepest part of the loch is near Eilean a'Ghiubhaid where it drops to 350 feet. From either shore dozens of small feeder burns cascade down the hills into the loch and these are the most productive areas to fish. Loch Arkaig holds brown trout, sea trout, occasional salmon and pike. Very large trout are taken from Arkaig but the average weight is in the order of ½–¾ lb. Most of the larger fish are taken by trolling but the standard loch fly patterns will do fine for their smaller brethren. Arkaig can be very dour and frustrating but on a warm June evening – fish or no – there are few more delightful places to fish.

14 *Loch Lochy.*

LOCH SHIEL   40/680680–905807
Fergie MacDonald, Clanranald Hotel, Acharacle, Inverness-shire.
Tel: Acharacle (098785) 622;
Loch Shiel Hotel, Acharacle, Inverness-shire.
Tel: Salen (096785) 224
Rod and Gun Shop, Fort William, Inverness-shire.
Tel: Fort William (0397) 2656

Loch Shiel lies to the north of Fort William and is one of the longest lochs in Scotland, being 17 miles long by half a mile wide. The loch is deepest by Meall nan Creag Leac (755m) where it drops to over 400 feet. Shiel is a wild, beautiful place with a seemingly unending range of mountians crowding the shore. The monument to the highlanders of the ill-fated '45 Rebellion at the north end sets the scene, although as far as fishing is concerned the southern end is the place to fish. It's a long road round, but the views are spectacular and make for a memorable drive. Shiel is best known and most fished for its sea trout and salmon. However, brown trout of 2–3 lb. are caught but the average weight is more in the order of ¾ –1 lb. Use standard patterns and fish the south end, especially the many small bays and islands. Creel Fishing offer a complete service including accommodation, hire of boats, outboard motors, rods and tackle, tuition and the services of an experienced gillie, if required. They will also arrange fishing on nearby hill lochs if Shiel is too windy to fish.

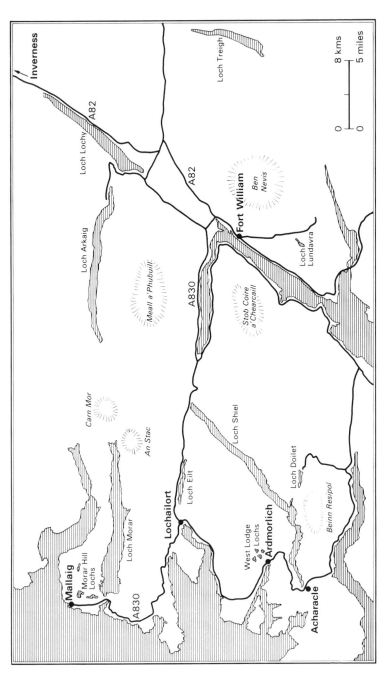

Map 17 *Fort William*

LOCH DOILET   40/810677

Permission: Ben View Hotel, Strontian, Sunart, Inverness-shire.
Tel: Strontian (0967) 2333

Loch Doilet is joined to Loch Shiel by the River Polloch and
contains sea trout and salmon. The loch is surrounded by forestry
plantations and hills and mountains of Sunart and Moidart.
Fishing is from the boat only and the eastern bay is the most
productive area. Sea trout of over 4 lb. have been caught and
salmon average 6–8 lb. Brown trout are in the 6–8 oz. class. This
is a very lovely loch to fish in a superb setting.

LOCH EILT   40/815825

Permission:
Lochailort Inn, Lochailort, Inverness-shire.
Tel: Lochailort (06877) 208;
Rod and Gun Shop, 18 High Street, Fort William, Inverness-
shire.
Tel: Fort William (0397) 2656;
Morar Hotel, Morar, by Mallaig, Inverness-shire.
Tel: Mallaig (0687) 2237

Loch Eilt is adjacent to the A830 and is 3¼ miles long by some
400 yards wide. The loch contains salmon, sea trout and brown
trout and is best known and most fished for the former rather
than the latter. Brown trout average ¾–1 lb. with the odd heavier
fish from time to time, but it is the sea trout which provide the
greatest attraction.

LOCH MORAR   40/690920–865905

Permission:
A. G. McLeod. Morar Hotel, Morar, by Mallaig, Inverness-shire.
Tel: Mallaig (0687) 2237;
The Superintendent, Alt an Loin, Morar, by Mallaig, Inverness-
shire.

Morar is the deepest freshwater loch in Europe and plunges to
over 1,000 feet between South Tarbet Bay and Camas Luinge Bay
where the River Meoble enters. At the end of the road to the isles
this desolate and magnificent water covers an area 12 miles long

15 *Loch Morar – the islands.*

by up to 1½ miles wide. The best way to explore Morar is by boat, the south shore being almost 'trackless' and the public road on the north bank ends after 5 miles at Bracorina. The loch has excellent brown trout and perhaps the odd salmon from time to time dependent upon water levels. The best fishing area is at the west end of the loch among the islands. Both boat and bank fishing are allowed and splendid results can be had from the bank. Because the water shelves so rapidly it isn't necessary to cast a long way out to cover the fish. Take great care when wading – it's a long way down. The trout average ¾ lb. and fight well. An average basket should bring you 4–6 fish and the best flies to use are Butchers, March Brown, Black Pennell, Greenwell's, and Grouse and Claret. The 1980 season saw a fish of 11 lb. 8 oz. caught and 1981 produced a trout of 7 lb. 11 oz. Other sample baskets contained 6 fish weighing 5 lb. 8 oz. and 4 trout weighing 2 lb. 10 oz. This is a splendid loch in magnificent setting. Get there if you can and fish its clear, clean waters. Keep a weather eye open for 'Morag' – Loch Ness has a rival here, and you never can tell what you might hook in the depths.

LOCH AN NOSTARIE	40/690955
LOCH EIREAGORAIDH	40/720957
LOCHAN A'MHEADHOIN	40/695947
LOCH A'GHOBAICH	40/686940

Permission: Not required

These hill lochs, and several others, lie to the north of Loch Morar at the end of the road to the isles and they contain trout which average ½–¾ lb. in weight. Fishing is from the bank only and excellent baskets are taken each year. All the lochs involve a good 'hike' out into the Morar Hills but they are well worth the effort and an ideal place for a day out in superb surroundings. Standard pattern loch flies will do. Hill loch fishing at its best.

LOCH NAM PAITEAN   40/725740

Permission: Mrs N. D. Stewart, Kinlochmoidart House, Kinloch-moidart, Lochailort, Salen, Inverness-shire.
Tel: Salen (096785) 609

This is a hill loch to the north of Ardmolich on the A861 from Acharacle to Lochailort in Moidart. A track leads off the minor road to the east of Ardmolich at Brunery and winds up Coire Mor and Leached Fheadancach. It is a stiff climb but worth the effort. The average weight of trout is 1 lb. and a reasonable day should produce 4–6 trout. The loch was stocked many years ago and the native population has thrived and is of really first-class quality. Best time to fish Paitean is May and June when good baskets are taken. The loch is a multitude of bays and points with a scatter of small islands. Trout of up to 2–3 lb. are sometimes caught and this is an excellent loch well worth visiting. Both boat and bank fishing are available and standard pattern loch flies work well.

LOCHAN A'MHUILLINN	40/700742
LOCH NA CAILLICH	40/705747

Permission: Mrs N. D. Stewart, Kinlochmoidart House, Kinloch-moidart, Lochailort, Salen, Inverness-shire.
Tel: Salen (096785) 609

Fishing on these and other nearby hill lochs all involve a good walk but they are delightfully remote and surrounded by some of the finest scenery in Scotland. Detailed directions will be given on booking and fishing is from the bank only. These lochs fish best during the early months of the season and standard pattern loch flies will do – and strong legs.

LOCHAN MEALL A'MHADAIDH 40/717750

Permission: Mrs N. D. Stewart, Kinlochmoidart House, Kinloch-moidart, Lochailort, Salen, Inverness-shire.

Tel: Salen (096785) 609

This lovely loch is at an altitude of 2,000 feet and is in a setting of supreme beauty. The walk up takes about an hour and a half and fishing is from the bank only. This is a classic hill loch with a scatter of small islands and trout are caught all round. The fish are a good weight, 1½ lb., but hard to catch. Larger fish are taken each year and this fine loch produces trout of up to 5–6 lb. You may puff and huff a bit on the way up but it's effort well spent. Directions will be given upon making your booking.

LOCH MUDLE 47/544660
LOCHAN A'MHADAIDH RIABHAICH 47/557656

Permission: Mike MacGregor, Glenmore Cottage, Glenborrodale, Salen, Inverness-shire.

Tel: Glenborrodale (09724) 263

Fishing on these lochs is managed by the Ardnamurchan Estate and they are situated midway between Kilchoan and Glenborrodale on the B8007. The lochs contain brown trout which average ½–¾ lb. with some larger fish of up to 1½ lb. being caught occasionally. Salmon are sometimes caught on Loch Mudle and permits are issued on the understanding that anglers make proper returns of catches. Both boat and bank fishing are available and baskets of 10–12 trout are often taken. A'Mhadaidh Riabhaich is the best for trout but both lochs are pleasant to fish and in lovely surroundings. Standard loch fly patterns.

THE ARDTORNISH ESTATE

LOCH ARIENAS	49/685510
LOCH DOIRE NAM MART	49/660525
LOCH TEARNAIT	49/750470
CROSBEN BLACK LOCHS	49/703530
EIGNIGG BLACK LOCHS	49/780454
LOCH NAN CLACH	49/785465
LOCH UISGE	49/805550
CAOL LOCHAN	49/780482

Permission: Ardtornish Estate, Estate Office, Morvern, by Oban, Argyll.

Tel: Morvern (096784) 288

These lochs all hold good stocks of wild brown trout and are

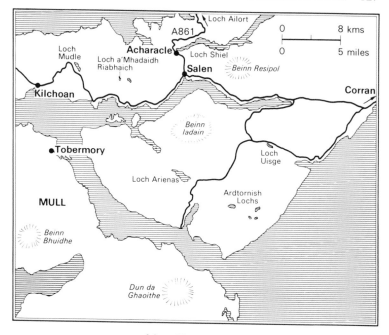

Map 18 *Ardtornish*

spread throughout the lovely hills and mountains of the Morvern peninsula. Approach from the Corran ferry or by the ferry to Lochaline from Oban or Fishnish on Mull. Loch Arienas and Loch Doire nam Mart are both adjacent to the minor Kinloch–Teacuis road (branching off the A884 at Claggan). Tearnait involves a walk of 2½ miles and the other lochs will all stretch the legs a bit, but it is worth the effort. Whilst there are boats on the first three lochs named, most trout are caught from the bank. The average weight is ½–¾ lb. but each season sees a number of fish between 2 and 3 lb. landed. These lochs fish best during the months of May and June, and again in September. Some 500–800 trout are taken each season. The best brown trout was a fish of 4 lb. and salmon and sea trout also enter Loch Arienas and Doire nam Mart. Salmon average 6–7 lb. with a best fish last season of 26 lb. and sea trout average 1 lb. with a best of 9 lb. Flies to use to attract them include Grouse and Claret, Alexandra, Peter Ross, Soldier Palmer, Invicta and Silver Invicta.

During 1985 the Ardtornish waters gave excellent sport, producing 80 salmon, 193 sea trout and nearly 400 brown trout. The estate also provides good self-catering cottages for anglers.

LOCHAN LUNN DA BHRA (Loch Lundavra)

41/090660

Permission: Mrs MacCallum, Lundavra Farm, Fort William, Inverness-shire.
Tel: Fort William (0397) 2582

This is a beautiful loch to the south of Fort William, high up on the slopes of Ben Nevis. A narrow, single track road leads up from the town into the hills and drivers should be very careful on some of the blind summits. It is important to establish which way the road turns before driving on! The loch is about a mile long by 250 yards wide and both boat and bank fishing are available. This is an exciting loch to fish and trout of 3–5 lb. are frequently taken. The heaviest fish caught on Lundavra was a trout of 8 lb. and the average weight is ¾ lb. Fish are caught all round the loch but the favoured areas are where the feeder burns enter at the west end and in the vicinity of the island. Book in advance and take along Peter Ross, Soldier Palmer and Black Pennell. A lovely loch, easily accessible and well worth a visit.

LOCH TREIGH

41/335720

Permission: British Alcan Highland Smelters Ltd, Estate Office, 33 High Street, Fort William.
Tel: (0397) 2433

Loch Treigh is 6 miles long by three-quarters of a mile wide and contains brown trout and pike. It is a distant, remote and dramatic water with Stob Coire Easain (1,116m) to the west and Stob Coire Sgriodain (960m) to the east. Turn south from the A86 at Inverlair Falls on the River Spean. This is a deep loch, over 300 feet in parts and great care should be taken when wading. The

16   *Loch Lundavra on the slopes of Ben Nevis.*

shallows are the most productive areas to fish, particularly at either end of the loch. There are very large trout in Loch Treigh but an average day should produce a basket of 3–4 fish weighing 2½–3 lb. Standard loch fly patterns should be used.

AVIELOCHAN LOCH 36/907165

Permission:
G. G. Mortimer, Fishing Tackle Shop, 61 High Street, Grantown-on-Spey, Morayshire.
Tel: Grantown-on-Spey (0479) 2684;
Mrs. M. McCook, Avielochan, Aviemore, Inverness-shire.
Tel: Aviemore (0479) 810450

Avielochan lies adjacent to the A95 2½ miles north of Aviemore. There are two sessions, 10.00 am–6.00 pm and 6.00 pm until dusk. The loch is stocked with both brown and rainbow trout with an average weight of 1 lb. Best fish taken during the 1981 season weighed 2½ lb. and in 1985 a trout of 2 lb. 4 oz. was caught. An average basket should produce 3 fish. No more than

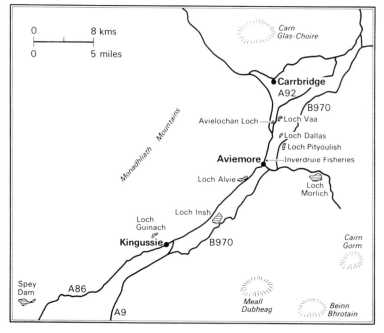

Map 19 *Aviemore*

ten rods are allowed on this small loch and because it is so easily accessible you would be well advised to book in advance. Standard loch fly patterns will do and in spite of its proximity to 'civilisation' Avielochan is a most pleasant venue for a few hours sport. Lovely views of the Cairngorms.

LOCH PITYOULISH   36/920135
Permission: Osprey Fishing School, Aviemore Centre, Aviemore, Inverness-shire.
Tel: Aviemore (0479) 810767

Pityoulish is to the east of Aviemore and is approached from the B970 Coylumbridge–Nethybridge road. This is a deep loch over half a mile long by quarter of a mile wide, surrounded by trees and nestling at the foot of Creag a'Ghreusaiche (435m). Fishing from the boat only and the loch contains brown trout. Excellent baskets are taken and the trout average ¾ lb. Fish of under 10 inches must be returned to the water.

LOCH MORLICH   36/965095
Permission: Camp Warden, Glenmore Forest Park, Glenmore, by Aviemore, Inverness-shire.
Tel: Cairngorm (047986) 271

It is many years since I fished Loch Morlich. Then it was a remote and peaceful place. Now it has become a major activity centre and attracts thousands each year. Nevertheless, it is still a beautiful loch and it contains brown trout and pike. On its day, good sport. Always very lovely to be near.

LOCH DALLAS   36/932160
Permission:
G. G. Mortimer, Fishing Tackle Shop, 61 High Street, Grantown-on-Spey, Morayshire.
Tel: Grantown-on-Spey (0479) 2684;
Mrs. M. McCook, Avielochan, Aviemore, Inverness-shire.
Tel: Aviemore (0479) 810450

Approach Loch Dallas from Kinchurdy Road in Boat of Garten and after leaving the 30 m.p.h. limit proceed for a further half mile, then turn left under the Strathspey railway line on the road to Kinchurdy Farm, where you will find the loch situated below semi-detached farm cottages, short of the farmsteading. The loch lies close to the River Spey with fine views of the Cairngorms and covers an area of 8 acres. Fishing is from the boat only and there is a bag limit of 10 fish per day. The loch is stocked with brown and rainbow trout and their average weight is 1 lb. The best fish taken during 1981 weighed 3 lb. and a brown trout of 2½ lb. was caught in 1985. The best rainbow taken during 1985 weighed 2 lb. Standard loch fly patterns bring results. Trout are caught all over the loch and excellent sport can be had.

LOCH VAA   36/913175
Permission:
G. G. Mortimer, Fishing Tackle Shop, 61 High Street, Grantown-on-Spey, Morayshire.
Tel: Grantown-on-Spey (0479) 2684;
Mrs M. McCook, Avielochan, Aviemore, Inverness-shire.
Tel: Aviemore (0479) 810450

Take the same farm road for Loch Vaa as for Loch Dallas but bear right at the first junction in the track. Loch Vaa is in the midst of the forest and covers an area of 35 acres. No bank fishing, but two boats available for visitors. This is a delightful, secluded loch with excellent fish, both brown and rainbow trout. The average weight is 1½ lb. and there is a limit of 10 fish per boat per day. Trout of over 4 lb. have been caught on Vaa and the fish respond well to the standard pattern loch flies. 1985 produced an excellent brown trout of 4 lb. 8 oz. and the heaviest rainbow trout weighed 2 lb. 8 oz. In calm weather good results will be had with dry fly also. Fish are taken all round the loch and there are many bays and points to explore. Book well in advance for, as you might imagine, this is a popular loch with local anglers.

LOCH ALVIE   36/865095
Permission: Alvie Estate, Estate Office, Kincraig, Kingussie, Inverness-shire.
Tel: Kincraig (05404) 255

Loch Alvie is one mile long by half a mile wide and lies close to the A9 8 miles north of Kingussie. This is a shallow loch of not more than 20 feet deep and the best fishing area is in the western end. It contains brown trout and pike with the trout averaging ½–¾ lb. A very lovely setting and a pleasant loch to fish. Boat only, bank fishing is not allowed.

LOCH INSH   35/830045
Permission: Cairngorm Sailing School, Kincraig, Kingussie, Inverness-shire.
Tel: Kincraig (05404) 272

Loch Insh is easily accessible and very lovely. It contains salmon, sea trout and brown trout and is an expansion of the River Spey. The best trout fishing area is at the southern end and round the islands at the northern end. Loch Insh is shallow over most of its area although there are parts where it drops to over 100 feet. Boat fishing only and the trout average ¾ lb. Larger trout have been caught and from time to time Loch Insh produces fish of up to 4 lb. Popular with canoe addicts.

INVERDRUIE FISHERIES   36/901112
Permission: Inverdruie Fishery, Rothiemurchus, Aviemore, Inverness-shire.
Tel: Aviemore (0479) 810703

This is a fish farm near Aviemore and over 300,000 trout are pro-duced each year for the commercial market. An 8 acre pond has been established for visitors and casting is easy since the banks have been cleared of trees. Something for all the members of the family with play area for children, refreshment bar and picnic area. Bank fishing and a limit of 4 fish per rod. Fishing is available from 10.00 am until dusk.

SPEY DAM   35/570935
Permission: The Paper Shop, Kingussie, Inverness-shire.
Tel: Kingussie (05402) 207

Spey Dam, on the upper reaches of the River Spey, is one mile long by half a mile wide. Approach via the minor road at Laggan Bridge. The loch is surrounded by magnificent hills and moun-tains and contains excellent brown trout. The local angling asso-ciation stocks Spey Dam and both boat and bank fishing is available. Trout average ¾ lb. although there are good numbers of larger fish. As always, the only problem is getting them out. Use standard pattern flies to try.

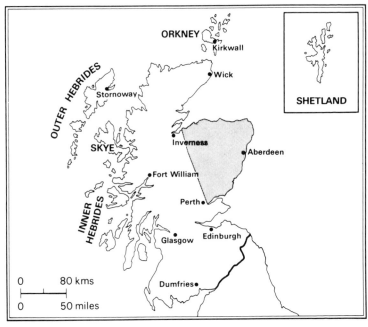

Map 20 *Angus and the North-East*

6 Angus and the North-East

All too often the potential of the trout fishing in this area is under-estimated. Most visiting anglers fish for increasingly rare salmon on the great rivers such as Don, Dee and Findhorn and very few try the many lovely trout lochs. There are few waters in Scotland that can match the excellent returns produced by Rescobie Loch near Forfar and few lochs in more remote and magnificent settings than Lochs Brandy and Wharrl in Glen Clova. The Loch of Strathbeg is one of the least known and most attractive lochs in Scotland whilst Lochindorb Loch, with its dramatic ruined castle, is a perfect place to spend a day. I began fishing in this area in the early 1960s and it was in the forests of Glen Isla that my wife and I saw our first wild cat. We spent an unforgettable few days walking and fishing amongst some of the most lovely scenery in all of Scotland. The Forth and Tay road bridges have made the area more easily accessible and I would highly recommend it to you.

LOCH OF LINTRATHEN   53/280550

Permission: Water Services Department, Ward Road, Dundee.
Tel: Dundee (0382) 21164
Club bookings available from
Dr Parratt, 91 Strathern Road, Broughty Ferry, Dundee.
Tel: Dundee (0382) 21164;
Club membership available from
J. Christie, 51 Broadford Terrace, Broughty Ferry, Dundee.
Tel: Dundee (0382) 736462

The Loch of Lintrathen lies to the north of Alyth and is 1½ miles long by three-quarters of a mile wide. Fishing is from boats only and 11 are available for anglers. The season extends from April to September and the loch is stocked with brown trout. Outboard motors are not allowed and two boats are held daily until 5.00 pm for the use of visitors who are not members of the Lintrathen Angling Club. There is an excellent clubhouse at the loch and a water bailiff is on hand to advise anglers on the best places to fish and which flies to use. Trout average ¾ lb. but a number of fish

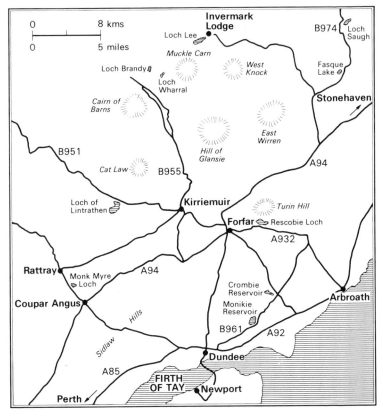

Map 21   *Dundee and Angus*

of 2 lb. are taken each season. Anglers are limited to 18 fish per boat and individual catches of 6–10 fish are common. Sample catches taken during the 1981 season will give you an indication of what to expect: May 6 fish weighing 9 lb., June 5 fish weighing 6¼ lb. The Lintrathen trout have a great reputation and fight hard and are of good quality. The most favoured fishing areas are around the island of the north-west shore and along the south shore. Standard loch fly patterns do well and in calm conditions great sport can be had using dry fly. This is a lovely loch in very pleasant surroundings, easily accessible and worth fishing. Bookings may be made up to seven days in advance.

MONK MYRE LOCH   53/210427

Permission: David Simpson, Post Office, Cupar, Angus.
Tel: Cupar (08282) 329

Monk Myre lies to the north of Cupar, east of the A923
Blairgowrie road and covers an area of 14 acres. Bank fishing is
not allowed but four boats are available for anglers. The loch is
stocked with both brown and rainbow trout and the average
weight is just over 1 lb. There is a limit of 8 fish per rod and the
best flies to use are Greenwell's Glory, Invicta, Grouse and Claret,
all in the 14–16 size. Trout of up to 3 lb. are taken each season and
an average basket would consist of 3–4 fish. Monk Myre fishes
best during June and July and the most productive area is in the
middle and then closer to the margins as darkness falls. The
season extends from May until the end of October and this is a
very popular little loch – so book early.

RESCOBIE LOCH   54/520515

Permission: The Rescobie Loch Development Association, Jack
Yule, The Bailiff, South Lodge, Reswallie, by Forfar, Angus.
Tel: Letham (Angus) (030781) 384

The object of the Development Association is to provide good
fishing at a reasonable price and these aims are being achieved
very well indeed if results from Rescobie are anything to go by.
Excellent provision is also made for disabled anglers – a facility
sadly lacking on most other waters. Rescobie Loch covers an area
of 190 acres and lies between Forfar and Friockheim on the A932.
This is an easily accessible loch in attractive surroundings of good
farming land and wooded slopes. Each year the loch is stocked
with 3,000 brown trout of 10 inches and 2,000 rainbow trout,
some of which are put into the loch weighing 3 lb. The brown
trout average 1 lb. 2 oz. whilst the rainbows average 1 lb. 4 oz.
Both boat and bank fishing are available and a limit of 6 fish per
rod per day is applied. An average basket should account for 2–3
fish. There are excellent trout in the loch and the best basket taken
during the 1981 season contained 6 fish weighing 9 lb. 12 oz. – all
caught from the bank. The best basket taken from the boat held
11 trout weighing 22 lb. The heaviest rainbow weighed 7 lb. 8 oz.
and the best brown trout 4 lb. 12 oz. Flies that do the damage on
Rescobie include Dunkeld, Black Pennell, Alexandra, Wickham's
Fancy, Cinnamon and Gold, and standard reservoir lures. Visitors
will find Jack Yule is an experienced and helpful angler and
Rescobie must be highly recommended as the best loch in the
area. Book in advance.

MONIKIE RESERVOIR   54/505380

Permission: Monikie Angling Club, Club Secretary, 30 Charleston
Drive, Dundee.
Tel: Newbigging (038235) 300

There are two waters here, separated by a narrow peninsula, and
they are within the confines of Monikie Country Park, to the
north of Monifieth. Fishing is from boats only and two are held
daily until 5.00 pm for the use of visitors who are not club
members. The lochs are stocked with brown trout and the
average weight of fish is ¾ lb. There is a bag limit – frequently
achieved – of 12 fish per boat and trout of 2 lb. are taken with fish
of over 1 lb. being common. Best flies include Wickham's Fancy,
Butchers, Black Pennell, Greenwell's and Invicta. Two sessions
operate, from 8.00 am–4.30 pm and from 5.00 pm until dusk.
Monikie fishes during the early months of the season and in mid-
summer, if it ever comes. Try the late evening for best results.
Man-made lochs, but nevertheless attractive and first-class fishing.

CROMBIE RESERVOIR   54/525407

Permission: Monikie Angling Club, Club Secretary, 30 Charleston
Drive, Dundee.
Tel: Newbigging (038235) 300

Crombie is in a woodland setting to the north of Carnoustie.
Approach from the B961 just past the junction with the A958
Forfar–Carnoustie road. Crombie Reservoir is in a country park
and wildlife sanctuary and is a long, narrow water which wends
its way through the trees for a distance of 1½ miles. The water is
stocked with brown trout and they average ½–¾ lb. The most
productive fishing area is around the large island at the western
end of the reservoir and in the 'Cut' where the feeder burn enters.
Boat fishing only and an average basket should produce 6–8 trout.
Fish of up to 1½ lb. have been caught and the most favoured flies
are Wickham's Fancy, Pennells, Greenwell's and Invicta. That great
northern fly the Ke-He also does well. Fishing is divided into two
sessions as at Monikie Reservoir and there is a deposit required
when you collect the key for the boat. This deposit is returned
after fishing – provided the key is also. An easily accessible and
very pleasant water to fish, well managed and worth a visit.

LOCH WHARRAL   44/358745

Permission: The Factor, Airlie Estate Office, Cortachy, Kirriemuir,
Angus.
Tel: Cortachy (05754) 222

Loch Wharral is 700 yards long by 200 yards wide and lies at an altitude of 1,800 feet. There is an invigorating two mile walk to get to Wharral and you should approach from the B966 at Wheen. The crags of Ben Tirran (896m) rise sharply from the margin of the loch and although the trout are not large they give a good account of themselves. Fishing is from the bank only and wading is reasonably comfortable – carrying the waders up the hill is not. Fish the north-east corner and the south shore using standard pattern loch flies. Loch Wharral is a very lovely loch, infrequently fished, and can give excellent sport. A trout of 1 lb. would be considered very large for this delightful water, but it is worth the effort required to get to it and is remote and peaceful.

LOCH BRANDY   44/340765
Permission: The Factor, Airlie Estate Office, Cortachy, Kirriemuir, Angus.
Tel: Cortachy (05754) 222

Loch Brandy lies at the head of Glen Clova in a horseshoe basin formed by the slopes of Green Hill (870m). This is a remote and lovely little loch and may be approached via a track which leaves the B955 just behind the Ogilvy Arms Hotel. Brandy contains a good stock of hard-fighting ½ lb. trout, but warm weather is really required before they can be tempted to rise. When they do, baskets of up to 30 fish can be taken and there are the odd 1 lb. trout from time to time – generally when you are lookng somewhere else. The best area is below the crags on the north-west shore and size 14–16 flies should be used. Try Butchers, Zulus and Black Pennell. A good walk up, but worth the effort. You will be rewarded with peace and quiet and surrounded by superb scenery.

LOCH LEE   44/420795
Permission: Fred Taylor, Invermark Estate Office, Glenesk, Angus.
Tel: Tarfside (03567) 208

Loch Lee is 1½ miles long by some 500 yards wide and lies in a hollow surrounded by Monawee (696m) to the north, Cairn Caidloch (647m) to the south and ragged Craig Maskeldie (687m) to the west. Loch Lee can be dangerously windy and at times fishing is cancelled due to high winds. Take along an outboard motor and a drogue. Bank fishing is not allowed and three boats are available for anglers. Lee is a deep loch and the best fishing area is at the western end of the loch where the water is shallow, and also round the western margins. The loch contains brown

17   *A fine hill loch basket.*

trout which average ½–¾ lb. and some char. The best trout caught during the 1981 season weighed 4 lb. and a char was caught which weighed 1 lb. 4 oz. Catches vary considerably according to weather conditions, but you should take home a basket of 6–12 fish and size 10–12 flies seem to do best. Flies to use include Blue and Black Zulu, Black Pennell, Grouse and Claret, and Kingfisher Butcher. The estate prefers to receive bookings by post giving at least two weeks notice. This is a most attractive loch to fish, out in the wilds amidst splendid scenery. Fishing on Sunday is not allowed.

LOCH SAUGH   45/676788
Permission: Drumtochty Arms Hotel, Auchenblae, Kincardineshire.
Tel: Auchenblae (05612) 210

This is a long, narrow loch between Thorter Hill (416m) to the west and Strathfinella Hill (414m) to the east. Approach from the B966 from Auchenblae or from the north via the B974, turning east at Clatterin Brig. The loch is managed by the Brechin Angling Association who have stocked it with both brown and rainbow trout. Fishing is from the bank only and the trout average ¾ lb. Fish of over 2 lb. are taken occasionally and standard loch fly patterns will do.

FASQUE LAKE   45/645747

Permission: Peter Gladstone, Fasque, Fettercairn Laurencekirk, Kincardineshire.
Tel: Fettercairn (05614) 201

Fasque Lake lies to the west of Laurencekirk and is approached via the B974 from Fettercairn. This is a man-made lake of about 20 acres in a beautiful setting within the Fasque Estate. The loch–sorry lake, was built in 1840 and has excellent natural spawning grounds. It contains brown trout, and rainbow trout have also been introduced. Average weight on Fasque is 1 lb. but fish of up to 5 lb. are caught. There is a bag limit of three fish, but should a trout of more than 3½ lb. be caught after this limit has been reached the angler is allowed to keep it. Boat fishing only and there are two available. The estate has first-class accommodation available and guests have priority on the fishing. If you wish for privacy, peace and quiet and excellent fishing in beautiful surroundings, then this is well worth considering. Highly recommended.

LOCH VROTACHAN   43/123785

Permission:
Ballater Angling Association, 59 Golf Road, Ballater, Aberdeenshire.
Countrywear, Ballater, Aberdeenshire.
Tel: Ballater (0338) 55365

This loch lies above the ski slopes at Spittal of Glenshee. It may be reached in relative comfort by hitching a ride up on the chair lift and then by striking out north-west for about one mile. Loch Vrotachan lies at an altitude of over 2,000 feet amidst the wild corries and crags of the mountains of Mar. Brown trout average ½ lb. and fishing is from the bank. The loch is closed after 11 August. A wonderful loch in lovely surroundings and worth a visit. Take along standard loch fly patterns, they all produce results.

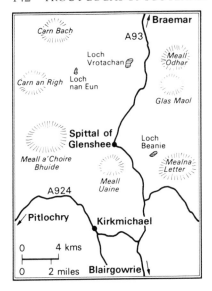

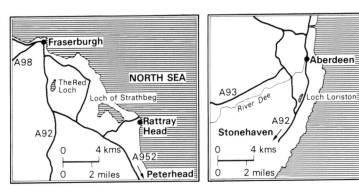

Map 22   *Aberdeen*

LOCH NAN EUN

43/063780

Permission: Estate Office, Invercauld Estate, Braemar, by Ballater, Aberdeenshire.
Tel: Braemar (03383) 224

Loch nan Eun lies at the head of Gleann Taitneach, 6 miles north-west of Spittal of Glenshee. Follow the track on the north side of the bridge at Spittal, where the A93 makes the sharp bend east.

The loch lies at an altitude of 2,000 feet and Beinn lutharan Mor towers a further 1,000 feet over the loch. Trout average ½ lb. with the odd larger fish, but visit Loch nan Eun as much for the beauty of the surroundings as for the fishing. The season closes on 11 August. Best flies are Butchers, Blue Zulu, Teal and Green, Black Pennell and Stoat's Tail.

LOCH BEANIE   43/160688
(sometimes called **Loch Shechernich)**
Permission: Estate Office, Invercauld Estate, Braemar, by Ballater, Aberdeenshire.
Tel: Braemar (03383) 224
To reserve the boat, contact the keeper, R. Hepburn, Wester Binzian, Glenshee, Perthshire.
Tel: Glenshee (025085) 224

Loch Beanie is 700 yards long by about 250 yards wide. It nestles in a hollow below Meatna Letter (702m) to the south and Craigenloch Hill (738m) to the north. Beyond, peaks and summits march into the distance and this is a really wonderful setting. The loch contains brown trout with an average weight of ½ lb. but larger fish are caught and a trout of 2¼ lb. was taken recently. There is a boat on the loch but bank fishing is just as rewarding. The season closes on 11 August. Approach Beanie from Runavey Farm (43/130690) and it's a walk of about 2 miles. Standard loch fly patterns will do fine.

LORISTON LOCH   38/940010
Permission: J. Somers and Sons, 40 Thistle Street, Aberdeen.
Tel: Aberdeen (0224) 50910

Loriston Loch lies 4 miles to the south of Aberdeen between the A92 and A956 roads. Fishing is from the bank only and the loch has been stocked with rainbow trout which average ¾ lb. Loriston is 700 yards long by 200 yards wide and can be a very windy loch. Wind direction dictates which shore to fish, but trout are taken all round the loch. An average basket should produce 3–4 fish and the heaviest trout caught during the 1981 season weighed 2¼ lb. Evening fishing is best and Red Buzzers and orange coloured flies, size 12–14, work well. An easily accessible loch. Bag limit, 6 trout per rod per day.

THE LOCH OF STRATHBEG   30/070590

Permission: Brown & McRae, Anderson House, 9–11 Firthside Street, Fraserburgh, Aberdeenshire.
Tel: Fraserburgh (03462) 4761

Strathbeg is one of the least well-known waters in Scotland and yet it is also one of the best trout lochs. It is also a paradise for the ornithologist and botonist and lies in an area of great natural beauty. The loch is separated from the sea by the Black Bar and covers an area extending to 2 miles long by some 600 yards wide, except in the northern bay where it is three-quarters of a mile across. The depth of the loch varies between 3 and 6 feet and there is one boat available for anglers. Bank fishing is not allowed. The loch has been stocked in years gone by and contains brown trout and Loch Leven trout. The average weight is about ¾ lb. and baskets of 6 fish are what to expect. It all depends upon the weather and larger baskets are frequently taken, including one last season (1981) of 18 fish. The southern end of the loch, where the boathouse is situated, fishes best and trout of 2½–3 lb. are caught here. Most fish are caught in the 'deeper' water and anglers should arrange their drift accordingly. Flies to use are size 14–16 and include March Brown, Blae and Black, Olive Duns and Butchers. This is the best loch in the area and you will find it a delightful place to fish. You must book in advance to make sure of getting the boat.

LOCH OF THE BLAIRS   27/023555

Permission: Department of Recreation, Moray District Council.
Local Agent: G. Lilley, 79D High Street, Forres, Morayshire.
Tel: Forres (0309) 72936

This is an easily accessible loch lying 2½ miles south of Forres. It is stocked regularly with both brown and rainbow trout and 3 boats are available for anglers. Bank fishing is not allowed. The loch is delightfully situated, surrounded by trees and has two small islands. Super bird life, squirrels and roe deer in the forest and the chance of an osprey proving that the fish are still there. There is a limit of 6 trout per rod per day – the osprey ignores this – and the fish average ¾ lb. Trout of up to 3 lb. are taken most seasons and an average basket should bring you 4 fish. Concentrate on the area round the islands and the margins of the loch, although fish can be taken all over. Most anglers use the standard loch fly patterns, but more and more are turning to reservoir lures and there is a restriction here on the size of lure permissible with 8

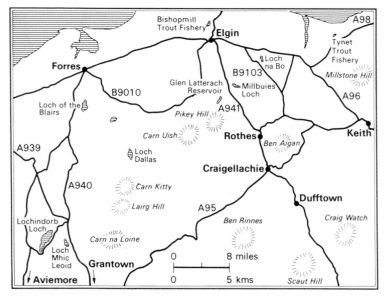

Map 23 *Morayshire*

being the largest allowed. Two sessions, 8.00 am–5.00 pm and 5.00 pm until dusk. Lovely loch and well worth a visit.

MILLBUIES LOCHS   28/242570
Permission:
Department of Recreation, Moray District Council, 30/32 High Street, Elgin, Morayshire.
Tel: Elgin (0343) 45121 Ext. 31;
The Warden, Millbuies Lochs, Elgin, Morayshire.
Tel: Longmorn (034386) 234

The Millbuies Lochs are 4 miles south of Elgin on the A941 Rothes road. There are two lochs covering an area of half a mile and they are in a woodland setting to the east of the main road. Four boats are available for anglers and bank fishing is not allowed. The District Council stock the loch with up to 2,000 rainbow trout each season and their average weight is just over 1 lb. Most outings should send you home with a basket of 2–3 fish (nothing is less certain than angling, however) and during the past three seasons fish of over 4 lb. have been caught each year. Trout are taken all over the lochs and the traditional loch fly patterns all do well. The Invicta seems to do best and also some of the reservoir lures which are becoming more popular. Millbuies is an excellent, well-managed fishery and, like Loch of the Blairs, a great credit to the enterprise of the District Council and an asset to the area.

LOCH-NA-BO   28/283600

Permission: D. Kinloch, Gardener's Cottage, Loch-Na-Bo, Lhanbryde, Elgin, Morayshire.
Tel: Lhanbryde (034384) 2214

This loch is near Elgin, half a mile east of Lhanbryde, and is approached via the A96 Fochabers road. Na-Bo is some 35 acres in extent and only boat fishing is allowed. Trout average ½ lb. and baskets of 3–4 fish is what to expect. This is a popular loch, so advance booking is advisable.

GLEN LATTERACH RESERVOIR   28/188525

Permission: Grampian Regional Council, Water Services Department, Grampian Road, Elgin, Morayshire.
Tel: Elgin (0343) 3361

Bank fishing only here, and the reservoir is 7 miles to the south of Elgin. Approach via the A941 at Whitewreath and turn right opposite the entrance to the Millbuie Lochs. Glen Latterach Reservoir is three-quarters of a mile long by 150 yards wide, easily accessible and contains brown trout which average ½–¾ lb. Fish are taken all round and they rise to standard loch fly patterns. Watch out for the odd larger fish but they are hard to catch and the water has a reputation for being dour.

BISHOPMILL TROUT FISHERY   28/247629

Permission: The Manager, Bishopmill Fisheries, Spynie Churchyard Road, Elgin, Morayshire.
Tel: Elgin (0343) 3875

This is a small commercial fishery 2 miles east of Elgin. Fishing is from the bank only and is for stock rainbow trout. They average 1 lb. and there is a bag limit of 4 fish per rod. Most flies catch fish.

TYNET TROUT FISHERY 28/393618

Permission: The Manager, Tynet Trout Farm, Buckie, Banffshire.
Tel: Clochan (05427) 295

This is a 1¼ acre pond adjacent to the A98 Buckie–Fochabers road. The pond is within the confines of the trout farm and fishing is for rainbow trout. There is a bag limit of 5 fish per rod and the average weight is 1 lb. Most flies catch fish.

LOCH MHIC LEOID (Loch McLeod) 27/009347

Permission: Strathspey Estate Office, Grantown-on-Spey, Morayshire.
Tel: Grantown-on-Spey (0479) 2529

Loch McLeod is a small loch of 4 acres and it is stocked with both brown and rainbow trout. It lies 4 miles to the north of Grantown on the A939 Forres road and a good track leads from the road to the loch. Fishing is from the bank only and the average weight of fish is 1 lb. There is a bag limit of 3 fish per rod and the best trout taken recently weighed 4 lb. The heaviest rainbow trout last season weighed 3 lb. This is a pleasant little loch, easily accessible and offering great sport. Standard loch fly patterns work well.

LOCH DALLAS 27/093475

Permission: P. McKenzie, 79 High Street, Forres, Morayshire.
Tel: Forres (03092) 2111

Loch Dallas lies at an altitude of 1,000 feet and is to the south of Forres on the A939 road to Grantown. Nine miles south of the town turn left at the Dunphail Viaduct (now demolished) and follow the rough track up into the hills. Spectacular views and hard-fighting trout which average ½–¾ lb. and rise to all the standard pattern loch flies.

LOCH LOCHINDORB 27/970360

Permission: J. Scott, Head Keeper, Lochindorb Lodge, Glenferness, Nairn.
Tel: Glenferness (03095) 270

Approach Lochindorb either from the B9007 Carrbridge–Ferness road or the A939 Grantown–Forres road. This is a shallow loch, 2 miles long by three-quarters of a mile wide. A windy place at times. It is also the lair of the Wolf of Badenoch and his ruined castle dominates the loch from the small island. Lochindorb is full of small, hard-fighting little trout and is a most pleasant loch to fish. It is a perfect place for the beginner and excellent baskets can be taken – even in high winds when the trout rise like express trains through the waves. Boat fishing only with the chance of larger fish from time to time, and all the standard loch fly patterns will produce results. Expect 12 fish to weigh about 5½ lb. Don't be put off though, I would recommend Lochindorb to anyone as a delightful loch to fish.

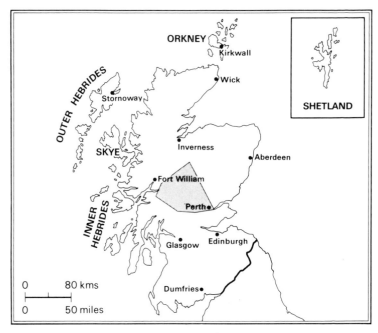

Map 24   *Perthshire*

7 Perthshire

Perthshire is a county of contrasts and offers the visiting angler every conceivable type of loch in almost every conceivable type of setting. They all have one thing in common, however, all contain good quality, hard-fighting trout. One of the reasons for this commendable state of affairs is, I think, the very excellent Pitlochry Angling Association and the waters which it manages and controls are carefully stocked and monitored. And Perthshire is such a lovely place to fish. From the desolation of Rannoch Moor to lovely, reed-fringed Butterstone, there is a loch to suit everyone. I first discovered Perthshire as a boy and from scout camps near Dunkeld we would wander into the hills sleeping out under the stars by some distant loch. We camped on the banks of the Tay to the north of Dunkeld and, in fact, I have worked out that the new motorway passes right over the spot where our tents were pitched. I always think of Perthshire as a wonderland of rowan and heather clad hills, huge sparkling waters and sudden breathtakingly beautiful little hill lochs and the smell of woodsmoke in the autumn air. Perthshire has just about everything any trout fisherman could desire – and more.

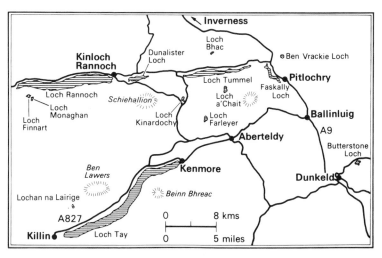

Map 25   *Rannoch and Pitlochry*

18   *A sudden rainstorm sweeps down Loch Tay.*

LOCH TAY   Sheet 51

Permission:
D. & S. Allan, Main Street, Killin, Perthshire.
Tel: Killin (05672) 362;
Ben Lawers Hotel, Aberfeldy, Perthshire.
Tel: Killin (05672) 436;
Loch Tay Guest House, Kenmore, Perthshire.
Tel: Kenmore (08873) 236
Killin Hotel, Killin, Perthshire.
Tel: (05672) 296;
Kenmore Hotel, Kenmore, Perthshire.
Tel: Kenmore (08873) 205

Loch Tay is over 14½ miles long by three-quarters of a mile wide. Its main interest for the angler is as a salmon fishery but it does contain good trout as well with fish of over 5 lb. sometimes being caught. However, I suspect that if you were out in a boat on this lovely loch you would be using flies somewhat larger than size 14s and looking for a fish of far more than the average weight of the trout which is ½ lb. If you do not have the time to catch a salmon – and these days it could take all week, have a go at the

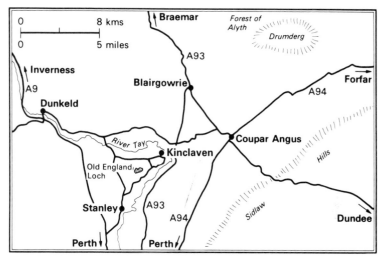

Map 26   *Blairgowrie*

trout, they fight well and are of good quality. The west and east ends fish best and you should keep to the margins and the shallow water.

LOCHAN NA LAIRIGE   51/600400
Permission: D. & S. Allan, Main Street, Killin, Perthshire.
Tel: Killin (05672) 362

Approach from the A827 and turn north at Edramucky towards Bridge of Balgie. Na Lairige lies to the west of the road and is easily accessible. The trout are not large but they give a good account of themselves and rise well, particularly to small black flies. If they are 'off', then why not have a quick canter up Ben Lawers (1214m) to pass the time? Or, for a less strenuous outing, follow the nature trail that begins by the visitor centre and mountain rescue post. Fish or no – a magnificent place to be.

OLD ENGLAND LOCH   53/123378
Permission: Ballathie Estate Office, Nr. Stanley, Perthshire.
Tel: Meikleour (025083) 250

Old England Loch lies to the north of Stanley and is approached from the Kinclaven–Murthly road. One boat is available and bank fishing is not allowed. The loch is stocked with brown and rainbow trout and the very good natural feeding makes for rapid

growth – ¾ lb. stock fish reach 2 lb. by their second season.
There is a bag limit of 8 fish and trout of over 4 lb. have been
caught. The Ballathie Estate can also offer well-appointed holiday
cottages on the estate, the rental of which includes a day's fishing
on Old England Loch. This is a very lovely area and a pleasant
place to spend some time – Old England Loch helps if you happen
to enjoy first-class trout fishing in beautiful surroundings.

LOCH OF BUTTERSTONE   52/060450
Permission: R. Knight, Lochend Cottage, Butterstone, Dunkeld,
Perthshire.
Tel: Butterstone (03504) 238

Butterstone is an easily accessible, well-managed fishery in lovely
surroundings. It lies to the north-east of Dunkeld on the A923
Blairgowrie road. The loch is stocked throughout the season and
contains brown and rainbow trout. The fishing day is divided into
two sessions, 9.00 am–5.00 pm and 5.30 pm–dusk. Bank fishing
is not allowed. There is a limit of 6 fish per rod and the trout
average 1 lb. Catches of 3–4 fish are normal and blank days
infrequent. We all have them though, and Butterstone is no
exception but generally speaking this loch is kinder than most to
us poor duffers. The heaviest trout taken recently weighed 7 lb.
8 oz. and most anglers tend to use reservoir lures. Nevertheless,
standard loch fly patterns work just as well and the old favourites,

19   *Loch Butterstone near Dunkeld.*

Black Pennell, Grouse and Claret, and Soldier Palmer produce good results. The loch fishes well all over and the visitor will be advised where to fish upon arrival. Butterstone has other fishers and you may be rewarded with the sight of an osprey showing you how it should be done or a heron stalking the banks. A lovely loch and highly recommended.

LOCH FASKALLY   52/935580
Permission: Mr E. Yule, The Boathouse, Loch Faskally, Pitlochry, Perthshire.
Tel: Pitlochry (0796) 2912/2938

In spite of its proximity to Pitlochry and the thousands of visitors that arrive each year, Loch Faskally is a charming, easily accessible loch and very pleasant to fish. Up to 75 bank and 54 boat permits are issued daily and it is also possible to hire outboard motors. Many excellent trout are caught and fish of over 10 lb. have been landed. The average weight is ¾ lb. and standard loch fly patterns will do. For the angler with an hour or two to spare, Faskally will make you very welcome and it is in a very lovely setting.

LOCH A'CHOIRS (Ben Vrackie Loch)   43/948627
*Permission:*D. Seaton, Gamekeepers House, Balsmund, Pitlochry, Perthshire.
Tel: Pitlochry (0796) 2273

Ben Vrackie Loch lies to the north of Pitlochry. It is a small loch which involves a steep climb but there are spectacular views to the south as you climb. Fishing is from the bank only and there are 6 daily permits available for visitors. Trout average ½–¾ lb. and standard loch fly patterns will bring good results. Just the place to work up an appetite before dinner – or to clear the head from the night before.

LOCH BHAC   43/823623
Permission: Airdaniar Hotel, Atholl Road, Pitlochry, Perthshire.
Tel: Pitlochry (0796) 2266

There are 6 boats on Loch Bhac and 12 bank fishing permits are available to visitors. The loch lies to the west of Pitlochry in the Allean Forest and covers an area of over 500 yards long by 200 yards wide. This is really a hill loch, lying at an altitude of 1,000 feet and it is managed by the Pitlochry Angling Club. The club stock the loch with brown trout, rainbow trout and brook trout. Fish rise and are taken all over the loch, particularly where the feeder burns enter the loch in the south-east and south-west corners. Average weight on Loch Bhac is 1 lb. and there is a bag limit of 6 fish per rod. There are much larger fish here as well and trout of up to 7 lb. have been taken. This is a first-class loch with excellent trout which fight very hard. It is in perfect surroundings and I would highly recommend it to you.

LOCH TUMMEL   52/820595–43/885603
Permission:
Forestry Commission Exhibition Centre, Queen's View, Loch Tummel, Killiecrankie, Perthshire.
Tel: Killiecrankie (079687) 223;
Port-an-Eilean Hotel, Strathtummel, Perthshire.
Tel: Tummel Bridge (08824) 233;
Queen's View Hotel, Strathtummel, by Pitlochry, Perthshire.
Tel: Killiecrankie (079687) 291
Loch Tummel, on 'the road to the isles' is 7 miles long by one mile wide. It is easily accessible from roads which run along both north and south shores. Tummel contains brown trout, pike and perch and both boat and bank fishing are available. Trout average ½ lb. but much larger fish are sometimes taken and fish of up to 4 lb. have been caught. Loch Tummel is a very popular area with visitors and campers but it is always possible to find a secluded corner somewhere and on its day Tummel can give great sport. Fish the shallows round the islands at the eastern end and at the bay below the 'Duns'. Depending upon wind direction, the south shore between Kynachan and Donlellan can be very rewarding. However, fish can be caught over most of the loch and there are a multitude of interesting bays and points to try.

LOCH A'CHAIT   52/846560
Permission: Major T. W. M. Whitson, Lick Foss, Strathtummel, Perthshire.
Tel: Tummel Bridge (08824) 208
This small loch lies at an altitude of over 1,500 feet and is approached from the road which runs along the south shore of Loch Tummel. About one mile past the Mains of Duntanlich there is a feeder burn which passes under the road. Follow this burn into the hills and you will come to the loch after about 2 miles – and a little short of wind. Fishing is from the bank only

and the average weight of fish is ½–¾ lb. Best flies include all the standard patterns and trout of under 9 inches must be returned to the water. Remote and perfect with superb scenery, and good trout.

LOCH KINARDOCHY   52/777550
Permission: Airdaniar Hotel, Atholl Road, Pitlochry, Perthshire. *Tel:* Pitlochry (0796) 2266

This loch lies between Tummel and Aberfeldy and is approached via the B846. Fishing is from the boat only and due to its exposed position Kinardochy can be a wild place to fish. It is easily accessible and there is a good hut and mooring bay. Bank fishing is not allowed. There is almost no natural spawning so the Pitlochry Angling Club stock the loch each year and stock fish quickly reach the ½ lb. mark during their first year. The average weight is ¾ lb. and the best fish taken recently weighed 3½ lb. Fish rise and are caught all over this shallow loch and it is very popular with local anglers – book early as there are only 4 boats. An excellent loch and worth a visit. Standard pattern loch flies will do just fine.

LOCH FARLEYER   52/810520
Permission: Major Neil Ramsey, Farleyer, Aberfeldy, Perthshire. *Tel:* Aberfeldy (0887) 20523

Loch Farleyer is a delightful hill loch to the north of Aberfeldy at an altitude of 1,000 feet. There is a good track out to the loch from Camserney on the B846 and the fishing is managed and controlled very strictly indeed. The loch has been stocked with both brown trout and Loch Leven trout and fish average ½ lb. in weight. Baskets of 5–8 fish are normal and all the standard pattern loch flies produce results. Fish are caught all over the loch but the most productive areas are in the vicinity of the two feeder burns which enter the north corner and the small bay on the eastern shore.

DUNALISTER LOCH   42/700585
Permission:
Dunalister Hotel, Kinloch Rannoch, Perthshire.
Tel: Kinloch Rannoch (08822) 323;
E. Beattie, 2 Schiehallion Place, Kinloch Rannoch.
Tel: Kinloch Rannoch (088220) 261

Dunalister is a large flooded area between Tummel and Rannoch covering an area of 1½ miles long by half a mile wide. It is a shallow loch and it is quite possible to run aground in the middle due to tree stumps lurking just below the surface. It is a very beautiful place to fish with Schiehallion (1083m) dramatically dominating the southern horizon, with Beinn a'Chuallaich (891m) to the north. The slopes of the hills are gently wooded and wild-life abounds. So do some rather large trout – but they are hard to catch. Fish of up to 6 lb. have been taken and the average is 1 lb. The best fish caught recently was a 5 lb. trout taken in 1986. This is a beautiful loch and a very pleasant place to fish. Standard loch fly patterns will do, although the Alexandra seems to catch a fair number of fish each year.

LOCH RANNOCH   42/600580
Permission:
Dunalister Hotel, Kinloch Rannoch, Perthshire.
Tel: Kinloch Rannoch (08822) 323;
The Bunrannoch Hotel, Kinloch Rannoch, Perthshire.
Tel: Kinloch Rannoch (08822) 367;
The Country Store, Kinloch Rannoch, Perthshire.
Tel: Kinloch Rannoch (08822) 306
Loch Rannoch is 10 miles long by three-quarters of a mile wide and is renowned for the steady stream of monster trout it has produced over the years; 1867–22 lb., 1904–21 lb., 1905–23 lb. 8 oz., 1912–18 lb. 8 oz. However, don't get too excited because the average weight is more in the order of ½–¾ lb. These larger fish are taken by trolling and are the exception rather than the rule. How is that for stating the obvious? No, a day on Loch Rannoch should produce a nice basket of about 10 trout but, of course, larger catches are common. During the 1981 season two rods had 34 trout weighing 19½ lb. for their day and the heaviest fish taken that same year weighed 5½ lb. This latter fish was caught from the bank and rose to a Wickhams Fancy. Apart from that, all the standard loch fly patterns will catch fish and the best area to fish is at the western end of the loch between Finnart and Eilan Mor. Loch Rannoch is one of the most delightful areas of Scotland and full of interest to the visitor. The Rannoch Conser-vation Association patrol and check the loch and every angler will encourage them and assist them in their task. A perfectly lovely loch and well worth a visit.

LOCH FINNART   42/523555
Permission: J. Brown, The Garage, Kinloch Rannoch, Perthshire.
Tel: Kinloch Rannoch (08822) 331
Loch Finnart lies to the south of Bridge of Gaur and is approached

20 *Loch Rannoch.*

via the B846. There is a good track from Little Finnart and the loch is beautifully situated on the edge of the forest. Finnart is 500 yards long by 500 yards wide and 'sprinkled' with small islands. Boat fishing only and the trout average ½ lb. A reasonable day should produce a basket of up to 15 fish and the best flies for this loch are Black Pennell, Grouse and Claret, and Peter Ross. A sample catch from the 1981 season accounted for 28 trout weighing 12 lb. and the heaviest fish weighed 1 lb. 4 oz. A most attractive loch in a lovely setting.

LOCH MONAGHAN 42/530550

Permission: J. Brown, The Garage, Kinloch Rannoch, Perthshire.
Tel: Kinloch Rannoch (08822) 331

Monaghan is to the east of Loch Finnart and is approached via a forest path through the Black Wood. Just as the trees end on your right a track leads on to the boathouse. The average weight of trout is again ½ lb. and fish are taken all over the loch. No bank fishing, and expect a basket of 10–15 fish. Standard loch patterns flies are fine and this lovely loch gives great sport. The heaviest fish to be taken during the 1981 season weighed 1 lb. 2 oz. and a sample basket included 20 trout weighing 9 lb.

LOCH EIGHEACH   42/450570
Permission: J. Brown, The Garage, Kinloch Rannoch, Perthshire.
Tel: Kinloch Rannoch (08822) 331

Loch Eigheach lies to the west of Loch Rannoch and is 1¾ miles long by one mile wide. Fishing is from the bank only and the loch is approached via the B846 and Rannoch Station. This is wild desolate country and the loch is full of small trout which average three to the pound. A few fish over 1 lb. are caught each season and the heaviest trout landed during 1981 weighed 1 lb. 2 oz. Eigheach has many delightful little islands and there are numerous bays and corners where fish can be caught. Grouse and Claret, Grouse and Green, and Black Pennell do well and a sample basket from 1981 produced 31 trout weighing 8½ lb. Just the place to take the beginner – or to restore your confidence, and very beautiful.

But take care, for Eigheach can produce the odd surprise – for instance, a perfect 4 lb. fish to a Black Pennell in 1986.

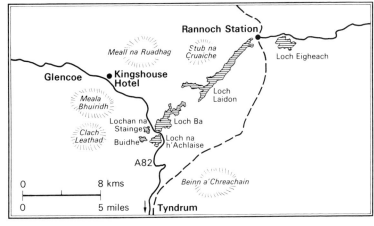

Map 27   *Rannoch*

LOCH LAIDON   41/360520–42/415570
Permission:
N. A. Thexton, Gaur Cottage, Rannoch Station, Perthshire.
Tel: Bridge of Gaur (08823) 248;
Moor of Rannoch Hotel, Rannoch Station, Perthshire.
Tel: Bridge of Gaur (08823) 238;
M. Pearson, The Barracks, Rannoch Station, Perthshire.
Tel: Bridge of Gaur (08823) 244

Loch Laidon is a long, narrow, shallow loch which runs for 5½ miles over Rannoch Moor. It is linked to Loch Ba in Argyll near to the A82 Glencoe road and ends in the north-east at Rannoch Station. The loch is surrounded by majestic peaks and desolate moorlands and is a paradise for fishermen and nature lovers. Both boat and bank fishing are available and the loch is a seemingly unending succession of bays and points and full of lovely trout. The average weight is ½–¾ lb. with much larger fish being taken from time to time – usually from the boat. Baskets of 30–40 trout are common and all the standard patterns of loch flies bring results. This is one of Scotland's great wildernesses and the scenery is magnificent. Try and pick a good day and you will remember it for a long time.

LOCH BA   41/330510–50/320495
Permission: The King's House Hotel, Glencoe, Argyll.
Tel: Kingshouse (08556) 259

Loch Ba, on Rannoch Moor, is a mad scatter of islands and bays to the east of the A82 Glencoe–Tyndrum road. The loch wanders over the moor for 2 miles before joining Loch Laidon via the Abhainn Ba Burn. Ba is easily accessible, being adjacent to the main road, but a few minutes dedicated walking takes you well out of the view of passers by. The trout average ½–¾ lb. and large baskets are often taken. The loch holds big fish as well; have a look at the trout in the King's House Hotel, it weighed an impressive 11 lb. and was taken from Loch Ba some years ago. Standard loch fly patterns work well on Loch Ba and this is a lovely loch to fish in very impressive surroundings.

LOCHAN NA H'ACHLAISE   50/310480
LOCH BUIDHE   50/298483
LOCHAN NA STAINGE   50/303490
Permission: The King's House Hotel, Glencoe, Argyll.
Tel: Kingshouse (08556) 259

These lochs lie close to the main A82 Glencoe–Tyndrum road and are the most southernly of the Rannoch Moor lochs. The lochs are all shallow, varying from 30 feet in h'Achlaise to between 3 and 4 feet in Buidhe. They are easily accessible and contain large numbers of small trout which rise well to standard pattern loch flies. A 1 lb. fish is a monster for these waters but the lovely setting makes up for it and therefore these little lochs are well worth a visit.

LOCH ERROCHTY   42/690650
Permission: Highland Guns and Tackle Shop, Blair Atholl, Perthshire.
Tel: Blair Atholl (079681) 303

Loch Errochty is 3 miles long by over half a mile wide and fishing is from the bank only. Approach from the B847 at Calvine to the north of Pitlochry. This is a hydro-electric loch but nonetheless attractive for being so, and the western end of the loch is the most productive area to fish. There is a track running the full length of both shores and the loch contains brown trout and pike. The average at present is ½–¾ lb. but there are proposals to stock it during the 1982 season. Good baskets can be caught and there is always the chance of the odd larger fish. Standard loch fly patterns will do. Loch Errochty is a remote loch and can be dour, but it is set amidst lovely scenery.

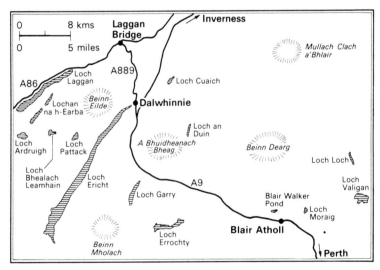

Map 28   *Loch Ericht and the Grampians*

THE BLAIR WALKER POND   43/867671

Permission: Highland Guns and Tackle Shop, Blair Atholl, Perthshire.
Tel: Blair Atholl (079681) 303

Blair Walker Pond is within the grounds of Blair Castle and is easily accessible. Fishing is from the bank only and there is a bag limit of 3 fish per rod. Four permits are available daily and the loch is stocked with trout which average ¾ lb.

LOCH MORAIG   43/907667

Permission: Major W. G. Gordon, Lude House, Blair Atholl, Perthshire.
Tel: Blair Atholl (079681) 240

This is an easily accessible loch lying to the north of Blair Atholl and the day is divided into two sessions. The evening period is reserved for local anglers from mid April until 12 August. Loch Moraig is a shallow loch of 350 yards long by 300 yards wide and there are 4 boats available. Trout are taken all round the loch but the west shore is a particularly productive area. The average weight of fish is ½–¾ lb. with the odd heavier fish from time to time. Standard loch fly patterns work well.

LOCH VALIGAN   43/975694

Permission: Major W. G. Gordon, Lude House, Blair Atholl, Perthshire.
Tel: Blair Atholl (079681) 240

Fishing on Loch Valigan is from the bank only and the walk out is about 4 miles. Four permits are issued each day but after 31 July the loch is closed for fishing. This is a classic hill loch with plenty of small, hard-fighting trout and it lies at an altitude of 1,800 feet. A glorious place to fish, deep amongst the mountains of Atholl and remote and peaceful. Standard loch fly patterns catch them.

LOCH LOCH   43/989745

Permission:
The Atholl Estate Office, Blair Atholl, Perthshire.
Tel: Blair Atholl (079681) 355;
Highland Guns and Tackle Shop, Blair Atholl, Perthshire.
Tel: Blair Atholl (079681) 303

Loch Loch involves a long walk into the mountains via Glen Tilt and access is restricted after 1 August because of salmon

21 *The upper Garry near Tomdoun.*

spawning. This is a most dramatic loch, 1¼ miles long by 250 yards wide. Carn nan Gabhar (1,121m) towers to the west and the crags of Braigh Feith Ghiubhaschain climb from the water's edge to the east. The trout average ½–¾ lb. although larger fish inhabit the 80 foot depths of this lovely loch. Small black flies produce best results and Loch Loch is a marvellous place to spend a day.

LOCH GARRY   42/630700

Permission: J. Kennedy, The Old School House, Dalnaspidal, by Pitlochry, Perthshire.
Tel: Calvine (079683) 202

Loch Garry is 3 miles long by some 500 yards wide. Its northern end may be glimpsed from the A9 Inverness road and fishing is from the bank only. Loch Garry is a dark, deep loch surrounded by mountains rising to 1,000m from the water's edge. Apart from the *ferox*, the loch contains trout and char and the average weight of trout is ½–¾ lb. In the right conditions good baskets are taken, and you don't have to cast very far out to be amongst the fish. The loch is closed after 31 July. Use standard loch pattern flies.

LOCH ERICHT   42/500640–630840
Permission:
The Grampian Hotel, Dalwhinnie, Inverness-shire.
Tel: Dalwhinnie (05282) 210;
The Loch Ericht Hotel, Dalwhinnie, Inverness-shire.
Tel: Dalwhinnie (05282) 257;
J. Brown, The Garage, Kinloch Rannoch, Perthshire.
Tel: Kinloch Rannoch (08822) 331

Most anglers have a quick look at Ericht as they speed northwards on the new road from Perth to Inverness. It lies to the west of the small village of Dalwhinnie, and what you see from the road is but the northern end of a 15 mile loch. It runs south-westwards towards Rannoch Moor through some of the most magnificent scenery in all of Scotland and is one of the most remote and attractive of all lochs. On either shore mighty peaks line the water's edge with Ben Alder (1,148m), Meall Liath (911m) and Meal Cruaidh (897m) to the north-west, whilst the wild slopes of the Dalnaspidal Forest crowd the south-east shore. Badenloch Angling Association have recently leased this mighty water and propose carrying out extensive restocking with brown trout. The present fish average ½–¾ lb. although the loch contains ferrox which reach the tens of pounds. Boats are available from the hotels at the northern end whilst it is only bank fishing from Kinloch Rannoch. The two extremities of the loch fish best along with the area round Alder Bay below Cluny's Cave, where that much travelled fugitive, Bonnie Prince Charlie, spent some of his last days in Scotland. Ericht is not much fished and is a very lovely loch and worth a visit. Vast, windy, wild and remote.

LOCH PATTACK   42/540790
LOCH A'BHEALAICH   42/500796
LOCHAN NA H'EARBA   42/480830
LOCH ARDRUIGH   42/455808
Permission: Osprey Fishing Centre, The Aviemore Centre, Aviemore, Inverness-shire.
Tel: Aviemore (0479) 810767

These lochs all lie between Loch Ericht and Loch Laggan and are delightfully remote and lovely. The Osprey Fishing School offer an inclusive fishing/camping holiday by land rover and foot which includes fishing them all, and Loch Laggan. This must be one of the best organised trips in Scotland and it passes through some really superb scenery. The trout are typical hill loch fish and average from ½ lb. to over 2 lb. The first camp is set up at Loch Pattack and thereafter the party walk on to the other lochs with the goods and chattels following in the vehicle. No further than two miles is traversed at a time – you won't be left behind. A well-organised outing and great fishing. Well worth considering.

LOCH LAGGAN   41/374809–42/536897
Permission: Badenloch Angling Association, Kingussie, Inverness-shire.
Tickets from Lochlaggan Estates, Estate Office.
Tel: Dalwhinnie (05282) 304

Fishing on Loch Laggan is from the north shore only, but access is easy since the A86 Kingussie–Spean Bridge road runs along the shore for the whole length of the loch. This is a 12 mile long water, by half a mile wide and there are many good bays and points for bank fishermen. Boats are also available and standard loch fly patterns will suffice. Don't expect too much, Loch Laggan can be a very dour loch indeed, and great skill is needed at times to bring results. Very lovely, nevertheless.

LOCH CUAICH   42/693877
Permission: The Keeper's House, Cuaich, Dalwhinnie, Inverness-shire.
Tel: Dalwhinnie (05282) 254

This is a small loch to the east of the A9 Perth–Inverness road. It is approached from the A9 some 2 miles north of Dalwhinnie. Access is via the Keepers House only and both boat and bank fishing are available. There is one boat and 8 bank permits are issued daily. The loch is not available to anglers between 12 August and 15 September.

LOCH EARN   51/640240
Permission:
The Post Office, St Fillans, Perthshire.
Tel: St Fillans (76485) 220;
The Post Office, Lochearnhead, Perthshire.
Tel: Lochearnhead (05673) 201

Loch Earn is one of the most popular lochs in Scotland and is the

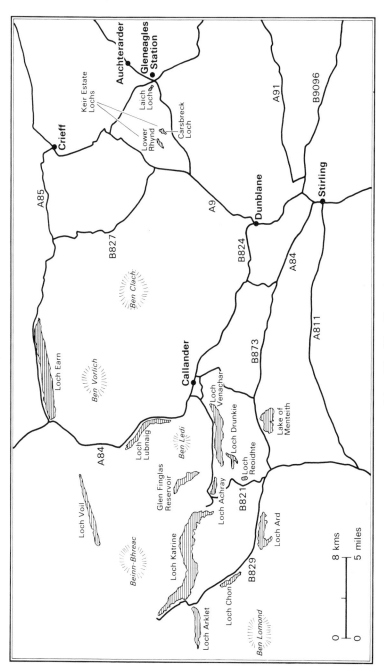

Map 29 *The Trossachs*

venue for all kinds of water sports. Approach from the A85. Most anglers seem to prefer bank fishing but boats are available and J. R. Wills, Rose Cottage, St Fillans, has boats available should you so wish. The loch is stocked every two years and contains both brown and rainbow trout. The brown trout average ½–¾ lb. whilst the rainbows average ¾ lb. Best flies include Blae and Black, Greenwell's Glory, Grouse and Claret, and Woodcock and Yellow. St Fillans is the most favoured fishing area but further down the loch, where the feeder burn enters at Ardvorlich, is also a good area to try. Fish the shallows and small bays and expect a basket of up to 8 trout. Larger fish are taken and trout of over 2 lb. are caught each season. Loch Earn is easily accessible and a delightful loch to fish.

LOCH VOIL   57/510200
Permission:
Harry Hilditch, Ledcreich Hotel, Balquhidder, Perthshire.
Tel: Strathyre (08774) 230;
Mrs Ferguson, Muirlaggan Farm, Loch Voil, Balquhidder, Perthshire.
Tel: Strathyre (08774) 219

Loch Voil and the Braes of Balquhidder are MacGregor Country and associated with the Scottish Robin Hood – Rob Roy MacGregor. The Braes extend northwards in an array of peaks and corries, culminating in Ben More (1,174m) whilst to the south are the tree-lined slopes of Ceann na Baintighearna (694m), with Ben Ledi (879m) and Ben Vorlich (983m) towering to the east. This is magnificent countryside and Voil is one of Scotland's most lovely lochs. It contains brown trout and the occasional salmon. The loch was stocked many years ago and both boat and bank fishing are available. Wading is difficult though and requires great care. Trout in Loch Voil average ½–¾ lb. and a basket taken in 1981 produced 14 trout weighing 8¾ lb. Another held 12 trout weighing 7¾ lb. Trolling brings up the larger fellows, and trout of 11 lb. have been caught. Fish of 2–4 lb. are taken often and Voil produces of its best in a south or south-west wind. Depending upon conditions there is often a hatch of mayfly during late June and early July and this is the time to fish the loch. All the standard loch fly patterns produce results. Scotland at its most beautiful.

LOCH LUBNAIG 57/570140

Permission: J. Bayne, Main Street, Callander, Perthshire.
Tel: Callander (0877) 30218

Loch Lubnaig lies to the west of the A84 Callander–Lochearnhead road. This road runs along the east shore and makes access easy and Loch Lubnaig is a popular fishing venue. It contains salmon and brown trout and the best fishing area is at the shallow northern end. This large sheltered bay often produces good baskets of ½ lb. trout but, as with most of the deep Trossachs lochs, much larger trout are frequently taken. Lubnaig has given up fish of 4–6 lb. but you may expect something more modest – 6 fish weighing 4 lb. Blae and Black, Black Pennell, Greenwell's all do well and the latter produces good results in a high wind. Lubnaig is a lovely loch, surrounded by majestic peaks with forest-covered lower slopes. Autumn particularly is a riot of colour and beauty and Lubnaig is worthy of a day or so fishing, regardless of size or weight of baskets.

LOCH VENACHAR 57/570055

Permission: J. Bayne, Tackle Shop, Main Street, Callander, Perthshire.
Tel: Callander (0877) 30218

Loch Venachar is to the west of Callander and is 4 miles long by three-quarters of a mile wide. The A821 is adjacent to the north shore and boats are available for the visitor. The loch contains brown trout with the occasional salmon and the best fishing area is to the western end of the loch where the Black Water enters from Loch Achray. Standard loch fly patterns work well and the trout average ½–¾ lb. with larger fish being taken from time to time. Venachar is in a lovely setting and a warm spring day, with the snow still on the mountains, makes a lasting impact – there are some days when the fish can do the same.

GLEN FINGLAS RESERVOIR 57/525090

Permission: Strathclyde Regional Council, Water Department, 419 Balmore Road, Glasgow.
Tel: Glasgow (041) 3365333

Glen Finglas is 1¾ miles long with a 'dog leg' of half a mile to the north-west. Approach from the Brig o' Turk on the A821. The reservoir is stocked by the council and trout average ¾ lb. in weight. Boat fishing only. An average day – for an average fisher-person in average conditions – should produce a basket of 4 fish and trout of up to 2 lb. are sometimes taken. This is grand fishing in a grand setting, easily accessible and well managed. The best area to fish is down the east shore and in the bay where the feeder burn enters the loch. Standard loch fly patterns work well.

LOCH ACHRAY   57/515065
Permission:
Loch Achray Hotel, The Trossachs, by Callander, Perthshire.
Tel: Trossachs (08776) 229;
Forestry Commission, David Marshall Lodge, Aberfoyle, Perthshire.
Tel: Aberfoyle (08772) 258

Loch Achray is 1¼ miles long by over 600 yards wide and lies between Loch Katrine and Loch Venachar. It is in a lovely wood-land setting and is a most attractive loch to fish. The loch is 100 feet deep at its deepest and in some areas as shallow as 4 feet. However, since it is bank fishing only, don't worry, you are not going to run aground. Achray contains brown trout, pike and perch and the best place to fish is from the north bank, especially where the Black Water leaves at the east end. Trout average ½–¾ lb. with some larger fish from time to time. Approach from the Loch Achray Hotel on the A821 for access to the south shore.

LOCH KATRINE   57/490075–56/382135
Permission: Strathclyde Regional Council Water Department, 419 Balmore Road, Glasgow.
Tel: Glasgow (041) 336 5333

Lovely Loch Katrine has attracted visitors and anglers to its tree clad, heather bedecked banks for several hundred years and it is one of the most beautiful lochs in all of Scotland. Katrine used to flow east to the River Forth until it was diverted to supply Glasgow with water. But this alteration has detracted little from the charm and character of the loch. Katrine is 8 miles long and an average of one mile wide. It is approached from the A821 Aberfoyle road or by Loch Venacher to the east. The Regional Council stock the loch and fishing is from boats only. The average weight of trout is ¾ lb. and the loch has a reputation for being very dour. A basket of 3–4 fish would be considered good

22 *A good day's work.*

but trout of more than 3 lb. are taken and who could wish for a more lovely place to spend the day? Best flies include Grouse and Claret, Peter Ross and Silver Butcher. The most favoured fishing area is at the western end of the loch from Glengyle down to the Black Island bay below Portnellan. Fish the shallows and cover both shorelines. Loch Katrine offers far more than fishing and is a place you will want to return to again and again.

LOCH ARKLET   56/380090

Permission: Strathclyde Regional Council Water Department, 419 Balmore Road, Glasgow.
Tel: Glasgow (041) 336 5333

Loch Arklet lies between Loch Katrine and Loch Lomand and is a long, narrow water of 2½ miles by 650 yards wide. On either side of the loch tower the heights of Ben Lomand (974m), Ben Venue (727m) and Beinn a'Choin (769m) and their shadows can make Arklet a dark and forbidding place at times. The Regional Council stock the loch and trout average ½ lb. Fishing is from the boat only and the best area to fish is in the vicinity of the Duke's boathouse of Corrieheichan Bay. The heaviest fish taken during the 1981 season weighed 1½ lb. and best flies to use include Grouse and Claret, Peter Ross and Silver Butcher.

LOCH DRUNKIE   57/545044

Permission: Forestry Commission, David Marshall Lodge, Aberfoyle, Perthshire.
Tel: Aberfoyle (08772) 258

Drunkie is in the Achray forest and is approached (on payment) via a forest road, by vehicle. Drunkie is to the north of Aberfoyle and drains into Loch Venachar. Loch Drunkie consists of a main section lying north/south, with a narrow neck running east/west. Another long, narrow bay runs south-west alongside the forest, from the southern bay. Drunkie can be a dour water and fishing is from the bank only. Trout average ¾ lb. and there are also pike in the loch. Standard pattern loch flies will suffice.

LOCH REOIDHTE   57/522035

Permission: Forestry Commission, David Marshall Lodge, Aberfoyle, Perthshire.
Tel: Aberfoyle (08772) 258

This small lochan is situated to the east of the A821 and the

Duke's Pass, just to the north of Aberfoyle. The loch is stocked with both brown and rainbow trout and fishing is from the bank only. Standard loch fly patterns work well and the trout average ¾ lb. in weight with the rainbow trout slightly heavier. The one ticket gives permission to fish Drunkie and Achray and this makes for a very pleasant day in the forest with good fishing.

LOCH ARD   57/465015
Permission:
Forest Hills Hotel, Aberfoyle, Perthshire.
Tel: Kinlochard (08777) 277;
Post Office, Kinlochard, Aberfoyle, Perthshire.
Tel: Kinlochard (08777) 261

Loch Ard is to the west of Aberfoyle on the B829 Stronachlachar road and is 3 miles long by one mile wide across the western bay. There are several boats available for visitors and Loch Ard contains trout which average ¾ lb. in weight. Fish of up to 4 lb. are also caught and the best fishing areas are in the bay along the south shore and round Eilan Gorm. Grouse and Claret, Pennells, Soldier Palmer and Butchers should do the trick. This is a lovely loch and the Forestry Commission have opened up wide areas to the south of the loch with forest walks and attractive paths. Loch Ard is a lovely place to spend a day and well worth a visit. The trout help too – the best basket during 1981 contained 22 fish and weighed 15 lb.

LOCH CHON   56/420050
Permission: I. Close, Frenich Farm, Aberfoyle, Perthshire.
Tel: Inversnaid (087786) 243

Loch Chon lies 8 miles to the west of Aberfoyle. The wooded slopes of Beinn Dubh (511m) are to the west with Benn Lomand towering in the distance. The loch is 1¾ miles long by some 600 yards wide. Both boat and bank fishing are allowed and the average weight on the water is ½–¾ lb. Larger fish can be caught – you will have to troll for them though. Pike are netted from the loch by the Forestry Commission and the average catch per visit is 1–2 fish. Standard loch fly patterns work. Best trout recently was a fish of 4 lb.

LAKE OF MENTEITH   57/580000
Permission: Lake of Menteith Hotel, Port of Menteith, Perthshire.
Tel: Port of Menteith (08775) 664

The Lake of Menteith is a lovely, gentle water surrounded by good farming land and fine forests. It has many historical links and each summer visitors make the short trip to the island of Inchmahome to the ruins of the Augustinian monastery. The lake is about one mile from north to south and 1½ miles from east to west. It is a well-managed and organised trout fishery and 20 boats are available for anglers. Bank fishing is not allowed. The average weight of trout is 1 lb. 4 oz. and the loch is stocked with brown trout, rainbow trout and some brook trout. Each year several very large fish are introduced and these weigh between 5 and 15 lb. During the 1981 season more than 1,000 fish were caught each month and the largest trout taken weighed 12 lb. 13 oz. Best flies to tempt the Menteith trout include Black Pennell, Peter Ross, Greenwell's Glory, Butchers, and Grouse and Claret. The best fishing areas vary during the season and anglers will be given this information by the fishery staff upon arrival. Lake of Monteith is one of the best fisheries in Scotland and well worth a visit. A fair estimate of an average day should bring you up to 4 trout – the experts might come in with up to 30. Have a go, it's a lovely loch.

LAICH LOCH   58/919113
Permission: The Sports Manager, Gleneagles Hotel, Auchterarder, Perthshire.

Laich Loch lies within the grounds of Gleneagles Hotel and fishing is reserved for the residents. The loch is stocked with brown and rainbow trout and there is one boat available for guests. The average weight is over 1 lb. and all the standard patterns work well. If you think you deserve a special treat, and can persuade your better half to go with you, you will not find a more attractive little loch to fish. First-class accommodation, first-class fishing.

CARSBRECK LOCH   58/868093
LOWER RHYND   58/857098
UPPER RHYND   58/863100
Permission: Blackford Farms Ltd, The Farmhouse, Burnside of Balhadie, Dunblane, Perthshire.
Tel: Dunblane (078682) 4000

Fishing on these small lochs is managed by Ardoch Farms Ltd and they lie to the north of the A9 between Blackford Village and Dunblane. They are easily accessible and stocked with brown trout averaging ½–1 lb. Seven boats are available for anglers and the best loch is Carsbreck. They average 1 lb. and fish of over 3 lb. are fairly frequently taken as well. Your average basket is not going to be large but any fish you do catch will be of excellent quality and will fight very well indeed. The best trout taken recently from Carsbreck weighed 4½ lb. The other two lochs contain smaller trout and they give themselves up a little more easily. A good day should produce a basket of up to 12 nice fish and larger baskets are sometimes taken. This is a well-managed and pleasant fishery where the visitor will be met with a friendly reception and given sound advice from the staff. Small flies, 14–16 size, and nymphing bring the best results. Patterns that arouse interest include, Greenwell's, Olives and Black Pennell. Excellent fishing and worth your attention.

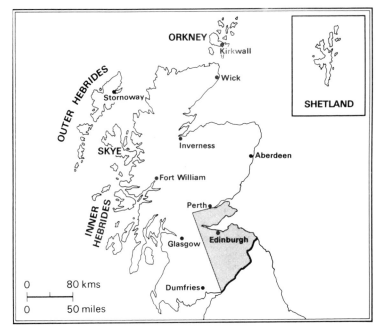

Map 30   *Edinburgh and the South-East*

8   Edinburgh and the South-East

My first attempts at fishing took place in the centre of Edinburgh, on the Water of Leith and the lochs of the King's Park. As the years passed I travelled further afield and soon discovered the many lochs and rivers which surround the city. The visiting angler has the best of all worlds in Edinburgh; excellent trout fishing on such waters as Loch Leven, Gladhouse and Portmore and all the delights of Scotland's capital. When I was a boy crossing the Forth at Queensferry was a real adventure and it could take up to three or four hours. Now, due to the road bridge, there are over one hundred trout lochs all within an easy drive of the city. Most of these waters are carefully managed and stocked. Consequently, although they may lack some of the scenic beauty of the more northern waters, they contain larger trout and are somewhat less unpredictable. There are many, however, that are really remote and if you want to get away from it all, climb the Grey Mares Tail waterfall and fish Loch Skeen, near Moffat – they don't come much more remote. Edinburgh is ringed with hills: to the south, east and west are the Pentlands, Lammermuir and Moorfoot Hills whilst over the Firth of Forth in Fife lie the Ochil Hills. All contain good trout waters which are readily available to visiting anglers. One small word of warning, however. Take great care if wading round some of the reservoirs. The margins can become soft and dangerous due to fluctuations in the level of the water as I have learned from bitter experience and one should be very careful indeed. My own favourite waters are Portmore, Gladhouse and Coldingham – and, of course, lovely Loch Leven – but there are many more excellent trout lochs in the region. I know that you will enjoy any time you spend in and around 'Auld Reekie'.

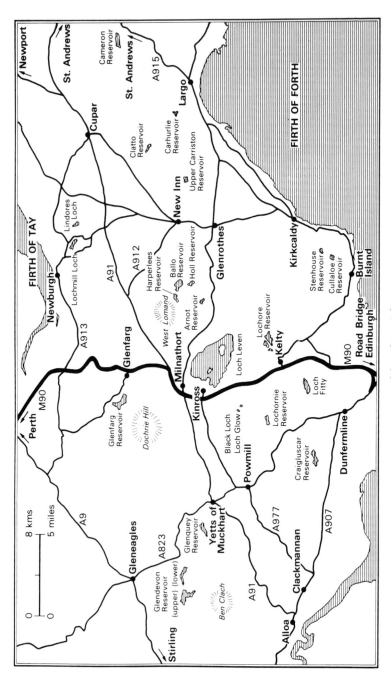

Map 31 *Fife*

GLENFARG RESERVOIR   58/105110

Permission: Fife Regional Council, Water Division, Flemmington Road, Glenrothes, Fife.
Tel: Glenrothes (0592) 756541

Glenfarg Reservoir is 600 feet up in the Ochil Hills and is approached via Glenfarg Village between Perth and Kinross. Five boats are available and bank fishing is not allowed. This is a very pleasant water and it has been stocked with brown trout. Average weight is ¾ lb. and the reservoir fishes best during May and June, although the larger fish are usually taken towards the end of the season. Two fish caught during the 1980 season weighed 9 lb. and a club competition had a catch of 20 fish to 6 rods. Best flies are Black Pennell, Greenwell's Glory and Butchers. The northern end, where the reservoir divides into two large bays, is the best fishing area, particularly the longer bay running directly north.

GLENQUEY RESERVOIR   58/976022

Permission: Castle Campbell Hotel, 13 Bridge Street, Dollor, Clackmannanshire.
Tel: Dollor (02594) 2519

This is a small reservoir high up in the Ochil Hills between Auchlinsky and Whitewhisp Hill (643m) to the south and north. Glenquey is triangular in shape and the fishing is managed by the Devon Angling Association who issue 5 daily permits to visitors. Approach from the A823 Yetts of Muchart–Glendevon road and park the car in the layby next to Castlehill Reservoir on the main road. The reservoir is stocked with brown trout and their average weight is ½–¾ lb. Good baskets are taken and a recent catch produced 18 trout weighing 10½ lb. Trout of 4½ lb. have been caught and these fish are of excellent quality and fight well. Best fishing area is at the top end of the reservoir and flies to use include Olives, Black Spider, Grouse and Claret, and Greenwell's. Book in advance.

UPPER GLENDEVON RESERVOIR   58/910045
LOWER GLENDEVON RESERVOIR   58/935048

Permission: Fife Regional Council, Water Division, Flemmington Road, Glenrothes, Fife.
Tel: Glenrothes (0529) 756541

Fishing on these two reservoirs is managed by the Regional Council. Approach from A823 Yetts of Muchart–Auchterarder road. The entrance is just to the north of Glenhead Farm. Boats are available on both reservoirs but bank fishing is only allowed on Lower Glendevon. These are hill lochs and lie at an altitude of 1,000 feet. Use standard pattern loch flies, there are good brown trout waiting to accept them.

CRAIGLUSCAR RESERVOIR   58/065905

Permission:
The Club Hut, Craigluscar Reservoir, Dunfermline.
Tel: Dunfermline (0383) 732891;
The Club Secretary, W. Dewer, 29 Alice Cox Walk, Dunfermline.
Tel: Dunfermline (0383) 732970

Fishing on Craigluscar is managed by the Dunfermline Artisans Angling Club and the reservoir lies to the north-west of the town, 2 miles along the A823. The club has been looking after this water since 1911 and brown trout are introduced twice each year. There are also some rainbow trout. The best trout to be caught recently was a fine fish of 7 lb. and the largest rainbow trout caught weighed 8¾ lb. However, the average weight is ¾ lb. and the club imposes a bag limit of 6 fish per rod. Bank fishing only. Due to the abundance of natural fly life anglers have to work hard for their fish, but it is considered to be well worth the effort – the 1981 season produced a trout of 3 lb. 5 oz. Flies to use are Black Pennell, Black Zulu, Black Spider during the early part of the season and Wickham's Fancy, Dunkeld, Invicta and Kingfisher Butcher during the 'back end'. This is a very well-managed and exciting loch to fish and worthy of your attention.

In 1984 a rainbow trout of 7 lb. 9 oz. was landed and the heaviest brown trout that year weighed 4 lb. 8 oz. Up until June 1986 more than 1,600 trout had been caught, with a best basket of 6 fish weighing 15 lb. and more than 200 of the fish caught weighing over 2 lb.

LOCH FITTY   58/120915

Permission: Game Fisheries Ltd, Loch Fitty, Kingseat, Dunfermline, Fife.
Tel: Dunfermline (0383) 23162

Loch Fitty lies 3 miles to the north-east of Dunfermline and extends to 160 acres. It is a shallow, water-filled open cast mining site and has been developed into an excellent trout fishery. Loch

Fitty produces very good results and trout average 1 lb. 3 oz. The best trout caught weighed 9 lb. and each season fish of over 3 lb. are frequently taken. The loch is stocked during the season with more than 20,000 brown and rainbow trout and there are 20 clinker built boats available for anglers. Bank fishing is also allowed. Trout are caught all over the loch and the visitor will be advised by the staff where to fish – and what to fish with. Lures which always do well include Ace of Spades, Sweeny Todd and Black Kelpie. Flies that produce results are Black Pennell, Grouse and Claret, Grouse and Green, Invicta and Wickham's Fancy. There is a small restaurant on site and the loch is well managed and visitors and anglers are well received and attended to.

LOCH LEVEN   58/150010
Permission: The Manager, The Pier, Kinross.
Tel: Kinross (0577) 63407

I was lucky in that the first loch I ever fished was Loch Leven, in 1952. That was in the days of no outboards and two boatmen. I was taken to Loch Leven as the guest of the late Mr and Mrs Kelly of Edinburgh and then, as always, we had as our boatman and gillie, Big Eck – I think. Anyway he was a charming man and a great encouragement to a small, over-excited boy. The day ended with 15 lovely trout in the boat, one of them mine, and I shall never forget the thrill of that first Loch Leven trout, or the kindness of my hosts. Now poor Loch Leven is beset with problems and controversy and hardly a good word to be said for it. However, it is, and always will be, the most famous trout loch in the country – indeed one of the most famous in the world. For years Loch Leven trout have been transported all over the world, being introduced to countless waters both at home and abroad, and the quality of these trout has gladdened the hearts and minds of anglers everywhere. The loch is 2½ miles long by 2½ miles wide and covers an area of some 4,300 acres. There are seven islands, the largest being St Serfs in the south-east and on it the remains of the dwellings of the two sects of monks which have lived there over the years. The other major island is Castle Island where Mary Queen of Scots was imprisoned. The castle is now in ruins but still retains its air of sadness and during the summer months it is open to visitors. The few words that I can devote to Loch Leven cannot do it proper justice but it is so well known that, at some time or another, most anglers visit it. When you get there, like me, you will fall in love with the place – fish or no fish – but these days you will have to adapt your technique to the

23 *The 'evening shift' setting out on Loch Leven.*

changed conditions. A rise of fish on Loch Leven is now as rare an event as it used to be commonplace. Therefore, many anglers are adopting reservoir tactics to tempt the trout. These seem to be working – there is no doubt that the fish are there – and it is a question of taking the flies/lures to them, rather than waiting for fish to come and get them on the surface. It has been estimated that Loch Leven can support and produce over 100,000 trout each season naturally, but plans are now in hand to reopen a hatchery and rear and introduce 70,000 trout to the loch starting in 1984. I am sure that every angler in the country wishes the scheme every possible success. In the meantime, the average weight of trout is 1½ lb. and the best fish caught during the 1981 season weighed 4 lb. 15 oz. Don't expect large baskets, and evening fishing is by far and away the best time to fish, but do visit this most lovely of lochs – you will come back again and again, I'm sure. Scotland without Loch Leven would be like Scotland with no lochs at all. All the information you require concerning flies and best places to fish is available at the pier. Tight lines.

BALLO RESERVOIR   58/225050
HOLL RESERVOIR   58/227036
Permission: Fife Regional Council, Water Division, Flemmington Road, Glenrothes, Fife.
Tel: Glenrothes (0592) 756541

Fishing on these reservoirs is managed by the Regional Council and is from boats only. There are two sessions, 10.00 am–4.00

pm and 4.00 pm–10.00 pm. Young persons, under 16, must be accompanied in the boat. These reservoirs are to the west of Leslie and are stocked with brown trout which average ¾ lb. On their day, great sport.

ARNOT RESERVOIR   58/207024
Permission: R. G. Tullis Newton of Strathenry, by Leslie, Fife.
Tel: Glenrothes (0592) 742317

Fishing on this 40-acre reservoir is by private permit only. It is regularly fished by two angling clubs and also visitors, some of whom have been loyal for many years. Trout on Arnot are very large indeed with the average weight being well over 1 lb., so it can be a most interesting loch to fish.

HARPERLEES RESERVOIR   58/213053
Permission: Constables Jewellers, 39a High Street, Kirkcaldy, Fife.
Tel: Kirkcaldy (0592) 60770

Harperlees Reservoir covers 44 acres and lies on the eastern slopes of the Lomand Hills. Approach from the A911 west of Leslie and drive past Holl Reservoir to Harperlees. Fishing is managed by the Fife Technical Teachers Association and the loch is stocked with brown trout. The average weight is ¾ lb. and 2–3 fish would represent an average basket. Trout of up to 2½ lb. are caught and since the water is very clear a good wind helps to disguise murderous intent from the well-educated inhabitants below the surface. Boat fishing only and at times an infuriating place to fish, but in lovely surroundings and well worth a visit. Best flies include Black Pennell, Blae and Black, and Greenwell's Glory.

LOCH ORE   58/160955
Permission: Park Centre, Lochore Medows Country Park, Crosshill, Nr. Lochgelly, Fife.
Tel: Ballingry (0592) 860086

Loch Ore was the site of an open cast mining operation and has been developed into the largest freshwater loch in Fife. It is one of the success stories of the 'seventies and the Lochore Medows Country Park is a most attractive and well-organised venture which offers a wide variety of activities in lovely surroundings. The loch is stocked with both brown and rainbow trout and their average weight is 1 lb. The heaviest fish caught recently weighed 5¾ lb. and the Fife Fly Fishing Championship was held over a period of three weeks during 1981 on Loch Ore. The best basket during the competition had 14 fish weighing 8 lb. 12 oz. Bank fishing is allowed but best results come from the boats. Flies to use include Black Spider, Black Pennell, Grouse and Claret, Woodcock and Yellow, Wickham's Fancy and Kingfisher Butcher. Loch Ore is rich in wildlife, there is a cafeteria, picnic area, golf course and sailing, and if it all sounds a bit overcrowded don't worry, the varying activities do not impinge upon one another and this is a delightful place to fish. Loch Ore is a credit to the Regional Council and a perfect place for a day out with the family.

UPPER CARRISTON RESERVOIR   59/327037
Permission: J. Caldwell, Newsagent, Main Street, Methilhill, Leven, Fife.
Tel: Buckhaven (0592) 712215

Upper Carriston is situated between Glenrothes and Markinch and is a pleasant water fringed by woods. Fishing is managed by the Methilhaven and District Angling Club and is all from the bank. Anglers are limited to 6 fish per rod and the reservoir contains brown trout with an average weight of 1 lb. The heaviest fish caught during the 1981 season weighed 2½ lb. and baskets during the same season included one of 6 fish weighing more than 10 lb. The best fishing areas are along the north dam wall and round the east bay. Flies to use include Greenwell's Glory, Dunkeld, Black Pennell, Wickham's Fancy and nymphs. There is good natural feeding in the reservoir and the growth rate of fish is exceptional. However, Upper Carriston is not for beginners, rather for the angler who likes a challenge, and evening fishing during the early months of the season can produce first-class results. At times the trout rise as though there were going to be no more flies tomorrow. It's just persuading them to accept what you offer that is the problem – isn't it always?

STENHOUSE RESERVOIR   66/210877
Permission: John McCracken, Newsagent, East Porte, Burntisland, Fife.
Tel: Burntisland (0592) 872292

Stenhouse lies adjacent to the A909 to the north of Burntisland and is a very pleasant loch with good trout. It is 900 yards long by 200 yards wide and the fishing is managed by the Burntisland Angling Club. The club stock the reservoir each year and the average weight is an impressive 1½ lb. Trout of 2–2½ lb. are unremarkable and fish of 4–4½ lb. are occasionally caught. The heaviest trout to come from this excellent water weighed 8 lb. There is a bag limit of 6 fish per rod and the loch fishes best in the evenings during the spring and during the day later on. Flies to use include all the standard pattern loch flies and this is an easily accessible water offering first-class sport in attractive surroundings.

LOCH GLOW   58/088958
BLACK LOCH   58/077963
Permission: L. Trim, Civil Service Sports Centre, Castle Road, Rosyth, Fife.
Tel: Inverkeithing (0383) 412507

Loch Glow is the principal water, fed from its smaller neighbour, Black Loch. These waters are situated in the Cleish Hills and often suffer from adverse weather conditions, making casting difficult. But well worth trying because the loch is well stocked with fish averaging 10–12 oz. The Black Loch regularly produces fish of over 3 lb. and, in 1983, a monster of 7 lb. 2 oz. was caught. Flies to use include Invicta, Connemara Black, Kingfisher Butcher, Whickham's Fancy and Greenwell's Glory.

CARHURLIE RESERVOIR   59/395050
Permission: Davesports, 14 Bridge Street, Leven, Fife.
Tel: Leven (0333) 25115

Carhurlie is a small reservoir to the north of Largo in the Wee Kingdom of Fife. Approach from the north by turning left off the A916 Cupar–Methill road at Montravie, or from the A921 Methill–Largo road by turning left at Sillerhole. The reservoir is 500 yards long by about 250 yards wide and is in the shape of a 'Y'. No bank fishing and only one boat, so you have the loch to yourself for the day. The reservoir contains brown trout and they have a reputation for being hard to catch. Average weight is ½–¾ lb. and the best time to fish is in the evenings. An average basket should account for 2–3 fish and trout of over 2 lb. are rare. Flies to try include Wickham's Fancy, Greenwell's Glory, Black Spider, Black Pennell and Butcher, all in size 14 dressings. Fish in the area of the boathouse for best results. Good hatches of flies in the summer months and a secluded, pleasant water to fish.

CLATTO RESERVOIR 59/360079
Permission: Crawford Priory Estate, Cupar, Fife.
Tel: Cupar (0334) 52678;

Clatto Reservoir lies between the A916 Kennoway–Cupar road to the south and the A92 Glenrothes–Cupar road to the north. Clatto Reservoir is 25 acres in extent and is a very pleasant, sheltered place to fish. There is a good stock of brown trout and an angling club has been formed to manage the water. There are 3 boats available and bank fishing is allowed. Fish over 3 lb. have been caught and the average weight is ¾ lb. Expect 2–3 fish for your efforts, but baskets of up to 6 trout are often taken. Small flies do best on Clatto and you should use size 14–16s. Try a cast with Black Pennell, Invicta and Kingfisher Butcher for starters. Clatto fishes best during May, June and September.

CAMERON RESERVOIR 59/470112
Permission: St Andrew's Angling Club, Cameron Reservoir, St Andrews, Fife.
Tel: The Fishing Hut, Peat Inn (033484) 236

This reservoir is three-quarters of a mile long by 250 yards wide and is easily accessible from the A915 via a minor road at Cameron School. The reservoir is stocked with brown trout and their average weight is just under 1 lb. The St Andrews Angling Club manages this excellent water and impose a bag limit of 9 fish per rod per day. Both boat and bank fishing are available but outboard motors are not allowed. Limit bags are not uncommon although the average basket is more likely to be in the order of 3–4 fish. Best flies are Wickham's Fancy, Greenwell's Glory, Black Spider, Dunkeld, Grouse and Claret and, of course, the Cameron Demon (gold body, Jungle cock eyes and blue hackle rather like an Alexandra). Cameron Reservoir tends to become weedy after July when boats always do better than bank fishers. New boats were introduced during the '81–82 season and there are now 12 available. This is a shallow water with good, natural feeding and excellent quality trout. Worth a closer look?

LINDORES LOCH 59/265165
Permission: F. G. Hamilton, 18 Strathview Place, Comrie, Perthshire.
Tel: Comrie (07647) 8221

Lindores Loch is 2 miles to the south-east of Newburgh and covers an area three-quarters of a mile long by 350 yards wide. It is a pleasant and well-managed fishery and contains rainbow trout and some brown trout. There are also pike in the loch but these are controlled by regular netting. Some escape, however, and a pike of 28 lb. has been caught on Lindores. There are 7 boats available for anglers but outboard motors are not allowed, nor is bank fishing. The average weight of fish is a very healthy 1½ lb. and a reasonable day should net you up to 4 fish. Sample baskets from the 1981 season will demonstrate the quality of the sport available at this excellent loch: 3 fish weighing 4½ lb., 2 fish weighing 3 lb. 4 oz. and the best result in recent years was a magnificent basket of 6 trout weighing 19½ lb. – hard to better anywhere in Scotland. Trout of 5 lb. are not uncommon and the best flies to use are Dunkeld, Black Pennell, Teal and Green, Wickham's Fancy, and Grouse and Claret. For reservoir lures, try Sweeny Todd, Whisky Fly and Muddlers. Easily accessible and great sport. Well worth a visit.

LOCHMILL LOCH   58/225163
Permission: Gina Crawford, Albert Bar, Newburgh, Fife.
Tel: Newburgh (03374) 439

Lochmill Loch is a small loch to the south of Newburgh and may be approached via the minor road which joins the A983 Auchtermuchty–Cupar road to the south or from Woodruffe Road in the town. The loch is 700 yards long by 200 yards wide and fishing is controlled by the Newburgh Angling Club which was formed in 1943. This is an easily accessible water and there is one boat available for visitors. Bank fishing is also allowed and can be quite productive though best results come from the boats. The loch has been stocked over the years with brown trout, Loch Leven trout and rainbow trout but it is now the policy to stock only with brown trout. One thousand trout were put in in October 1980 and a further 800 were introduced in October 1981. There is excellent natural feeding in Lochmill and these fish, introduced at 7 inches, reached 1 lb. by the following September. The average weight for the loch is ¾ lb. and fish of 2½ lb. are occasionally caught. Fishing is best in the small bays and in the area of the reed beds at the western end of the loch. Best flies include Blae and Black, Soldier Palmer, Greenwell's Glory, March Brown and Black Spider.

BEECRAIGS LOCH 65/010744

Permission: Beecraigs Country Park, Linlithgow.
Tel: Linlithgow (050684) 3121

Beecraigs is a small and very popular reservoir to the south of Linlithgow. It has been stocked with brown and rainbow trout and their average weight is ¾ lb. Trout of up to 4 lb. have been caught here as well and standard loch pattern flies will produce results. More than 1,500 fish are taken each season so book your boat well in advance.

BONALY RESERVOIR 66/210662

Permission: Not required.

This was a favourite walking tour stopping-off place for me many years ago and Bonaly is an attractive little water high up in the Pentland Hills. It has brown trout and fishing is from the bank. Hard to pass it by if you are in the hills and a pleasant place to stop for a few casts. The trout are small, but fight well.

CLUBBIEDEAN RESERVOIR 66/200668

Permission: Lothian Regional Council, Department of Water Supply Services, Comiston Springs, 55 Buckstone Terrace, Edinburgh.
Tel: Edinburgh (031) 4454141

Clubbiedean covers 12 acres and is near Colinton on the outskirts of the city. This reservoir had the best average weight for the 1980 season of the Regional Council waters and 470 trout were recorded averaging 14 oz. each. The best fish taken weighed 2 lb. 15 oz. The reservoir was not fished so much during the 1981 season when only 116 trout were recorded caught. The Regional Council planned to re-stock Clubbiedean during the 1982 season. Bank fishing is not allowed and there are 3 boats available, bookable up to one month in advance. Two casting platforms have been constructed for the use of disabled anglers – a very welcome added facility.

CROSSWOOD RESERVOIR 65/060575

Permission: Lothian Regional Council, Department of Water Services, Comiston Springs, 55 Buckstone Terrace, Edinburgh.
Tel: Edinburgh (031) 4454141

This is a delightful reservoir of some 62 acres, within easy reach of the city and it has been stocked with brown trout and brook

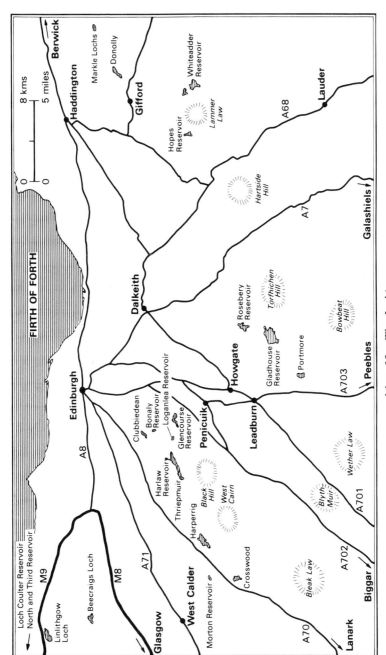

Map 32   *The Lothians*

trout. Crosswood was very popular during the 1981 season and a bag limit has now been introduced of 6 fish per rod per day. During 1981, 145 anglers accounted for 368 trout. One thousand additional brook trout were introduced during 1982 and there are now 3 boats available for visitors. Book in advance.

DONOLLY RESERVOIR 67/577688
Permission: Lothian Regional Council, Department of Water Supply Services, Alderston House, Haddington, East Lothian.
Tel: Haddington (062082) 4131

Donolly is a small, remote water near Gifford, at the foot of the Lammermuir Hills. It is a very pleasant place to fish and there are 2 boats available. Bank fishing is not allowed. This reservoir is not fished as much as the other Regional Council waters but the average weight is good, ¾ lb., and it is well worth a visit. Boats will not be given to single anglers – so pack a friend – and all the usual standard patterns loch flies. The 1980 season produced over 200 trout with a best fish of 2 lb.

FRUID RESERVOIR 78/100190
Permission: Lothian Regional Council, Department of Water Supply Services, Comiston Springs, 55 Buckstone Terrace, Edinburgh.
Tel: Edinburgh (031) 4454141

Fruid is a wild, remote place, surrounded by hills and covering an area of 290 acres. The road from Tweedsmuir stops at the dam where there are 2 boats available for anglers. Fish the shallow areas at the southern end where Fruid Water enters the reservoir and in the vicinity of Catchope and Priestehope along the south shore. 1980 saw 285 trout averaging 11 oz. caught and the best fish weighed 2 lb. 10 oz. Fewer anglers fished Fruid during 1981 but 194 trout were caught. Standard loch fly patterns – and skill on the oars – this can be a windy place.

GLADHOUSE RESERVOIR 66/300535
Permission: Lothian Regional Council, Department of Water Supply Services, Comiston Springs, 55 Buckstone Terrace, Edinburgh.
Tel: Edinburgh (031) 4454141

Gladhouse has always had an excellent reputation for the quality of the trout fishing and for the past 25 years at least, an average of

1,500 fish have been caught each season. The reservoir covers an area of 400 acres and is delightfully situated to the south of Edinburgh. The Regional Council has 4 boats available for anglers, one having a modified seat to accommodate disabled anglers, and during the busy months the fishing day is divided into two sessions, 8.00 am–4.00 pm and 4.30 until one hour after dusk. Gladhouse is also a nature reserve and is an important resting place for geese during the winter. The boathouse at the reservoir has a full list of all the different species which visit Gladhouse and it makes very interesting reading. Anglers must avoid disturbing nesting birds and should note that landing on the two islands is not permitted. During the early 'sixties, whilst visiting Gladhouse one spring, I witnessed the remarkable sight of some 50,000 seagulls resting on the loch – at least that was my estimated rough count. The best areas to fish on Gladhouse are round the islands and along the south-west shore. No bank fishing by the way. Fish of 3 lb. are sometimes caught but the average weight is in the order of ¾ lb. Standard loch pattern flies all work well but a good cast to start off with might be Black Pennell, Grouse and Claret, and Cinnamon and Gold. Expect a

24   *A hard row on Gladhouse Reservoir.*

basket of 5 trout to weigh about 4 lb. and a catch for the day of up
to 6 fish. Yes, it can be dour like anywhere else but good baskets
are taken each year and catches of 10 fish are frequent. The 1981
season recorded some 1,310 trout being caught for the Regional
Council boats – the total for all 8 boats on the loch was 3,500.
This is an easily accessible water, one of my favourites and highly
recommended.

GLENCOURSE RESERVOIR   66/215638
Permission: Lothian Regional Council, Department of Water
Supply Services, Comiston Springs, 55 Buckstone Terrace,
Edinburgh.
Tel: Edinburgh (031) 4454141

Glencourse is in a valley in the Pentland Hills, just outside the city
boundary. This is a popular place for a day out and so it can be
quite busy. As children, my parents used to take us there on
Sundays for a special treat, as parents today still take their off-
spring. Glencourse is in a delightful situation and offers first-class
trout fishing. There are brown trout and brook trout, and the
Regional Council introduced a further 1,000 brook trout during
the 1982 season. There is a bag limit of 6 fish per rod per day and
some really excellent trout have been caught during recent
years. 1979 produced a fish of 2 lb. 14 oz., 1980 2 lb. 5 oz. The
average weight is ½–¾ lb. and during 1981 196 anglers caught
362 trout. Standard loch pattern flies will do fine. No bank
fishing.

LOGANLEA RESERVOIR   66/195624
Permission: Logan Cottage, Milton Bridge, by Penicuick.
Tel: Penicuik (0968) 72826

Drive on past Glencourse Reservoir and you will find Loganlea at
the end of the road, sheltering between Black Hill and Carnethy
Hill. Loganlea Cottage, the keeper's house, is situated mid-way
between Glencourse and Loganlea. Trout are not very large here,
but they fight well.

HARLAW RESERVOIR   66/180650
Permission: Lothian Regional Council, Department of Water
Supply Services, Comiston Springs, 55 Buckstone Terrace,
Edinburgh.
Tel: Edinburgh (031) 4454141

Harlaw Reservoir is adjacent to Thriepmuir and is easily accessible from either Balerno or Currie to the south of Edinburgh. The reservoir was stocked by the Regional Council in 1979 and again in 1980 and holds both brown and rainbow trout. Two boats are available and bank fishing is allowed. There is a bag limit of 6 fish per rod per day and the best brown trout caught so far weighed 4 lb. 3 oz. The heaviest rainbow trout weighed 3 lb. 5 oz. It should be noted that wading can be very dangerous since the water is deep close to the shore, so take care. Two sessions operate from May to August, 8.00 am–4.00 pm and 4.30 pm until one hour after dusk. Standard pattern loch flies.

HARPERRIG RESERVOIR 65/095610

Permission: Lothian Regional Council, Department of Water Supply Services, Comiston Springs, 55 Buckstone Terrace, Edinburgh.
Tel: Edinburgh (031) 4454141

This is a wild, windy loch out on the Lang Whang, the local name of the moorland, off the A70 road to Lanark. It is a very popular fishing water, nevertheless, and 1980 saw 1,749 anglers catch 1,931 trout, The average weight of trout is ¾ lb. and the best fish taken recently weighed 3 lb. There are 4 boats available for anglers and all of the shore line is used for bank fishing. Take care when wading, since due to the variations in the level of the water, margins tend to become soft. The Council warns anglers not to land on exposed 'islands' and caution fishermen about the quicksands at the north-west corner. Don't be put off – but do take care. This is a first-class water and well worth a visit. Standard loch pattern flies work well, and dry fly in calmer conditions – when they happen.

MORTON RESERVOIR 65/075635

Permission: Morton Fisheries, Morton Reservoir, Mid Calder, West Lothian.
Tel: Mid Calder (0506) 880087

Another well managed brown and rainbow trout fishery lying to the north of Harperrig. Fly fishing only, boat and bank fishing and a limit of 3 fish per rod. Sunday fishing is allowed and there are seven boats available. Book well in advance.

HOPES RESERVOIR 66/547620

Permission: Lothian Regional Council, Department of Water Supply Services, Alderston House, Haddington, East Lothian.
Tel: Haddington (062082) 4131

This is a lovely reservoir covering an area of 35 acres and lying high up in the Lammermuir Hills, south of Haddington. The average size of the trout is not large, ½ lb., but great sport can be had and good baskets are taken. The heaviest fish caught during the 1980 season weighed 1 lb. 3 oz. and fishing is from boats only, of which there are two. Anglers must be accompanied since no boat is let to a single fisherman. Get married or take a friend – and standard loch pattern flies. This is a very pleasant loch and worth a visit.

ROSEBERY RESERVOIR 66/308565

Permission: Lothian Regional Council, Department of Water Supply Services, Comiston Springs, 55 Buckstone Terrace, Edinburgh.
Tel: Edinburgh (031) 4454141

I first fished Rosebery Reservoir in a howling gale in 1957 and still remember the difficulty of rowing the heavy boat round the first headland. I also remember it as a lovely loch and it still is. It covers an area of 52 acres and 2 boats are available for anglers. Bank fishing is also allowed. The 1980 season accounted for 1,417 trout being caught by nearly 1,000 anglers and the averge weight of trout is ¾ lb. The best fish taken from the reservoir that season weighed 3 lb. 12 oz. The Regional Council planned to re-stock Rosebery Reservoir during 1982 and this is a popular water for local anglers. Boats can be booked up to one month in advance and visitors would be well advised to do so. Use the usual standard pattern loch flies and watch out for the wind.

TALLA RESERVOIR 72/110220

Permission: Lothian Regional Council, Department of Water Supply Services, Comiston Springs, 55 Buckstone Terrace, Edinburgh.
Tel: Edinburgh (031) 4454141

Talla Reservoir can be a very windy loch and it covers an area of 300 acres. Approach from Tweedsmuir. The loch has a native population of brown trout and both boat and bank fishing are available. Permits for bank fishing can be obtained at the reservoir from the Water Superintendent. The average weight of trout is

½–¾ lb. but fish of over 2 lb. are sometimes caught. Best place to fish are where the burns enter the reservoir at the southern end of the loch. It is shallower here, although a long row to get to. Bank fishing is considered best early on in the season and a good basket from Talla would amount to 7 fish, the average catch is probably going to be 4 trout. Remote and wild and lovely.

THRIEPMUIR AND HARLAW RESERVOIRS
Permission: 66/175640
The Factor, Dalmeny Estate Office, South Queensferry, West Lothian.
Tel: South Queensferry (031331) 1888;
Alexander Flemming, 42 Main Street, Balerno, Edinburgh.
Tel: Edinburgh (031) 4493833

Permits are available on Thriepmuir by ballot and intending visitors should write to the Factor at the above address to be included. A limited number of day tickets for fly fishing from the bank are available from Alexander Flemming in the village. Thriepmuir covers an area of 246 acres and opinions vary widely concerning it – from magnificent to very, very dour. It is a very lovely water and is easily accessible. Boat fishing is controlled by the Thriepmuir Angling Club. The loch is stocked with both brown and rainbow trout and there is a bag limit of 6 fish per rod per day. The bank fishing area is from the boathouse to Black Springs and anglers must use thigh waders only – no chest waders are allowed. The eastern end of the reservoir is an SSI designated area of special interest and visitors must take great care not to disturb wildlife. The average for this water is ¾ lb. but each season several fish of between 3–3½ lb. are caught. Two fish would be considered an average basket and any more a red-letter day. But the quality of these trout is very good indeed and they fight hard. The best fishing areas are in the vicinity of Black Springs and around the margins. Thriepmuir fishes best from the bank during the early months of the season and again during August and September when evening fishing is most likely to produce results.

WHITEADDER RESERVOIR   67/655635
Permission: Lothian Regional Council, Department of Water Supply Services, Alderston House, Haddington, East Lothian.
Tel: Haddington (062082) 4131

Whiteadder Reservoir is 193 acres and is to the south-east of

Gifford. It lies between Starleton Edge and Penshiel Hill near to Cranshaws on the B6355. The reservoir was built in 1969 and there are 4 boats available for anglers. Two persons per boat due to high winds so do not go alone. Bank fishing is not allowed and the average weight of trout is ½ lb. The heaviest fish caught recently weighed 2 lb. 3 oz. and 1981 saw increased use by anglers of this water with 469 trout caught. There is a good boathouse in which to take shelter if things get too rough for fishing and boats may be booked up to one month in advance.

LINLITHGOW LOCH   65/000775
Permission: The Garden Shop, 2 The Cross, Linlithgow, West Lothian.
Tel: Linlithgow (050684) 2943

This is an easily accessible and dramatic loch, dominated by the Palace of Linlithgow and in a very lovely setting. The loch is stocked with both brown and rainbow trout and fish of up to 9 lb. have been caught. But it is a dour water and anglers have to work hard for a fish. It is worth it, nevertheless, and fish of 3–5 lb. are often taken. The natural feeding in the loch is very good and trout grow fast. These fish tend to feed on the bottom and so more and more anglers are turning to reservoir lures, rather than standard pattern loch flies. Boats are available and bank fishing is also allowed. Bank fishing is best early on in the season since, being a shallow loch, it becomes weedy as the season advances. Fish are caught all over the loch – sometimes – and in the evenings nymphs can bring results. Don't be too disappointed if you have a blank day, it happens to the best of us. However, Linlithgow Loch is an excellent fishery and deserves to be visited. It might just bring you that 'one for the glass case'.

LOCH COULTER RESERVOIR   57/765860
Permission: Andrew Patterson, 6 Wheatlands Avenue, Bonny-bridge, Stirlingshire.
Tel: Bonnybridge (032481) 2643

Coulter lies to the west of the intersection of the M80 and M9 motorways at Bannockburn House. This is a well managed fishery offering fishing for both brown and rainbow trout in an attractive setting.

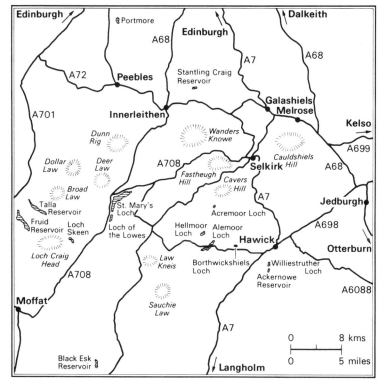

Map 33 *Borders*

NORTH AND THIRD RESERVOIR 57/755890

Permission: George Holdsworth, Greathill, Cambusbarron, Stirling.

Tel: Stirling (0786) 71967

North and Third Part is an excellent, well managed commercial fishery lying to the north of Coulter. Brown and rainbow trout fishing is offered and the loch, with its three small islands, is a very pleasant place to fish.

PORTMORE LOCH 73/260500

Permission: W. McGeachie, 101 John Street, Penicuik, Midlothian.

Tel: Penicuik (0968) 74345

Portmore covers an area of 104 acres and lies 14 miles to the south of Edinburgh. Approach via the A703. This is one of the loveliest lochs in the area and offers really good trout fishing in gentle, peaceful surroundings. Portmore lies on the western slopes of the Moorfoot Hills below Dundreich Hill and is partly shielded from winds. There are small woods of 'proper' trees and on a warm spring evening there are few more pleasant places to fish. During 1980 over 7,500 trout were caught with an average weight of 1 lb. 8 oz. Sixty-one of these fish weighed over 6 lb. and 2 trout weighed over 8 lb. As you can imagine with results like that Portmore is a popular water and it is advisable to book in advance. The fishing day is divided into two sessions as follows: 10.00 am–5.00 pm and 5.30 pm until 11.00 pm. Standard loch patterns will produce results as will reservoir lures and trout are caught all round the loch. The Tweed Valley Hotel used to offer half a gallon of whisky for the best brown trout of the season. If they still do, and you should happen to be the lucky winner, spare a small dram for yours truly.

STANTLING CRAIG RESERVOIR   73/430395
Permission: Tweed Valley Hotel, Walkerburn, Peeblesshire.
Tel: Walkerburn (089687) 220

Stantling Craig is a small reservoir on the south-east slopes of the Moorfoot Hills. Fishing is managed by the Tweed Valley Hotel and Charles Miller stocked it during 1982 with brown trout. The reservoir has an excellent gravelly feeder burn running into it from Craig Head Hill and it is hoped to improve the native stock. Beautiful surroundings, and easily accessible.

MARKLE LOCHS   67/579774
Permission: R. Wallace, Markle Fisheries, East Linton.

A new fishery created and managed by Bob Wallace. Well stocked with both brown and rainbow trout, Markle fish have an excellent growth rate and provide great sport. Trout of up to 8 lb. have been caught and this fishery has an ever-increasing reputation for easily accessible, quality fishing.

ST MARY'S LOCH   73/250230
LOCH OF THE LOWES   79/237195

Permission:
Rodono Hotel, Yarrow, Selkirk.
Tel: Cappercleuch (07504) 232;
Glen Cafe, St Mary's Loch, Yarrow, Selkirk.
Tel: Cappercleuch (07504) 241;
Tibbie Shiels Inn, St Mary's Loch, Yarrow, Selkirk.
Tel: Cappercleuch (07504) 226;
Gordon Arms Hotel, Yarrow, Selkirk.
Tel: Yarrow (07508) 222

These two lochs are separated by a narrow neck of land and they
lie to the south of Innerlethen. They contain brown trout, pike
and perch and are stocked occasionally. St Mary's Loch is 3 miles
long, half a mile wide and at its deepest, 150 feet. The most productive areas to fish are round the shallow bays – Megget Bay,
Bowerhope Bay, and Tibbie Shiels Bay in particular. Another
good area is along the March Woods. Most anglers, when fishing
from the boat, 'keep the bottom in sight'. Bank fishing is also
allowed and can be good as well. But St Mary's has a reputation
for being dour and at times trout are hard to catch. Recently the
St Mary's Angling Club had a competition and 38 anglers caught
33 trout weighing 17 lb. However, a very good basket was taken
last September (1981) and contained 6 trout weighing 7 lb. Flies to
use include Black Pennell, Black Spider, Black Gnat, Blue Zulu,
March Brown and Kingfisher Butcher. The adjacent Loch of the
Lowes is, if anything, even more dour than St Mary's, but the fish
are larger and if you do get one it will probably be over the 1 lb.
mark and heavier fish are sometimes caught. Same flies as for St
Mary's. The best area for Lowes is the roadside bank. These lochs
are in a lovely area, the land of Sir Walter Scott and James Hogg,
the Ettrick Shepherd, and are a perfect place for a day out. There
are other activities on the loch such as sailing but plenty of room
for all.

LOCH SKEEN   79/170165

Permission: Not required

Skeen is a beautiful loch 6 miles to the north of Moffat on the
A708. This is lovely country and some of the wildest in Scotland,
remote, yet easily accessible. There is one problem with Skeen,
however, and it is that the loch lies above the Grey Mares Tail.
This is a spectacular waterfall which plunges 200 feet to the road,

and the quickest way to the loch is by the track up the side of this waterfall. To folks like you and me, I suppose that a few hundred feet here or there is nothing – a quick scamper a few moments to recover and we are soon casting. (Believe it if you can.) But if you do attempt the steep way, be careful, it can be dangerous. Better to take a little longer and approach from further up the valley in easy stages. Skeen lies at an altitude of 1,700 feet and is full of small, hard-fighting trout. The average weight is 6–8 oz. but it is said that a 2 lb. fish was caught a few years back. Bank fishing only and the end of the loch which is furthest away fishes best (it always does). Ten trout would weigh about 5 lb. and all the standard pattern loch flies produce results. It's not so much the fish that make Skeen so attractive, rather its remoteness and lovely situation. Waders are a great help when fishing this loch, but not so handy on the way there. Do visit it if you can, it's very pleasant indeed.

ACREMOOR LOCH   73/407210
Permission:
Hawick and District Angling Club, 5 Sandbed, Hawick, Roxburghshire.
Tel: Hawick (0450) 73771;
Stotharts, 6 High Street, Hawick, Roxburghshire.
Tel: Hawick (0450) 72231;
Pet Store, 1 Union Street, Hawick, Roxburghshire.
Tel: Hawick (0450) 73543;
David Dickman, Main Street, Denholm, Hawick, Roxburghshire.
Tel: Denholm (045087) 320;
Horse & Hounds Inn, Bonchester, Hawick, Roxburghshire.
Tel: Bonchester Bridge (045086) 645

Acremoor is probably the best loch in the Hawick area and lies to the north of the town, below Belmanshaws (353m). Approach via the A7 at Ashkirk village and follow the road out to Longhope Farm. There is a track from the farm and the walk takes about half an hour. The loch contains brown trout and their average weight is 1¼ lb. but Acremoor has a reputation for much heavier fish. Trout of between 2–3 lb. are not uncommon and fish of over 5 lb. have been caught. One boat is available and bank fishing is also allowed. Indeed many anglers prefer to fish from the bank and achieve excellent results so doing. A first-class loch in a delightful setting and well worth visiting. Take along Greenwell's Glory, Wickham's Fancy, Olives and Butchers. They all take fish.

HELLMOOR LOCH   79/385170

Permission:

Hawick & District Angling Club, 5 Sandbed, Hawick, Roxburghshire.
Tel: Hawick (0450) 3771;
Stotharts, 6 High Street, Hawick, Roxburghshire.
Tel: Hawick (0450) 2231;
Pet Store, 1 Union Street, Hawick, Roxburghshire.
Tel: Hawick (0450) 3543;
David Dickman, Main Street, Denholm, Hawick, Roxburghshire.
Tel: Denholm (045087) 320;
Horse & Hounds Inn, Bonchester, Hawick, Roxburghshire.
Tel: Bonchester Bridge (045086) 645

Hellmoor covers an area of 25 acres and lies at the end of the forestry road to the north of Alemoor Loch. Approach from the B711. Keys for the gate should be obtained from the club premises in Hawick and must be returned the same day. This is a beautiful loch and the Hawick Angling Club have stocked it with brown trout. It also contains pike and a monster of 28 lb. has been caught here. Brown trout average over 1 lb. in weight and fight hard, and fish over 4 lb. have been caught. Expect 3–4 fish for your day and a March Brown seems to do very well on this loch.

25   *Safely 'on'.*

ACKERNOWE RESERVOIR   79/495106
Permission:
Hawick & District Angling Club, 5 Sandbed, Hawick, Roxburghshire.
Tel: Hawick (0450) 3771;
Stotharts, 6 High Street, Hawick, Roxburghshire.
Tel: Hawick (0450) 2231;
Pet Store, 1 Union Street, Hawick, Roxburghshire.
Tel: Hawick (0450) 3543;
David Dickman, Main Street, Denholm, Hawick, Roxburghshire.
Tel: Denholm (045087) 320;
Horse & Hounds Inn, Bonchester, Hawick, Roxburghshire.
Tel: Bonchester Bridge (045086) 645

Ackernowe lies half a mile to the south of Williestruther Loch, just outside Hawick. There is one boat on the loch and bank fishing is also allowed. The water has been stocked with 10 inch trout by the Hawick Angling Club and the flies that can catch them – the fish, not the Angling Club – are March Brown, Olives and Black Spiders. The best fishing area on the loch is at the north end and trout of up to 5 lb. have been caught. Easily accessible and very pleasant to fish. Boat available.

WILLIESTRUTHER LOCH   79/492115
Permission:
Hawick and District Angling Club, 5 Sandbed, Hawick, Roxburghshire.
Tel: Hawick (0450) 3771;
Stotharts, 6 High Street, Hawick, Roxburghshire.
Tel: Hawick (0450) 2231;
Pet Store, 1 Union Street, Hawick, Roxburghshire.
Tel: Hawick (0450) 3543;
David Dickman, Main Street, Denholm, Hawick, Roxburghshire.
Tel: Denholm (045087) 320;
Horse & Hounds Inn, Bonchester, Hawick, Roxburghshire.
Tel: Bonchester Bridge (045086) 645

Williestruther Loch is a small water to the south of Hawick. Fishing is from the bank only and no boats are allowed. The Hawick Angling Club has stocked the loch with brown trout and their average weight is 1 lb. Williestruther is a difficult loch to fish due to the strong weed growth near the margins. There are large trout in the loch and due to its ease of access it is a popular place for a few casts in the evening. Standard loch pattern flies do well.

ALEMOOR LOCH   79/400155

Permission:
Hawick and District Angling Club, 5 Sandbed, Hawick, Roxburghshire.
Tel: Hawick (0450) 3771;
Stotharts, 6 High Street, Hawick, Roxburghshire.
Tel: Hawick (0450) 2231;
Pet Store, 1 Union Street, Hawick, Roxburghshire.
Tel: Hawick (0450) 3543;
David Dickman, Main Street, Denholm, Hawick, Roxburghshire.
Tel: Denholm (045087) 320;
Horse & Hounds Inn, Bonchester, Hawick, Roxburghshire.
Tel: Bonchester Bridge (045086) 645

Alemoor is a lovely loch on the edge of the Carrick Forrest 8 miles west of Hawick on the B711. It is 1½ miles long and is divided by the road. There are two boats available for anglers and the boathouse is at the north end of the loch. Hawick and District Angling Club has stocked the loch with brown trout but it also holds pike and perch. Alemoor Loch has a reputation for large trout and fish of up to 5 lb. have been caught. Fishing is best in the evenings and most productive flies are March Brown, Greenwell's Glory and Silver Butcher. Dour, but worth a go.

BLACK ESK RESERVOIR   79/205965

Permission: For details of fishing available to the public, contact J. W. Crowson, Sandyford Cottage, Boreland, Lockerbie, Dumfries-shire.

This reservoir lies in the Eskdale Moor Forest between Eskdalemuir in the north and Lockerbie to the south. Access is

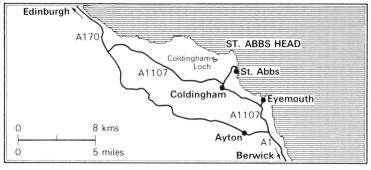

Map 34 *Duns and Dunbar*

from the B723 at Sandyford. This is a popular area with visitors and of great natural beauty. The Black Esk Reservoir is one mile long by 500 yards wide and several feeder burns enter from Cairn Knowe and Kilburn Hill. Three boats are available for anglers and bank fishing is not allowed. The loch has been stocked with brown trout and their average weight is ½–¾ lb. The last record of catches was in 1978, when 701 trout were caught, the heaviest fish weighing over 1 lb. Fish rise and are caught all over the loch but the best area is at the northern end. Use standard pattern loch flies. You will not break any records but you will have a most pleasant day.

COLDINGHAM LOCH   67/896685
Permission: Dr E. J. Wise, West Loch House, Coldingham, Berwickshire.
Tel: Coldingham (03903) 270

This is a beautifully situated little loch and one of the oldest, and best managed fisheries in Scotland. As early as the late 'forties rainbow trout had been introduced and I remember being told, as a boy, tales of these strange and lovely fish. The loch is 22 acres in extent and contains both brown trout and rainbow trout. There is a good boathouse and boats can be booked either for a full day when the bag limit is 7 fish per rod, or for a morning or evening only when the bag limit is 3 trout. Fish rise and are caught all over the loch and there is no one area better than another. The average weight is 1½ lb. Coldingham has always had a reputation for large fish and in 1980 a brown trout of 6 lb. 7 oz. was caught and in the following year a lovely fish of 7 lb. 7 oz. was taken. Flies to use include Black Pennell, Greenwell's Glory, Wickham's Fancy, Black Spider, Soldier Palmer and 'buzzers'. Visitors will be well received at Coldingham and given advice concerning which flies to use. Be warned, however, it can be very dour – I know – but for the man who likes a challenge there are few better places to fish. Turn east off the A1107 north of Coldingham village and look out for large trout. One of the best lochs in Scotland. Advance booking is essential since numbers of anglers are strictly limited; there are only 4 boats but good bank fishing is also available.

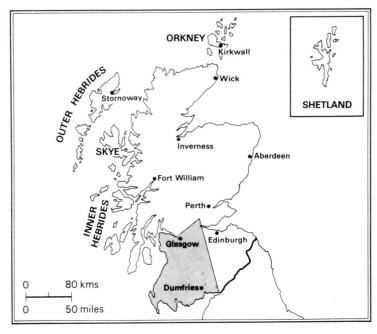

Map 35   *Glasgow and the South-West*

9 Glasgow and the South-West

Within easy reach of Glasgow are hundreds of trout lochs and no other major industrial centre in Europe can offer such a diversity of fine sport. Wander deep into the Galloway Forest Park to fish Loch Dee or Bradan, climb the boulder-scattered screes of Merrick – you will hardly see another soul all day. Visit scenic little Morton Castle Loch near Thornhill, or the wild moorlands to the north of Stranraer in Wigtownshire. You are never very far from the 'shades' of Robert Burns. From Ellisland Farm, near Dumfries, to the Auld Kirk at Alloway the presence of the great man dominates the countryside. But if I were forced to choose one area it would have to be the 'little highlands' and the area of the Galloway Forest Park. Here there is an abundance of everything that makes fishing my favourite pastime; forest tracks and secret places, wild and beautiful hills, peace and great trout.

LOCH LOMOND   Sheet 56

Permission:
Inverbeg Inn, Luss, Dunbartonshire.
Tel: Luss (043686) 678;
Ardlui Hotel, Ardlui, Loch Lomond, Arrochar, Dunbartonshire.
Tel: Inveruglas (03014) 243;
Rowardennan Hotel, Drymen, Glasgow.
Tel: Balmaha (036087) 273;
R. A. Clement & Co., 224 Ingram Street, Glasgow.
Tel: (041) 2210068

The main interest here for the angler is salmon and sea trout and most visitors fish for them. Loch Lomond is, however, a good trout loch and well worth a visit. On such a vast water it would be difficult to give more than a very brief outline in the space allotted to me, but I think most people who know the loch would agree with me when I say that you could walk down to the shore at almost any point and catch trout. The western shore line is the most easily accessible. If you want to really get away from it all, explore the east shore. It is all very beautiful, and Loch Lomond is

Map 36   *Kilsyth*

one of the best known and best loved lochs in Scotland. The trout average ½ lb. and, depending upon where you are fishing, tend to be beautifully marked and well shaped. The northern end of the loch produces the best results and all the standard pattern loch flies will bring fish. In spite of being so close to Glasgow and popular for all kinds of water sports and other activities, there is room for everyone on the lovely loch.

MOUNT DAM/WHITEFIELD POND   64/644774

Permission: Caurnie Pets & Tackle, 105 Cowgate, Kirkintilloch, Glasgow.
Tel: Glasgow (041) 7764458

These two waters lie in the Campsie Fells midway between Lennoxtown and Milton of Campsie. Fishing is from the bank only and the lochs are stocked with brown trout. Average weight is ¾ lb. Mount Dam is considered to be the most productive of the two and baskets of up to 5 trout are often taken. Standard loch fly patterns work well as does a Grey Duster. A lovely area to fish, redolent with old castles, ancient forts and wild hills.

BANTON LOCH   64/740785
Permission:
Members of the Committee of Kilsyth Fish Protection Association in attendance at the loch;
R. Brown, Colzium Motor Sales & Service, Stirling Road, Kilsyth, Glasgow.
Tel: Kilsyth (0236) 822003;
Coachman Hotel, Park Foot Street, Kilsyth, Glasgow.
Tel: Kilsyth (0236) 821649
Banton Loch lies one mile to the east of Kilsyth and is over half a mile long by 250 yards wide. The loch is managed by the Kilsyth Fish Protection Association whose Secretary is S. Gillies, 13 Findly Street, Kilsyth. The club stock the loch with brown trout and both boat and bank fishing are available to visitors. The average weight of the fish is in the order of ½–¾ lb. but several trout of 1 lb. and more are taken each season. The heaviest fish caught during the 1980 season weighed 2½ lb. Boats should be booked from the Coachman Hotel and there are 5 available. Two sessions operate, from 8.00–5.00 pm and 5.00 pm until midnight. Fishing is good all round the loch and the trout seem to prefer dark coloured flies. This is a well-managed and organised loch and worth a visit.

SPRINGFIELD RESERVOIR   72/904520
Permission:
Clyde Valley Tackle Shop, 28 Kirkton Street, Carluke, Lanarkshire.
Tel: Carluke (0555) 72183;
William Robertson & Co. (Fishing Tackle) Ltd, 27 Wellington Street, Glasgow.
Tel: Glasgow (041221) 6687
Springfield Reservoir lies to the east of Carluke in Lanarkshire and is 700 yards long by nearly 300 yards wide. Fishing is managed by the United Clyde Angling Protective Association whose address is 20 Cunningham Street, Motherwell. The reservoir contains brown trout and is easily accessible being adjacent to the B7056, 2½ miles out of town, at Easterseat.

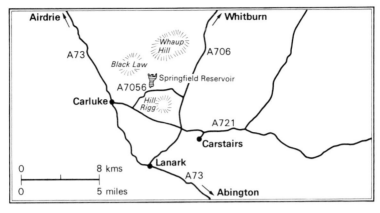

Map 37   *Upper Clyde Valley*

CARRON VALLEY RESERVOIR   57/690840

Permission: The Director of Finance, Central Regional Council, Viewfirth, Stirling.
Tel: Stirling (0786) 3111

Carron Valley Reservoir lies to the south of the B818 road between Denny and Fintry. It is 3 miles long by three-quarters of a mile wide and is almost surrounded by the Carron Valley Forest. The lovely Fintry Hills lie to the north and the Campsie Fells to the south, and Carron Valley is a most pleasant loch to fish. The loch is stocked from time to time and fishing is from boats only, of which there are 12 available for visitors. There is a bag limit of 30 fish per boat per day, but before you get too excited I hasten to add that the average basket is about 6 trout. Nevertheless, they average 1 lb. and fight very hard indeed. This is a loch for small flies, I think, and the best patterns to use are Black Pennell, Woodcock and Yellow, Grouse and Claret, Greenwell's Glory and Butchers. Fish are caught all round the loch but one of the best areas is the tree-fringed south shoreline. Heavier fish are also caught, so look out for the 2-pounder and concentrate, Carron Valley is a popular water so you would be well advised to book early. Easily accessible and good fishing in lovely surroundings. Can be windy but the Council, thoughtfully, have outboard motors for hire.

WHINHILL RESERVOIR   63/277746
Permission:
Findlay & Co., 25 West Stewart Street, Greenock, Renfrewshire.
Tel: Greenock (0475) 24056;
J. Rankin, Water House, Loch Thom Reservoir, Greenock,
  Renfrewshire.

Whinhill is a small brown trout reservoir to the south of Greenock
and fishing is managed by the Greenock and District Angling
Club. Approach from the hill road to Largs which leaves the
B7054 near the golf course.

LOCH THOM   63/260720
GRYFE RESERVOIR   63/280719
Permission: Findlay & Co., 25 West Stewart Street, Greenock,
Renfrewshire.
Tel: Greenock (0475) 24056

Loch Thom and the Gryfe Reservoir are the largest trout waters in
the area and lie in the Renfrewshire Hills above Greenock. In spite
of the fact that they are close to major urban centres, they remain
secluded and remote. They are easily accessible and a welcome
facility for local anglers. Fishing is controlled by three separate
angling clubs: Loch Thom and the Compensation Reservoirs Nos
6/7/8 by Greenock and District Angling Club, B. Paterson, 56
Pentland Court, Greenock; Gryfe Reservoir No. 1 by Dunrod
Angling Club, T. Rae, 36 Margaret Street, Greenock and Gryfe
No. 2 by the Port Glasgow Angling Club, P. Graham, 12 Skye
Road, Port Glasgow. Permits are also issued by J. Rankin, Water
House, Loch Thom, N.Bowes, Water House, Loch Thom and
Mrs A. Baird, Cornalees Farm, Loch Thom and A. Caskie,
Garvocks Farm, Loch Thom. I suggest that the visitor would be
best advised to contact Findlay & Co. who will give directions
and advice.

HARELAW RESERVOIR   63/310733
Permission: P. Graham, 12 Skye Road, Port Glasgow,
Renfrewshire.
Tel: Port Glasgow (0475) 43143

Fishing is controlled by the Port Glasgow Angling Club and this
small reservoir lies adjacent to the B788 on Burnhead Moor. The
loch is stocked with brown trout and is easily accessible.

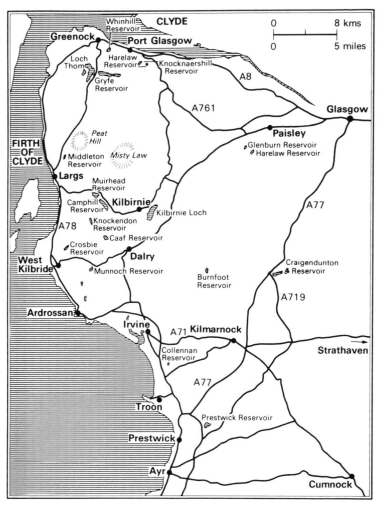

Map 38   *Ayrshire and Renfrewshire*

KNOCKNAERSHILL RESERVOIR   63/307733

Permission: P. Graham, 12 Skye Road, Port Glasgow,
Renfrewshire.
Tel: Port Glasgow (0475) 43143

This is another of the Port Glasgow Angling Club waters and it
lies close to Harelaw Reservoir and is approached by the same
route. Fishing is for brown trout which average ½–¾ lb.

HARELAW RESERVOIR   64/485596

Permission: J. Cuthbertson, 68 Bellfield Crescent, Barrhead, Glasgow.

The St Mirin Angling Club manage this reservoir and membership of the club is restricted to 70 members. There are generally a few memberships vacant and you should contact the Secretary whose name is given above. Harelaw is to the south of the B774 Barrhead–Paisley road and the club has a good boathouse with lighting and cooking facilities. The loch is stocked with 500 2-year old brown trout each season and the average weight of trout is ¾ lb. Whilst a catch of 2–3 fish would be considered good, trout of 2–3 lb. are occasionally caught and fishing is all from the bank. Size 10–14 flies do best and the trout are always in excellent condition. Try Black Pennell, Greenwell's and Silver Butcher for your first cast.

GLENBURN RESERVOIR   64/475600

Permission: The Lower Clyde Water Board, 19 Underwood Road, Paisley, Renfrewshire.
Tel: Paisley (041887) 5161

Glenburn lies to the south of Paisley in the Fereneze Hills and may be approached through the Glenburn housing estate from either B774 or B775. This small reservoir is stocked occasionally with brown trout and the average weight is ¾ lb. Fishing is all from the bank and the south and west banks produce the best results. An average basket would consist of 2 fish and the best flies to use are Greenwell Glory and Olive Dun. Summer evenings are the best time to fish.

CRAIGENDUNTON RESERVOIR   64/526457

Permission: McCririck & Sons, 38 John Finnie Street, Kilmarnock, Ayrshire.
Tel: Kilmarnock (0563) 25577

There are 2 reservoirs here, in a delightful woodland setting amidst the Whitelee Forest. The lochs are stocked with brown trout and their average weight is ¾ lb. The main part of the reservoir is 700 yards long by 200 yards wide and the best fishing area is along the south shore. Bank fishing only. Average catches amount to 3–6 fish and the best trout taken recently weighed 4 lb. Blae and Black, Teal and Green, and Greenwell's Glory do most of the damage and fishing is good throughout the season. Approach via the A719 Glaston road at Amlaird. The road up to the reservoirs is about 2½ miles. A secluded and pleasant place to spend the day.

BURNFOOT RESERVOIR   64/453450–70/450448

Permission: McCririck & Sons, 38 John Finnie Street, Kilmarnock, Ayrshire.
Tel: Kilmarnock (0563) 25577

This is a small reservoir to the west of the A77 Kilmarnock–Glasgow road. It is stocked with brown trout and their average weight is ¾ lb. Fishing is from the bank only and there is a bag limit of 6 fish per rod. Fish rise and are caught all over the loch and the best flies to use include Greenwell's Glory, Pennells, Teal and Red, and Teal and Green. An average day should bring you 3–6 trout and the best fish taken recently weighed 3 lb. Evening fishing is most productive.

CROSBIE RESERVOIR   63/219505

Permission: P. M. Shepherd, Dunruadh, Bowfield Road, West Kilbride, Ayrshire.
Tel: West Kilbride (0294) 822182
Also from tackle shops in Largs. Fly only with fly rod and reel.

Crosbie Reservoir is a small brown trout water to the north of West Kilbride, below Caldron Hill (329m). Approach via B781 West Kilbride–Dalry road just north of the town and follow the minor road a few hundred yards north. The road up to the reservoir is on your right. Fishing on Crosbie is managed by the Largs Angling Club. Best flies to use are size 12 and 15 Black Pennell, Blae and Black, Invicta and Butchers.

MIDDLETON RESERVOIR   63/215625

Permission: P. M. Shepherd, Dunruadh, Bowfield Road, West Kilbride, Ayrshire.
Tel: West Kilbride (0294) 822182
Also from tackle shops in Largs. Fly only with fly rod and reel.

Fishing is managed by the Largs Angling Club and this reservoir is to the east of the Largs–Loch Thom hill road. The loch is stocked with brown trout. Best flies are size 14 Grouse and Claret, Greenwell's Glory, spiders and Invicta.

KILBIRNIE LOCH   63/330549
Permission: Ian Johnstone, 12 Grahamston Avenue, Glengarnoch, Ayrshire.
Tel: Kilbirnie (0505) 682154

Kilbirnie Loch is stocked every year with brown trout and fishes best during the months of March–June and late September. The east shore is the most productive fishing area and trout of up to 4 lb. in weight have been taken.

MUIRHEAD RESERVOIR   63/255570
CAMPHILL RESERVOIR   63/270555
Permission: The Lower Clyde Water Board, 19 Underwood Road, Paisley, Renfrewshire.
Tel: Paisley (041887) 5161

These reservoirs lie to the south of the A760 Largs–Kilbirnie road and are easily accessible. They have been stocked with brown trout and fishing is managed by the Largs Angling Club.

MUNNOCH RESERVOIR   63/252477
Permission: Starks (newsagents), Dockhead Street, Saltcoats, Ayrshire.

Munnoch Reservoir is at the junction of the B781 and B780 and covers an area of 450 yards by 230 yards. Fishing is managed by the Munnoch Angling Club and the reservoir contains brown trout.

CAAF RESERVOIR   63/250503
Permission: The Secretary, The Dalry Angling Club, 8 Peden Avenue, Dalry, Ayrshire.

This is a long, narrow reservoir to the south of the minor road between Glenside on the A78 and to the west of Giffordland on the B780 Ardrossan—Dalry road. Fishing is managed by the Dalry Angling Club and it contains brown and rainbow trout.

PRESTWICK RESERVOIR   70/395272
Permission:
Red Lion Hotel, Prestwick, Ayrshire.
Newalls Newsagents, Monkton, Ayrshire.
Wheatsheaf Inn, Monkton, Ayrshire.
Gamesport Shop, Ayr.
C. Hendrie, Secretary, Prestwick Angling Club, 12 Glenpark Avenue, Prestwick, Ayrshire.
Tel: Prestwick (0292) 70203

Prestwick Reservoir is a 12-acre fishery which lies 3 miles to the east of Prestwick Airport. The loch is well managed and controlled and considered to be the best trout water in Ayrshire. The club stocks every month with 11–12-inch rainbow trout and their average weight – when caught – is 1½ lb. Season is from 15 March until 15 November, and there is a bag limit of 6 fish per rod per day.

KNOCKENDON RESERVOIR   63/244524

Permission: J. M. Currie, Sports Goods, 32 High Street, Irvine, Ayrshire.
Tel: Irvine (0294) 78603

Fishing on Knockendon Reservoir is managed by the Munnoch Angling Club and it contains brown trout. This is a hill water and lies at an altitude of 700 feet. Approach from the minor road between Glenside on the A78 or from the B780 at Giffordland.

COLLENNAN RESERVOIR   70/350332

Permission: Club Secretary, 1 Fairhaven, Brassie, Troon, Ayrshire.
Tel: Troon (0292) 315466

This small reservoir lies to the east of the A78, between Loans and the Brassie B746 turn off. Collennan is stocked each year with 1,500 brown trout which are introduced to the reservoir weighing 1 lb. The average weight of fish in Collennan is therefore the best in the area and is an impressive 1½ lb. Fishing is from the bank only and trout of up to 5 lb. are taken. The south-east shore is the most productive area and good flies to try are Blae and Black, and Black Pennell. Sedge imitations do well also, particularly at dusk. There is excellent feeding in the reservoir so the trout are highly selective but an average basket should produce 2–3 fish. The members go to great lengths to protect and preserve their fishing and the loch is under continual surveillance including patrols using two-way radios. This is a delightful, well-managed water and an asset to the area.

MORTON CASTLE LOCH   78/890993

Permission: Buccleuch Estates Limited, Estate Office, Drumlanrig Mains, Thornhill, Dumfries-shire DG3 4AG.
Tel: Marrburn (08486) 283/284

This small loch covers an area of 8 acres and it lies to the north of

Map 39   *Kirkcudbrightshire*

Thornhill. The loch is dominated by the ruins of Morton Castle which stand on a hill overlooking the water. There is one boat on the loch and bank fishing is not allowed, so you have the loch to yourself for the day – apart from time to time when the estate gives permission to local Scouts to camp there. The loch has been stocked with brown and rainbow trout and their average weight is ¾–1¼ lb. There is a limit of 4 fish per rod per day, up to a maximum of three rods. The estate can also provide first-class accommodation in self-catering cottages and lodges. Morton Castle Loch is one of the most scenic and lovely little waters in the south-west and really deserves your attention. Book well in advance.

26   *Morton Castle Loch.*

STARBURN LOCH 78/851980

Permission: Buccleuch Estates Limited, Estate Office, Drumlanrig
Mains, Thornhill, Dumfries-shire DG3 4AG.
Tel: Marrburn (08486) 283/284

Starburn is a small, sheltered loch covering an area of 4 acres. It
lies to the north of Thornhill and the season extends from
1 April–11 August. Starburn is stocked with both brown and
rainbow trout and their average weight is ¾–1¼ lb. Fishing is
from the boat only and there is a limit of 4 fish per rod per day up
to a maximum of three rods. Starburn Loch fishes best during the
early months of the season and standard pattern loch flies will do
fine. A perfect place to fish and the Estate can provide accommodation also.

The loch is situated in an attractive mixed woodland setting and
has beautiful water-lilies growing round the edge.

AFTON RESERVOIR 77/635040

Permission:
Superintendent, Filter Station, Afton Reservoir, New
Cummnock, Ayrshire;
Stanley Stores, Unit 9, Glaisnock Shopping Centre, Cummnock,
Ayrshire.
Tel: Cummnock (0290) 22467

Fishing on Afton Reservoir is managed by the New Cummnock Anglers Association and the reservoir is approached via Afton Road in Afton Bridgend on the A76. This is very lovely country-side and the quality of the scenery is matched by the quality of the fishing. The water contains both brown and brook trout and an average basket from Afton should amount to 5–7 fish. Baskets of 10–15 are common and the average weight of fish is ½–¾ lb. The reservoir is stocked at least once in every eighteen months with about 1,000 trout and both boat and bank fishing are available. The most productive fishing area is at the top end of the loch where Montraw Burn and Afton Water enter. Two further feeder burns come in on the south-west shore and this is also a good fishing area. Afton is almost completely surrounded by forest with Carsphairn (797m) and the scar of Gairy Cairnsmor to the south and Cairshairn Forest covering the slopes to the west. A beautiful loch offering good sport.

LOCH ETTRICK   78/945938

Permission: The Keeper, Blawbare Cottage, Thornhill, Dumfries-shire.
Tel: Thornhill (0848) 31304

Loch Ettrick is a small loch below Sowens Knowe and bordering the forest of Ae to the south. Approach from Kirkpartick on the A76 from the west, or from Ae Bridgend and Ae village on the A701 from the east. The loch has been stocked and contains brown trout and rainbow trout. The average weight of fish is ¾ lb. and good baskets are regularly taken. Standard pattern loch flies should be offered.

KETTLETON RESERVOIR   78/897005

Permission: Messrs Pollock & Oag, 1 West Morton Street, Thorn-hill, Dumfries-shire.
Tel: Thornhill (0848) 30207

This small reservoir lies to the north of Thornhill between Parr Hill (423m) and Nether Hill (393m) to the west. Bank fishing only and small flies do best. Kettleton is now a well managed fishery and regularly stocked with rainbow trout throughout the season. Can be very windy, but beautifully situated amidst the Lowther Hills.

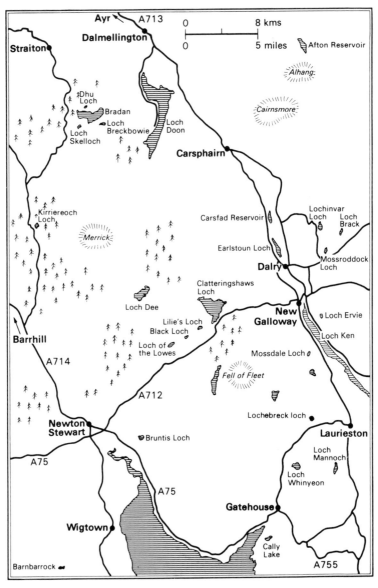

Map 40   *Dumfries-shire*

LOCH DOON
77/490990

Permission: Not required

This is the largest and deepest loch in the area and is 7½ miles long by 1¼ miles wide. The Ayrshire Angling Association manage the fishing and hold their annual competition on the loch. This is usually won with a basket of 8–10 fish weighing 3–4 lb. Fish of over 1 lb. are very rare and the loch also contains pike, char and perch. This is a hydro-electric water and wading requires great care due to the unstable nature of parts of the margin. Best areas to fish include Starr Bay in the north-east, Graple Burn – the outfall for Loch Finlas – on the west shore, and where the Carrick Lane enters the loch south of Graples. Another good area is at the south end of the loch round Loch Head Burn. Best flies to use include Black Pennell, Teal and Yellow, and Butchers. The trout are not all that ready to give themselves up, but Loch Doon is a pleasant place to fish, popular with local anglers and visitors alike.

DRUMLAMFORD LOCH
76/280775

Permission: A. McKeand, Head Keeper, The Kennels, Barrhill, Girvan, Ayrshire.
Tel: Barrhill (046582) 256

This is a small, tree-fringed loch to the south of Barhill and it offers excellent sport in lovely surroundings. Drumlamford is stocked each season with up to 3,000 brown trout and there are also rainbow trout and brook trout. The average weight of fish is 1 lb. 3 oz. and there is a bag limit of 6 fish per rod. Fishing is best from the boat and trout rise and are caught all over the loch. Best cast is Blae and Black, Wickham's Fancy and Silver Butcher. Trout of over 2 lb. are not uncommon and the loch produces of its best early on in the season. The estate also have fishing available on several other lochs which contain wild brown trout averaging ½–¾ lb. Drumlamford is the most popular and is easily accessible. Book in advance.

PENWHAPPLE RESERVOIR
76/260970

Permission: Reservoir Superintendent, Penwhapple Reservoir, Girvan, Ayrshire.
Telephone bookings not accepted.

Penwhapple Reservoir is three-quarters of a mile long by 500 yards wide and lies 5 miles south of Girvan on the B734. The water is stocked, and each year up to 1,000 11 inch brown trout are put in. During the past ten years Penwhapple has produced an average of 1,200 fish per season and their average weight is ¾ lb. Trout of over 2 lb. are taken and the largest fish caught recently weighed 2 lb. 9 oz. There are 5 wooden boats available but the use of outboard motors is not permitted. Bank fishing is allowed, but Penwhapple fishes best from the boat. Dependent upon the weather, the north end, where the feeder burn enters, can be very good. Catches of 10–15 trout are common but the average basket is usually about 4–6 fish. Flies to try include Greenwell's Glory, Grouse and Claret, Black Pennell, Wickham's Fancy, Blae and Black, and Butchers. Best months are April, May and June. This is a well-managed fishery in pleasant surroundings and worth a visit.

LOCH BRADAN   77/425970
Permission:
Forestry Commission, Ayrshire Forest District, Forest Office, Dalmellington Road, Straiton, Ayrshire.
Tel: Straiton (06557) 637;
R. Heaney, Taliminnoch, Straiton, Maybole, Ayrshire.
Tel: Straiton (06557) 617

Loch Bradan is the largest of the lochs to the west of Loch Doon and lies to the south of Straiton on the road to Newton Stewart. Five boats are available for anglers and bank fishing is also allowed. Bradan used to be two separate waters, Bradan Reservoir and Loch Lure, but were joined together during the hydro-electric development. The water has been stocked with brown trout and their average weight is ½–¾ lb. with the occasional fish of over 1 lb. being taken from time to time. The largest fish to come from the reservoir so far weighed 4 lb. 4 oz. Take care when wading, especially to the east of the dam where underwater tree stumps can present difficulties. The headland round Craig Dhu is a good area for bank fishing although fish are caught round most of the loch. Flies to use include Black Pennell, Peter Ross, Grouse and Claret, and Butchers. A weekly ticket is available which includes fishing on nearby Loch Skelloch as well. The water is restocked twice yearly and outboard motors are not permitted.

LOCH SKELLOCH   77/410962
Permission:
Forestry Commission, Ayrshire Forest District, Forest Office, Dalmellington Road, Straiton, Ayrshire.
Tel: Straiton (06557) 637;
R. Heaney, Taliminnoch, Straiton, Maybole, Ayrshire.
Tel: Straiton (06557) 617

Loch Skelloch lies to the south of Loch Bradan and is approached via a track from Stinchar Bridge on the Straiton–Newton Stewart road. The Water of Girvan passes through Loch Skelloch on its way down Shalloch of Minnoch from tiny Loch Girvan Eye. One boat is available for anglers and the loch contains hard-fighting, small brown trout in the ½–¾ lb. class. A delightful little loch to fish in very attractive surroundings. Standard loch pattern flies do well. Outboard motors are not permitted on the loch.

LOCH DEE   77/470790
Permission:
Forestry Commission, Galloway Deer Museum, New Galloway, Castle Douglas, Kirkcudbrightshire.
Tel: New Galloway (06442) 285;
Forestry Commission, Caldons Camp Site, Bargrennan, Newton Stewart, Wigtownshire.
Tel: Bargrennan (067184) 218;
Forestry Commission, Creebridge, Newton Stewart, Wigtownshire.
Tel: Newton Stewart (0671) 2420;
Forestry Commission, Castle Douglas Forest District, 21 King Street, Castle Douglas, Kirkcudbrightshire.
Tel: Castle Douglas (0556) 3626;
Forestry Commission, Talnotry Caravan Park, Newton Stewart, Wigtownshire.
Tel: Newton Stewart (0671) 2170

Loch Dee is remote, yet easily accessible and lies amidst the beauty of the Galloway hills surrounded by boulder strewn granite crags. This is a delightful place to fish and the loch is stocked each year with native Loch Dee trout. Their average weight is 1 lb. 3 oz. Access is from Clatteringshaws and the visitor will be given detailed directions when he obtains his permit. All fishing is from the bank and the most productive areas are the peninsula and points round the south and west shore. Several trout of over 3 lb. are caught each year and the flies that do most damage include Blae and Black, Greenwell Glory and Wickham's Fancy. A sample basket taken during the 1981 season had 2 trout weighing 2¾ lb. for the visit. The best fish caught during 1985 weighed 6 lb. and several trout of over 2 lb. were taken.

THE DHU LOCH 77/422986

Permission:
Forestry Commission, Ayrshire Forest District, Forest Office, Dalmellington Road, Straiton, Ayrshire.
Tel: Straiton (06557) 637;
R. Heaney, Taliminnoch, Straiton, Maybole, Ayrshire.
Tel: Straiton (06557) 617

This lovely small loch is in the forest to the north of Loch Bradan and near Craig Dhu (415m). It is stocked with brown trout and they average ½–¾ lb. in weight. Bank fishing only and small flies work best, particularly olives, sedges and all in 14–16 size. The Dhu Loch is a 'special' place and very attractive.

LOCH BRECKBOWIE 77/433960

Permission:
Forestry Commission, Ayrshire Forest District, Forest Office, Dalmellington Road, Straiton, Ayrshire.
Tel: Straiton (06557) 637;
R. Heaney, Taliminnoch, Straiton, Maybole, Ayrshire.
Tel: Straiton (06557) 617

Loch Breckbowie lies to the south of Loch Bradan, in the Carrick Forest. The track out to the loch has been marked for the first mile over the moor and there is one boat available for anglers. Bank fishing is also allowed. Breckbowie can be windy but shelter can generally be found round the shore and this is a pleasant loch to fish. Trout average ¾ lb. and the flies to use to tempt them are Black Pennell, Grouse and Claret, Greenwell's Glory and Peter Ross.

LILIE'S LOCH 77/517747

Permission:
Forestry Commission, Galloway Deer Museum, New Galloway, Castle Douglas, Kirkcudbrightshire.
Tel: New Galloway (06442) 285;
Forestry Commission, Caldons Camp Site, Bargrennan, Newton Stewart, Wigtownshire.
Tel: Bargrennan (067184) 218;
Forestry Commission, Castle Douglas Forest District, Castle Douglas, Kirkcudbrightshire.
Tel: Castle Douglas (05560) 3626;

Forestry Commission, Creebridge, Newton Stewart, Wigtown-shire.
Tel: Newton Stewart (0671) 2420;
Forestry Commission, Talnotry Caravan Park, Newton Stewart, Wigtownshire.
Tel: Newton Stewart (0671) 2170

Lilie's Loch is a small forest loch to the north of the A712 between Clatteringshaws and Murray's Monument. It lies on the line of the Pulran Burn close to the old Edinburgh road. Approach through the forest along a good track, an easy and very pleasant walk. The loch has been stocked and contains brown trout with an average weight of ½–¾ lb. Bank fishing only and small flies of the Blae and Black/Black Spider do best.

LOCH OF THE LOWES   77/469705
Permission:
Forestry Commission, Galloway Deer Museum, New Galloway Castle Douglas, Kirkcudbrightshire.
Tel: New Galloway (06442) 285;
Forestry Commission, Caldons Camp Site, Bargrennan, Newton Stewart, Wigtownshire.
Tel: Bargrennan (067184) 218;
Forestry Commission, Creebridge, Newton Stewart, Wigtown-shire
Tel: Newton Stewart (0671) 2420;
Forestry Commission, Castle Douglas Forest District, 21 King Street, Castle Douglas, Kirkcudbrightshire.
Tel: Castle Douglas (0556) 3626;
Forestry Commission, Talnotry Caravan Park, Newton Stewart, Wigtownshire.
Tel: Newton Stewart (0671) 2170

Loch of the Lowes is a mile to the south of the Black Loch and is a small forest loch full of good ½ lb. trout. There is a limit of 5 fish per rod and the loch is stocked each year by the Forestry Commission. Fishing is from the bank only and the south bank is the most productive area. The term 'free rising' really does apply to these small forest lochs and they are a perfect place to take a newcomer to boost his ego – your own as well I shouldn't wonder, if your casting is anything like mine.

THE BLACK LOCH   77/497728

Permission:
Forestry Commission, Galloway Deer Museum, New Galloway,
Castle Douglas, Kirkcudbrightshire.
Tel: New Galloway (06442) 285;
Forestry Commission, Caldons Camp site, Bargrennan, Newton
Stewart, Wigtownshire.
Tel: Bargrennam (067184) 218;
Forestry Commission, Creebridge, Newton Stewart, Wigtown-
shire
Tel: Newton Stewart (0671) 2420;
Forestry Commission, Castle Douglas Forest District, 21 King
Street, Castle Douglas, Kirkcudbrightshire.
Tel: Castle Douglas (0556) 3626;
Forestry Commission, Talnotry Caravan Park, Newton Stewart,
Wigtownshire.
Tel: Newton Stewart (0671) 2170
This is another delightful forest loch close to the A712 road south
of Clatteringshaws. It has been stocked with brown trout and
their average weight is ½ lb. Fishing is from the bank only and is
best from the north bank. Small black flies do best and the trout
rise well, with good baskets regularly being taken. Ticket also
includes Loch Dee, Loch of the Lowes and Lilie's Loch.

BRUNTIS LOCH   83/447654

Permission: Gun and Tackle Shop, 40 Queen Street, Newton
Stewart, Wigtownshire.
Tel: Newton Stewart (0671) 2570
Bruntis Loch lies close to Newton Stewart and is beautifully
situated amidst tree-covered Auchannoch Hill. Two miles east of
the town on the A75, turn left at Craig Hall on to a rough forestry
road. The car may be parked at the top of the hill and from this
point it is a half mile stroll through the forest to the loch. The
loch does not have natural spawning so the Newton Stewart
Angling Club, who manage the water, introduce rainbow trout
each year. The average weight of fish is ¾ lb. and there is a bag
limit of 4 fish per rod. Fishing is from the bank only and the loch
covers an area of 10 acres. The occasional trout of up to 2 lb. is
caught. Pleasant fishing in attractive surroundings.

KIRRIEREOCH LOCH   77/365866

Permission: R. W. McDowall, 9 Victoria Street, Newton Stewart,
Wigtownshire.
Tel: Newton Stewart (0671) 2163

This loch lies between Rowantree Toll and Glentrool village and can be approached either from Straiton in the north or from the A714 Newton Stewart–Girvan road to the south at Bargrennan. Fishing is from the bank only and there is a limit of 4 fish per rod. The loch has been stocked with brown trout and their average weight is ¾ lb., although several fish of over 1 lb. are taken each season. The treeless west bank is the preferred fishing area but trout can be caught all round the loch as well. Make sure you have a Mallard and Claret, and Teal and Black in your fly box before you go, since these two patterns do very well on this loch. Kirriereoch fishes best in August and September, particularly in the evening – the midges like it too – and you may expect 2–4 fish. The trout are of excellent quality, well marked and yellow-bellied.

LOCH OCHILTREE   76/315745
Permission: R. W. McDowall, 9 Victoria Street, Newton Stewart, Wigtownshire.
Tel: Newton Stewart (0671) 2163

Ochiltree is 6 miles to the north of Newton Stewart between the A714 and B7027. The loch is three-quarters of a mile long by half a mile wide and fishing is managed by the Newton Stewart Angling Association. The loch is stocked each year and contains brown trout, rainbow trout and brook trout. Anglers are limited to 4 fish per rod and both boat and bank fishing are available. Bank fishing is best during the early months of the season but after June the best baskets are taken from the boat. The average weight of the trout is 1 lb. and you may expect to catch 2 fish. Trout of 5 lb. have been taken from this lovely loch and 3 lb. fish are caught each season. Can be very windy. Standard pattern loch flies bring results.

MOSSRODDOCK LOCH   77/632815
Permission: Milton Park Hotel, Dalry, Castle Douglas, Kirkcudbrightshire.
Tel: Dalry (Kirk) (06443) 286

This loch is controlled by the Milton Park Hotel and guests have priority. It is stocked with brown and rainbow trout and lies to the north of the A702 just outside the town. Easily accessible from the road and visitors should inquire at the hotel for permits.

LOCH BRACK   77/685821

Permission: Milton Park Hotel, Dalry, Castle Douglas, Kirkcudbrightshire.
Tel: Dalry (Kirk) (06443) 286

This is a small loch in the Corriedoo Forest below Tarquhain Hill. It is 3 miles to the east of the town and may be approached via the A702 via Drummanister. Hotel guests have priority and visitors should inquire at the hotel for further details. The loch has been regularly stocked for some years and contains both brown and rainbow trout. The average weight is over ¾ lb. and baskets of 5 fish are common. Trout of up to 2 lb. are taken and the best flies to try are standard patterns and Cow Dung and Bluebottle Fly. Best place to fish is down the east bank though trout rise all over the loch. There are also reported to be char in Loch Brack.

EARLSTOUN LOCH   77/615830

Permission: Glenkens Cafe, 14 Main Street, Dalry, Castle Douglas, Kirkcudbrightshire.
Tel: Dalry (Kirk) (06443) 427

Earlstoun Loch lies adjacent to the A713 north of Dalry. Fishing is managed by the Dalry Anglers Association and the loch is stocked each year. Boat fishing only. The loch contains brown trout and they average ½–¾ lb. Best flies to use are Blae and Black, Grouse and Claret, Greenwell's Glory and Coch-y-Bonddu, and the area to concentrate on is the far side from the main road. Earlstoun is one of the 'head ponds' in the Loch Doon Water System and easily accessible.

CARSFAD RESERVOIR   77/607860

Permission: Glenkens Cafe, 14 Main Street, Dalry, Castle Douglas, Kirkcudbrightshire.
Tel: Dalry (Kirk) (06443) 427

Carsfad is the second of the head ponds for the Galloway power scheme and fishing is managed by the Dalry Anglers Association who regularly stock Carsfad. The water lies adjacent to the A713 and fishing is allowed from the west bank only. There is no boat fishing. Trout average ½–¾ lb. and you may hope for a basket of 3–4 fish.

LOCHINVAR LOCH   77/658854
Permission:
Lochinvar Hotel, Dalry, Castle Douglas, Kirkcudbrightshire.
Tel: Dalry (Kirk) (06443) 210;
Kenmure Hotel, New Galloway, Castle Douglas,
Kirkcudbrightshire.
Tel: New Galloway (06442) 360;
Ken Bridge Hotel, New Galloway, Castle Douglas,
Kirkcudbrightshire.
Tel: New Galloway (06442) 211

This is a really delightful loch to the north-east of Dalry and may
be approached from the A702 Dalry–Thornhill road. The loch has
been stocked with both brown and rainbow trout and boats are
available for visitors. Bank fishing is also allowed. The average
weight of fish is ¾ lb. and good baskets of trout are frequently
taken. Best fishing area is in the north end of the loch and also
round Donald's Island in the south. Standard pattern loch flies
work well.

BARSCOBE LOCH   77/670812
Permission:
Mrs Kirk, Barscobe Cottage, New Galloway, Castle Douglas,
Kirkcudbrightshire.
Tel: New Galloway (06442) 245;
Milton Park Hotel, Dalry, Castle Douglas, Kirkcudbrightshire.
Tel: Dalry (Kirk) (06443) 286

Barscobe Loch is 3 miles to the east of Dalry and covers an area of
13 acres. It is in a very lovely setting midst the Galloway Hills and
is one of the best lochs in the south-west. The loch is on the estate
of Sir Hugh Wontner of Barscombe and the estate is strict about
casual access, litter and picnickers. Barscobe is stocked with
brown trout, rainbow trout and brook trout and their average
weight is ¾–1 lb., although several trout of over 2 lb. are taken
each season. Standard loch pattern flies will produce results and
fishing is mostly from the boat. Some bank fishing may be
allowed. An excellent loch in delightful surroundings and well
worth visiting.

CLATTERINGSHAWS LOCH   77/540770
Permission: Forestry Commission, Galloway Deer Museum, New
Galloway, Castle Douglas, Kirkcudbrightshire.
Tel: New Galloway (06442) 285

Clatteringshaws was formed in the 1930s as part of the Loch

Doon hydro-electric scheme and is a large loch adjacent to the A712 road. This is a popular loch and it contains brown trout and pike. The trout average ½–¾ lb. and you may expect a basket of 2–3 fish. Access is easy all round the loch and standard pattern loch flies should produce results. Black flies and Cinnamon and Gold do particularly well.

JERICHO LOCH   78/990810
Permission:
M. N. Gordon Pattie & Sons, Queensberry Street, Dumfries.
Tel: Dumfries (0387) 2891;
Baird & Stevenson, Lochanbriggs, Dumfries.
Tel: Amisfield (0387) 710237

This is a new fishery, established in 1981 and it is situated 3 miles to the north of Dumfries on the A701 Moffat road. The loch covers an area of 10 acres and has been stocked with brown trout, rainbow trout and brook trout. There is a limit of 4 fish per rod and so far the average weight has been 1¾ lb. The best fish taken during the first season weighed 3½ lb. and it looks as though this little water is going to become a very popular place to fish. Too early to say what flies – I would think standard patterns and probably reservoir-type lures.

LOCH MANNOCH   83/665605
Permission: G. M. Thomson & Co., 27 King Street, Castle Douglas, Kirkcudbrightshire.
Tel: Castle Douglas (0556) 2701/2973

This loch is about 3 miles to the north of Twynholm, a village 27 miles west of Dumfries on the A75. It is part of the Lairdmannoch Estate, a small sporting estate which is easily accessible, but yet in beautiful unspoilt upland scenery, completely secluded. The loch is narrow, being over one mile in length and about 72 acres in area. It has not been stocked for many years but, due to the excellent spawning burns and a level of fertility which is unusually high for a hill loch, the number and size of brown trout is very satisfactory. In the first months of the 1986 season the average catch was over 12 fish per boat with two rods (there are four boats) at an average weight of just under ½ lb. It is an interesting loch to fish with a varied shoreline but the chief joy is peaceful beauty.

27 *The sweet smile of success.*

LOCH ERVIE   84/677728
Permission: G. M. Thomson & Co., 27 King Street, Castle Douglas, Kirkcudbrightshire.
Tel: Castle Douglas (0556) 2701/2973

Ervie is a small loch, unmarked on the map but easily accessible and quite private. It lies close to Loch Ken, off the A713 north of Castle Douglas. It is stocked regularly, mainly with rainbow trout, which grow to a good size. Bank fishing only – but in a setting of great beauty.

MOSSDALE LOCH   77/657710
Permission: Cross Keys Hotel, New Galloway, Kirkcudbrightshire.
Tel: New Galloway (06442) 494

Follow the A762 south from New Galloway with Loch Ken on your left and the Cairn Edward Forest to the right. As the forest ends, to the right of the road lies Mossdale Loch. Fishing is from boats only and the loch holds some good brown trout. Standard pattern flies get them out – sometimes.

LOCH KEN   77/650740
Permission: Cross Keys Hotel, New Galloway, Kirkcudbrightshire.
Tel: New Galloway (06442) 494

Loch Ken lies to the south of New Galloway and is famous throughout Scotland for the size of pike caught. What is less well known is that it can also provide good sport with brown trout. The loch also holds rainbow trout and occasional salmon. Boat fishing is best and these may be hired from the Loch Ken Holiday Centre. Most productive area for brown trout is at the New Galloway end of the loch.

DALBEATTIE RESERVOIR   84/806615
Permission: N. Parker, 30 High Street, Dalbeattie, Kirkcudbrightshire.
Tel: Dalbeattie (0556) 610448

This reservoir covers an area of 10 acres and is 2 miles to the west of the town on the A745 Castle Douglas road. The reservoir has a reputation for being dour and a basket of 2–3 trout would be considered good. Nevertheless, it is a popular place to fish and in an attractive setting. It contains both brown and rainbow trout and fishing is from the bank only. Flies to use are Black Pennell, Greenwell's Glory, Grouse and Claret, and Peter Ross. Dalbeattie Reservoir fishes best during the early months of the season.

LOCH ROAN   84/744693
Permission: Tommy's Sports Shop, 178 King Street, Castle Douglas, Kirkcudbrightshire.
Tel: Castle Douglas (0556) 2851

Loch Roan lies 3 miles to the north of Castle Douglas on the A713 approach via Crossmichael and Wallbutt. There are 4 boats on the loch and bank fishing is not allowed. Roan is stocked with brown and rainbow trout and the average weight is 1 lb. There is a limit of 8 fish per boat and an average day should account for 4–6 fish. The best fish taken during the 1981 season weighed 2¼ lb. and all the usual standard pattern loch flies work well. This is a popular loch so book well in advance. Heaviest trout caught recently was a fish of 4 lb. 4 oz. taken in 1984.

GLENKILN RESERVOIR   84/845780
Permission:
The Water Engineer, South-West Scotland Water Board, 70 Terreglas Street, Dumfries.
Tel: Dumfries (0387) 63011;
William Logan, 1 Killylour, Shawhead, Dumfries-shire;
Killylour Filter Station, Shawhead, Dumfries-shire.
Tel: Dumfries (0387) 73234;
Galloway Arms Hotel, Crocketford, Dumfries.
Tel: Crocketford (055669) 240

Glenkiln Reservoir lies to the north of the A75 Dumfries–Castle Douglas road and is approached via Shawhead village. Boats are available and bank fishing is also allowed. Glenkiln has been stocked with brown trout and the average weight of fish is ¾ lb. Standard loch pattern flies will produce results and although Glenkiln has a reputation for being dour good baskets are taken.

LOCH WHINYEON   83/624608
Permission: Murray Arms Hotel, Gatehouse of Fleet, Castle Douglas, Kirkcudbrightshire.
Tel: Gatehouse (05574) 207

Loch Whinyeon is to the north of Gatehouse of Fleet and covers an area of 104 acres. There is a one mile walk along a forestry track to get to the loch and visitors should approach from Laghead on the Gatehouse–Laurieston minor road. Four boats are available and bank fishing is also allowed. The most productive areas are the small bays in the north-west and south-east corners. The loch has brown trout and is stocked with rainbow trout. There are a few fish of over 1 lb. and an average day should bring you up to 7 trout. Size 12–14 flies do best and all the standard pattern loch flies will bring results. This is a good loch, very pleasantly situated and recommended.

LOCHENBRECK LOCH   83/645655
Permission:
D. Twiname, 52 High Street, Gatehouse of Fleet.
Tel: Gatehouse (05574) 222
Watson McKinnel, 15 St Cuthbert Street, Kirkcudbright.
Tel: Kirkcudbright (0557) 30693;
Lochanbreck Farm, Nr. Laurieston, Castle Douglas, Kirkcudbrightshire.
(Evenings only)

This is a lovely loch to the west of the little minor road from Laurieston to Gatehouse of Fleet. It is a sheltered water, surrounded by the forest, with Kenick Hill to the east and Slogarie, Clack and Laughenghie Hills to the west and north. This is a well-established fishery and is regularly stocked with rainbow trout. The average weight is ¾ lb. and a day should produce for you up to 6 trout. The loch covers an area of 70 acres and the most productive places are in the bays at the south-east and south-west corners. Small flies work best, particularly Blae and Black, Black Spider and Black Pennell. There is a road to within 200 yards of the loch.

BARNBARROCH LOCH   83/400514
Permission: Forestry Commission, Hazelbank, Kilsture, Sorbie, Newton Stewart, Wigtownshire.
Tel: Sorbie (098885) 238

Barnbarroch is a tiny loch to the south of Wigtown and may be approached via the A714. The loch is set in a small wood and has been stocked with rainbow trout. Average weight of fish is ¾ lb. and they rise to standard pattern loch flies. Very pleasant little loch.

BAREND LOCH   84/880550
Permission: Barend Properties, Sandyhills, Dalbeattie, Kirkcudbrightshire.
Tel: Southwick (038778) 663

This is a small loch of 6 acres and it forms part of a holiday village. The loch is stocked with 500–700 rainbow trout each year and the average size of fish is ¾ lb. The best fish to come from the loch weighed 4 lb. Fishing is from the bank only and there is a limit of 3 fish per rod.

SOULSEAT LOCH   82/100590
Permission: J. L. Johnstone, 13 Dalrymple Court, Stranraer, Wigtownshire.
Tel: Stranraer (0776) 4554

This is the most popular loch in the area and it is managed by the Stranraer and District Angling Association. Approach via the A75 Stranraer–Glenluce Road. Two boats are available and bank fishing is also allowed. The loch covers an area of 72 acres and holds brown trout and rainbow trout. The average weight of fish is 1–1½ lb. and the best fish caught recently weighed 5 lb. 1 oz. This is an easily accessible loch and offers excellent sport.

PENWHIRN RESERVOIR   82/125697
Permission: J. L. Johnstone, 13 Dalrymple Court, Stranraer, Wigtownshire.
Tel: Stranraer (0776) 4554

Penwhirn lies to the north of Stranraer and is at the end of the New Luce road. The loch covers an area of some 150 acres and fishing is from the bank only. The fish are native brown trout and they rise well to standard pattern loch flies. The north shore fishes best and the loch is in a most attractive setting.

LOCH REE   82/104699
Permission: J. L. Johnstone, 13 Dalrymple Court, Stranraer, Wigtownshire.
Tel: Stranraer (0776) 4554

Loch Ree is a small loch to the west of Penwhirn Reservoir and is approached via the New Luce road. A track follows the south shore of Penwhirn to Awies Farm at the end of the reservoir and Loch Ree is a walk of one mile from this point. Bank fishing only, for hard-fighting ½–¾ lb. trout. Remote and beautiful and well worth a visit. Standard pattern loch flies work well.

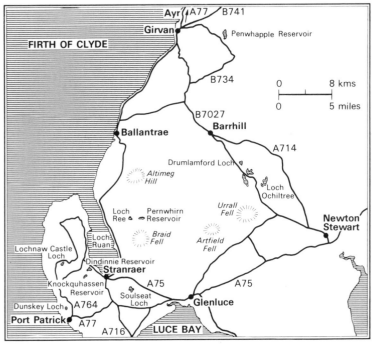

Map 41   *Wigtownshire*

DINDINNIE RESERVOIR   82/022607
Permission: J. L. Johnstone, 13 Dalrymple Court, Stranraer, Wigtownshire.
Tel: Stranraer (0776) 4554

Fishing on Dindinnie is managed by the Stranraer and District Angling Association and the loch has been stocked with brown trout which average 1 lb. in weight. Best flies are Black Spider, Black Pennell, Greenwell's Glory and Butchers. Fishing is from the bank only. The south end of the loch, where the feeder burn enters, is a good fishing area although fish are caught all round the shore. Approach via Stranraer–Kirkcolm on the A718 and turn left at Auchneel. Leave the car at Dindinnie Farm.

KNOCKQUHASSEN RESERVOIR   82/020595
Permission: J. L. Johnstone, 13 Dalrymple Court, Stranraer, Wigtownshire.
Tel: Stranraer (0776) 4554

This reservoir is to the south of Stranraer and it is full of little bays and interesting points. The west end of the reservoir fishes best, especially near the small island. Although the trout are not monsters, they give a good account of themselves and fight well. Follow the old Portpatrick road from Stranraer and at the top of Auchtralure Hill turn right to Greenfield Farm. Standard pattern loch flies work well. A windy place to fish but a very pleasant water.

LOCHNAW CASTLE   82/993630

Permission: Lochnaw Castle Hotel, Leswalt, by Stranraer, Wigtownshire.
Tel: Leswalt (077687) 227

Lochnaw is a small loch of 46 acres within the grounds of the hotel. Guests have priority. Follow the A718/B798 road to Leswalt and then turn left. Lochnaw Castle Hotel is 2 miles further on along the B7043. The loch has been stocked with Loch Leven trout and their average weight is ¾ lb. Fishing is from the boat only and visitors may choose to fish all day or either morning/evening only. The most favoured fishing area is round the small island. This is a very lovely loch to fish and the castle stands at the edge of the loch amidst acres of rhododendron bushes and mature beech woods. Fish with standard pattern loch flies, but make sure that you have a Black Spider on the cast. Trout of up to 2½ lb. are often caught and the fish are of an excellent quality.

DUNSKEY LOCH   82/006565

Permission: The Keeper, Dunskey Kennels, Portpatrick, Wigtown-shire.
Tel: Portpatrick (077681) 486

Two small lochs in the grounds of Dunskey Estate, 2 miles from Portpatrick on the A764. Both are sheltered by trees and are stocked, one with brown trout and the other with rainbow trout and brook trout. The average weight is 1 lb. but much larger fish are in evidence. Fishing is fly only and normally from boats. The maximum basket is 2 brace per rod. Day tickets are available; special arrangements can be made for visitors staying in the Estate 'Country Holiday Homes', which are of an excellent standard and self-catering.

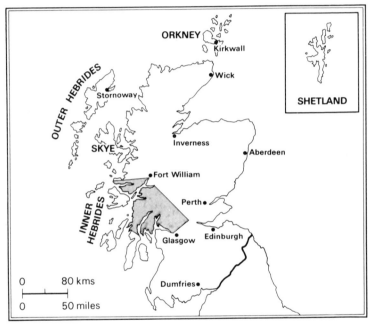

Map 42   *Argyll*

10 Argyll

Loch Awe is the fishing centre of Argyll and one of the most popular lochs in Scotland. It produces very large fish indeed and escaped rainbow trout from local fish farms seem to have firmly established themselves in the loch's vast waters. In the hills around Loch Awe are dozens of small lochs all containing good trout, and to the north lie the waters controlled by the Oban and Lorn Angling Association. During the winter, when we are comfortably installed before a warm fire, somewhere out in the hills club members will be quietly carrying on the task of stocking the waters and they, and so many others like them, deserve our highest praise and support. The Forestry Commission in Argyll also does great work in making fishing more accessible to members of the public, and one of their lochs, Loch Collie Bhar, is my favourite loch in this area. It is easy to get to and in a delightful setting, and the trout are some of the most beautiful and hard-fighting fish I have ever caught. Argyll has a lot to offer the angler, from mighty Loch Awe to well-managed fisheries such as Inverawe Fisheries and the lovely Enderline hill lochs. Take your pick, pack your bag and tight lines.

THE HOSPITAL LOCHAN   41/105597

Permission: Forest District Manager, Lorne Forest District, Mill Park Road, Oban.
Tel: Oban (0631) 66155

The Hospital Lochan lies behind the hospital in the village of Glencoe with the Pap of Glencoe to the east and sea loch Leven to the north. Approach through Glencoe village and the hospital grounds. This is a really delightful loch in a perfect woodland setting, easily accessible and a delight to fish. It is a small loch surrounded by trees and bushes with several small islands so can be sheltered when the wind rages elsewhere. Hospital Lochan is stocked and the trout average ¾ lb. with good baskets being taken, especially during the month of June. Standard loch fly patterns work well and the dry fly should also be used when it is calm. A most lovely, secluded little loch and should be visited and fished if you are in the area.

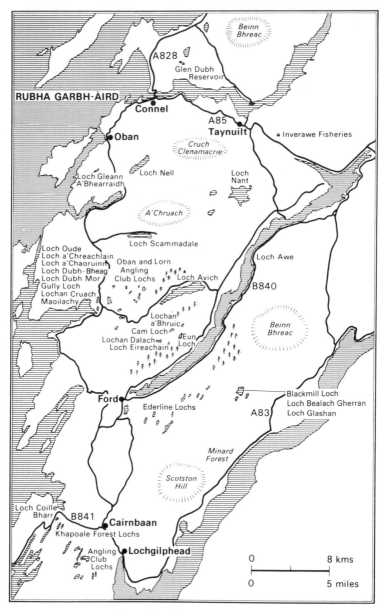

Map 43   *Oban and Loch Awe*

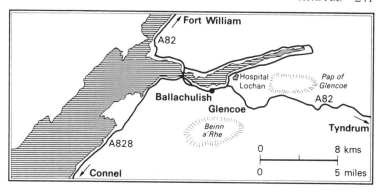

Map 44 *Ben Nevis*

GLEN DUBH RESERVOIR 49/977423

Permission: Forest District Manager, Lorne Forest District, Mill Park Road, Oban.

Tel: Oban (0631) 66155

These two small lochs lie within the Barcaldine Forest to the north of Connel. Glen Dubh Reservoir has a boat and bank fishing is allowed. Trout average ¾ lb. and best flies include all the standard patterns. The Forestry Commission plans to stock Glen Dubh and Hospital Lochan at regular intervals and selective felling of trees has made the fishing more accessible.

LOCH NELL 49/890273

Permission: David Graham, 9/15 Combie Street, Oban, Argyll.

Tel: Oban (0631) 62069

This is the largest loch in the vicinity of Oban and covers an area of 150 acres. Fishing is managed by the excellent Oban and Lorn Angling Club and one boat is available to visitors. The day is divided into two sessions, 9 am–6 pm and 6 pm–dusk. The loch drains into the sea by the River Nell and holds the occasional salmon and sea trout and also brown trout and char. The average weight of sea trout is 1 lb. and brown trout average ½–¾ lb., although fish of up to 1½ lb. are sometimes caught. The angling club stress to visitors the importance of observing the Country Code. Loch Nell is a very pleasant loch to fish and can produce some surprises – a 10¼ lb. sea trout was caught during the 1981 season on a size 12 Kingfisher Butcher. For the brown trout, standard loch fly patterns will do fine. Boats are included with permit for fishing on a first-come-first-served basis.

LOCH A'PHEARSAIN   55/855137

Permission: David Graham, 9/15 Combie Street, Oban, Argyll.
Tel: Oban (0631) 62069

Loch a'Phearsain is half a mile long by over 400 yards wide and
lies to the east of the A816 near Kilmelford. This shallow loch lies
in a natural basin, surrounded by hills to the north and east. One
boat is available and bank fishing is also allowed. The loch is
stocked by the Oban and Lorn Angling Club and trout average
¾ lb. There are larger fish as well and the 1981 season produced a
fine fish of 2 lb. plus several of over 1 lb. The best fishing areas
are in the north-east corner where the feeder burn enters and in
the vicinity of the small island in the southern bay. A'Phearsain
also contains char and during 1981 three fish were caught
weighing 4 lb. 8 oz. Use standard loch fly patterns and return all
fish under 10 inches to the water.

LOCH OUDE   55/850160

Permission: David Graham, 9/15 Combie Street, Oban, Argyll.
Tel: Oban (0631) 62069

Loch Oude is to the south of Oban, adjacent to the A816. It is
easily accessible but in a very pleasant situation with forestry

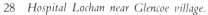

28   *Hospital Lochan near Glencoe village.*

plantation covering the crags and corries of Cnoc nan Larach-cloiche (265m) to the west. Fishing is managed by the Oban and Lorn Angling Club and the loch is stocked with rainbow trout. The present (1986) policy of the club is to cull all brown trout in order to improve the average weight on the loch. The best brown trout caught during 1986 weighed just under 1 lb. whilst the best rainbow weighed 3½ lb. There is no limit to fish caught and all fishing is from the bank only.

LOCH A'CHAORUINN	55/884137
LOCH DUBH-BHEAG	55/890140
LOCH A'CHREACHAIN	55/888143
LOCH DUBH MOR	55/892147
THE GULLY LOCH	55/890145
LOCHAN CRUACH MAOILACHY	55/895139

Permission: David Graham, 9/15 Combie Street, Oban, Argyll.
Tel: Oban (0631) 62069

This delightful series of small lochs and lochans lies to the northeast of Kilmelford and is managed by the Oban and Lorn Angling Club. The lochs are linked by small streams and are in a beautiful and peaceful corner of the Kilmelford Forest. They all contain good trout which fight well and average ½–1 lb. in weight. The first of the series, Loch a'Chaoruinn, has the largest fish and trout of over 1 lb. are often caught. As you walk up the valley, Creachain and Dubh-bheag come next and are full of bright ½ lb. fish. The Gully Loch and Dubh Mor hold fish which average ¾ lb. The club has a shelter on the east side between Gully and Creachain – it has been known to rain in these parts. Standard loch fly patterns work well and this is a lovely area in which to spend a day. Great sport and the chance of a 2 lb. trout. All bank fishing, so take care whilst wading.

LOCH A'MHINN	55/865128
LOCH NA CURRAIGH	55/865130

Permission: David Graham, 9/15 Combie Street, Oban, Argyll.
Tel: Oban (0631) 62069

Fishing is managed by the Oban and Lorn Angling Club and the lochs are stocked with both brown and rainbow trout. The present policy (1986) of the club is to cull the brown trout and there is a limit of 6 per angler on the rainbow trout. Fishing is from the bank only and the brown trout average ½ lb. The rainbow trout thrive and average 1½ lb. Best rainbow taken recently weighed 2 lb. 6 oz. Loch na Curraigh is joined to a'Mhinn by a short stream and the same rules apply to brown trout. The brown trout are slightly larger then a'Mhinn and the rainbows average 2 lb. Lovely lochs and well worth fishing. Standard loch fly patterns work well.

THE FEINN LOCHS   55/870145
Permission: David Graham, 9/15 Combie Street, Oban, Argyll.
Tel: Oban (0631) 62069

These two lochs involve a good walk into the hills and lie at an altitude of 700 feet on Cruach an Nid. The walk out is well worth while and the trout average over ¾ lb. There is a boat available on Big Feinn but like most of the lochs in the area very good sport can be had from the bank as well. The best fish from Big Feinn during the 1981 season weighed 2 lb. 6 oz. whilst Wee Feinn produced a fish of 1¼ lb. These lochs are a delight to fish and can produce really excellent sport. Standard loch fly patterns, return all fish under 10 inches and travel light. Approach from the minor road from Kilmelford on the A816 to Loch Avich.

LOCH NA SAILM   55/877146
LOCH A'CHEIGEIN   55/876140
LOCH IASG   55/874150
Permission: David Graham, 9/15 Combie Street, Oban, Argyll.
Tel: Oban (0631) 62069

These three lochs lie to the east of the Feinn Lochs and are approached from the same direction. Fishing is managed by the Oban and Lorn Angling Club and there is a boat available on Sailm whilst the other lochs are fished from the bank. The average weight is ½ lb. although a number of 1 lb. fish are caught each season. Use standard loch fly patterns and expect good baskets and good sport.

LOCH AN LOSGAINN   55/865120
Permission: David Graham, 9/15 Combie Street, Oban, Argyll.
Tel: Oban (0631) 62069

The minor road from Kilmelford to Loch Avich is adjacent to the north shore of the loch making it an easily accessible water. There is a parking place at the west end and fishing is from the bank only. The loch is stocked and managed by the Oban and Lorn Angling Club and holds both brown and rainbow trout. The 1980 season produced a 2 lb. 10 oz. rainbow and a 1½ lb. brown trout and during 1985 rainbow trout of up to 5 lb. have been caught. Best flies include Black Pennell, Grouse and Claret, and Greenwell's.

LOCH AN DAIMH 55/860111

Permission: David Graham, 9/15 Combie Street, Oban, Argyll. *Tel:* Oban (0631) 62069

This small loch lies to the south of the Kilmelford–Loch Avich road and is managed by the Oban and Lorn Angling Club. The present policy (1981) of the club is to cull all trout in order to improve the average overall weight. A ¾ lb. trout would be very large for this water but its remote setting makes it a lovely loch to fish.

LOCH AN LOSGAINN BHEAG 55/860127

Permission: David Graham, 9/15 Combie Street, Oban, Argyll. *Tel:* Oban (0631) 62069

This small loch lies close to the Kilmelford–Loch Avich road and is managed by the Oban and Lorn Angling Club which stocks it with brown and rainbow trout. Fishing is from the bank only and there is a bag limit of 6 rainbow trout per angler. The best brown trout caught during the 1980 season weighed 1¼ lb. and the heaviest rainbow trout 2 lb. 11 oz. They don't give themselves up exactly, but a good loch to visit. Again, use standard loch fly patterns.

LOCH GLEANN A'BHEARRAIDH 49/846270

Permission: The Barn Bar, Cologin, Lerags, Oban, Argyll. *Tel:* Oban (0631) 4501

This is a long, narrow loch three-quarters of a mile long by 150 yards wide. It lies to the south of Oban and visitors should turn right at the signpost at Lerags 2 miles out of town on the A816. There is a good track out to the loch which starts about a mile down this road. Boats are available and bank fishing is also allowed. The loch is stocked and contains good trout with an average weight of ¾–1 lb. There are fish of over 2 lb. as well and standard loch fly patterns should be used.

SIOR LOCHS 49/965230
LOCHAN AIRIGH SHAMHRAIDH 49/954208
LOCH A'BHARRAIN 49/966241
Permission: David Graham, 9/15 Crombie Street, Oban, Argyll.
Tel: Oban (0631) 2069

These remote lochs lie 5 miles out into the hills to the east of the A816 and for the angler who likes walking and wildlife with his fishing, this is the place to head for. Approach from Kilmore, south of Oban. The trout average three to the pound and large baskets are caught. Fishing is managed by the Oban and Lorn Angling Club and standard pattern loch flies will bring results. Choose a good day.

LOCH SCAMMADALE 49/890205
Permission: Mary McCorkindale, Glenann, Kilninver, by Oban, Argyll.
Tel: Kilninver (08526) 282

Loch Scammadale lies 9 miles south of Oban and is approached from the A816 by following up the River Euchar in Glenann. The loch is 1½ miles long by one third of a mile wide and contains salmon, sea trout and brown trout. The loch is over 120 feet deep towards the eastern end and is in a remote and lovely setting. Both boat and bank fishing are available and the most productive fishing area is along the north bank, particularly where the Eas Ruadh burn enters the loch. The loch is stocked and the average weight of trout is 1 lb. Baskets vary depending upon conditions but a good one should produce 3–4 fish. Larger fish are taken and the sea trout average over 2 lb. Standard loch fly patterns work well.

LOCH AWE Sheets 50–55
Permission:
Chief Forester, Forest Office, Dalavich, by Taynuilt, Argyll.
Tel: Lochavich (08664) 258;
Portsonachan Hotel, by Dalmally, Argyll.
Tel: Kilchrenan (08663) 224;
Carraig Thura Hotel, Loch Awe village, by Dalmally, Argyll.
Tel: Dalmally (08382) 210;
Ardanaiseig Hotel, Kilchrenan, by Taynuilt, Argyll.
Tel: Kilchrenan (08663) 333

Loch Awe is the longest loch in Scotland and would require a book on its own to do it full justice. The loch is nearly 26 miles long by ½–¾ mile wide and very popular with anglers and country lovers who make full use of its vast area. Sailing is enthusiastically pursued and during the summer months visitors crowd the banks. Nevertheless, in spite of all the activity, it is generally possible to find a quiet corner somewhere and Loch Awe is a very beautiful place to spend some time. The loch contains salmon, sea trout, brown trout, rainbow trout, char, pike and no doubt one or two other 'things' hidden within its 300 foot depths. Loch Awe fishes best from the boat and trout are caught all over the loch, mostly in the shallows and near to the side. Concentrate round the islands in the south end and all the bays and points. The north-east bay, where Teatle Water enters, is also a good area at the other end of the loch. The brown trout on Loch Awe average ½–¾ lb. and an average basket should contain 8–10 fish. Having said this, it must be added that Loch Awe is noted for its much larger ferrox which may be tempted by trolling. The (unofficial) all-time record brown trout came from Loch Awe and was caught in 1866 and weighed 39 lb. 8 oz. More recently trout of great proportions have been caught: 1973, 15 lb. 3 oz.; 1975, 13 lb. 1980, 19 lb. 8 oz., and rainbow trout of over 10 lb. have also been landed. Treat every offer with great respect – you never know, it might be that 'trout of a lifetime'. Early on in the season is the best time to fish Loch Awe, and there are few more delightful settings. Visitors to Loch Awe are respectfully reminded that there is no public right of free fishing in the loch. You must seek permission before fishing and must also comply with the law relating to fishing methods. Obtain a copy of the excellent Loch Awe Improvement Association Guidelines for Visiting Anglers from Jonathan Brown, Secretary, LAIA, Hayfield, Kilchrenan, Argyll, PA35 1HE.

INVERAWE FISHERIES 50/024316
Permission: Inverawe Fisheries, Inverawe Barn, Taynuilt, Argyll. *Tel:* Taynuilt (08662) 262

There are three trout lochs here managed as a commercial fishery and stocked with rainbow trout. The average weight is 1½ lb. and fishing is from the bank only. An average day should produce up to 5 trout and this fishery has a reputation for producing much larger trout. The 1981 season saw a trout of 12 lb. landed. Best flies to use here are Dunkeld, Black Pennell and reservoir lures. Easily accessible and set in pleasant surroundings, Inverawe offers good sport and good quality trout. The best trout landed during 1985 weighed 12 lb. Open from April until October.

LOCH NANT   50/008240

Permission: Kilchrenan Trading Post, Kilchrenan, by Taynuilt, Argyll.

Tel: Kilchrenan (08663) 232

Loch Nant covers an area of 1½ miles by one mile and may be approached from north of Kilchrenan. There is a locked gate by the roadside and a good track leads from here to the loch, which is due west. Trout average ¾ lb. and an average day should produce a basket of 3–4 fish. The shoreline of Loch Nant wanders round dozens of bays and points and the largest of these is in the north-east corner. This is the best fishing area and also where the burn from Loch Stor comes in. Standard pattern loch flies are fine. Access to the loch is by 'hoof' only; cars are not allowed, so be prepared for a bit of a hike.

CAM LOCH   55/905095
EUN LOCH   55/917091
LOCHAN DALACH   55/916103
LOCHAN A'BHRUIC   55/920105
LOCH EIREACHAIN   55/927095

Permission: David Murray, Ford Hotel, Ford, Argyll.

Tel: Ford (054681) 273

These small forest lochs all lie to the north of Loch Awe and fishing is from the bank only. They are not fished very much because there is a fair walk involved, but do not let that put you off. They are delightful lochs full of small hard-fighting brown trout and give great sport in lovely surroundings. When the wind is raging down Loch Awe, in the depth of the forest relative peace and quiet reigns. Loch Cam, the largest, holds the best fish and they average ½–¾ lb. However, trout of up to 4 lb. have been caught here, so be prepared. Best flies on Loch Cam include Peter Ross, Soldier Palmer and Butchers and the most productive fishing area is in the western end of the loch and the bay opposite the old boathouse. Expect a basket of 8–10 fish.

LOCH AVICH   55/935145

Permission: Loch Awe Forest District, Whitegates, Lochgilphead.

Tel: Lochgilphead (0546) 2518.

Boats may be hired from Mr S. Davren at Lochavich.

Tel: Lochavich (08664) 216

Loch Avich lies to the west of Loch Awe, into which it drains. At the eastern end, near the island, the loch drops to nearly 200 feet deep and the trout rise and are caught all round the shoreline. Fishing on Avich is managed by the Forestry Commission and both boat and bank fishing are allowed. Two boats are available and anglers may also hire an outboard motor – a great help since Avich is 3½ miles long by half a mile wide, and windy. Trout average ½–¾ lb. and excellent baskets are taken from boat and bank. An average basket should produce up to 10 fish and baskets of 20 or more are not unusual. Smaller flies do best on Avich and all the standard pattern loch flies will produce good results. A delightful loch in a delightful setting.

THE EDERLINE LOCHS 55/870025

Permission: The Ederline Estate, Estate Office, Ford, Argyll.
Tel: Ford (054681) 284

The Ederline Lochs are managed by the Ederline Estate and lie to the south of Ford village. There are over 30 lochs on the estate, some stocked and all containing good trout. The nearest of the hill lochs involves a walk of 3 miles but excellent baskets are taken of ½–¾ lb. wild brown trout. Catches of 20–30 fish are unremarkable and from time to time a fish of 2–3 lb. is landed. But the real beauty of fishing these lochs lies in the lovely surroundings and remote setting. This is a wild area, where the angler can lose himself and most of his worries for a short time. Some of the lochs have boats but most are fished from the bank and all the usual flies produce results. It you want a little peace and quiet – and a good walk – contact Ford 284.

LOCH COILLE BHARR 55/785905

Permission: Chief Forester, Knapdale Forest, Cairnbaan, Barnluasgan, Lochgilphead, Argyll.
Tel: Lochgilphead (0546) 2304

Coille Bharr lies 7 miles to the west of Lochgilphead via the B841/B8025 road to Tayvallich. The loch is just under 1¼ miles long by 200 yards wide and there are 2 boats available for visitors. Bank fishing is not allowed. Standard loch fly patterns work well and the loch fishes best in a good south-west wind. Although fish are caught over most of the loch the small bay, just before the south end, is a favoured area. Drift down, about 15 yards out, and as you pass the headland dividing the small bay from the end of the loch, look out for fireworks. The trout on this loch are some of the hardest fighting fish I have ever come across and are beautifully shaped and average about 1¼ lb. Excellent fishing and highly recommended.

LOCH BARNLUASGAN 55/793913
Permission: Chief Forester, Knapdale Forest, Cairnbaan, Barnluasgan, Lochgilphead, Argyll.
Tel: Lochgilphead (0546) 2304
This loch is adjacent to the B841 road to the west of Lochgilphead. Fishing is from the boat only and outboard motors are not allowed. Trout average ¾–1 lb. and fight well. An average basket should account for up to 6 fish and all the standard loch fly patterns do well. This is a small, pleasant loch, easily accessible and ideal for a few casts if Collie Bharr is busy.

LOCH LINNHE 55/798910
Permission: Chief Forester, Knapdale Forest, Cairnbaan, Barnluasgan, Lochgilphead, Argyll.
Tel: Lochgilphead (0546) 2304
Loch Linnhe is a short walk from the main road and is 800 yards long by 300 yards wide. Boat fishing only and no outboards, but plenty of sport on this lovely loch with trout averaging ¾ lb. The best drift is down the west shore, but you will catch fish all over to standard loch fly patterns. A very pleasant, secluded little loch well worth a visit.

LOCH LOSGUNN 55/791898
LOCH BUIE (Seafield) 55/789890
Permission: Chief Forester, Knapdale Forest, Cairnbaan, Barnluasgan, Lochgilphead, Argyll.
Tel: Lochgilphead (0546) 2304
Set in the midst of the Knapdale Forest, these two small lochs can be fished on the one permit. Fishing is from the bank only and standard loch fly patterns do fine. The trout average ½–¾ lb. and good baskets are taken. However, the best part about these lochs is their lovely setting and they are well worth seeking out.

CAM LOCH 55/824877
LOCH CLACHAIG 55/813870
GLEANN LOCH 55/815880
THE DUBH LOCH 55/810878
LOCH NA FAOILINN 55/815887
LOCH AN ADD 55/805888
LOCH NA BRIC 55/804892
Permission: H. MacArthur, The Tackle Shop, Lochnell Street, Lochgilphead, Argyll.

All these lochs are managed by the Lochgilphead and District Angling Club which restricts access. Fishing is strictly private but a certain number of day tickets may be available for visitors. The lochs named are a fair walk from the road and are approached via the B841 a mile or so west of Cairnbaan. Loch an Add and Loch na Bric are in the Knapdale Forest whilst Loch na Faolinn, the Dubh Loch and narrow Gleann have the forest as their western boundary. All the lochs contain brown trout but the club restricts visitors to bank fishing only, the boats being reserved for members. If you do obtain permission, I should use standard loch fly patterns. If not head for Coille Bharr.

BLACKMILL LOCH   55/950958
Permission:
Loch Awe Forest District, Whitegates, Lochgilphead, Argyll.
Tel: Lochgilphead (0546) 2518;
At weekends, contact Mr R. Hardie, No. 1 Nursery Cottages.
Tel: Minard (05466) 86630

Blackmill Loch offers brown trout fishing from the south bank and a boat is also available for hire. The loch is surrounded by forest and therefore sheltered from high winds.

LOCH BEALACH GHERRAN   55/949949
Permission: As for Blackmill Loch above

Another small forest loch in the heart of the Minard Forest. Brown trout fishing, fly only, and a boat is also available.

LOCH GLASHAN   55/915930
Permission: As for Blackmill Loch and Loch Bealach Gherran above

Glashan is surrounded by forest and a perfect place to escape from it all. A boat is available and best results come fishing from the boat rather than from the bank. Fish may be caught all over the loch. However, one of the most productive areas is along the west shore and towards the point before the large north-west bay. Trout average 10 oz. with the odd fish of up to 1½ lb. Use standard pattern flies.

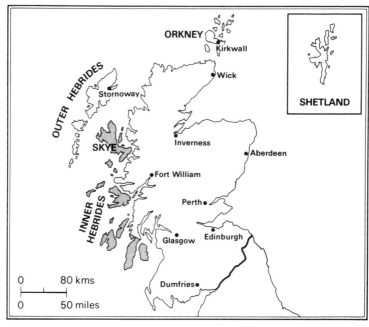

Map 45   *Inner Hebrides*

11 Inner Hebrides

Skye is a popular and romantic island much visited and easily accessible. For the trout fisherman, the best lochs are in the north of the island to the north of Portree. A few days fishing here will be most rewarding and all the lochs are in magnificent settings. Mull and Islay offer really first-class sport and the smaller islands are self-contained, remote and delightful. Arran has very few decent trout lochs. Visit this lovely island for its sea trout and marvellous scenery rather than for trout fishing. On Bute, if you havn't already discovered it, you are in for a pleasant surprise when you fish Loch Fad, whilst over to the west of Kintyre the tiny island of Gigha can offer excellent trout fishing and a perfect and peaceful holiday. The islands of the Inner Hebrides will give you great pleasure and exciting trout fishing. There are also many interesting and delightful local malt whiskies to sample – great for dulling the pain of a lost fish and brightening the perception of days to come.

ISLE OF SKYE
LOCH CONNAN   23/388430
Permission: Ullinish Lodge Hotel, Struan, Isle of Skye.
Tel: Struan (047472) 214

North of the B885 Struan–Portree road, Connan is a circular loch about 500 yards across. The hotel has a boat available and guests have priority. Trout average ¾ lb. and catches vary from a few fish to baskets of 20 trout weighing 20 lb. It depends upon your skill and the weather. Take standard loch fly patterns and try, it's an excellent loch. During 1984/85 a good number of trout weighing over 2 lb. were taken.

LOCH DUAGRICH   23/400400
Permission: Ullinish Lodge Hotel, Struan, Isle of Skye.
Tel: Struan (047472) 214

All fishing has been from the bank, but it was proposed to put a boat on the loch during 1982 season. The loch is three-quarters of a mile long by 400 yards wide and the loch is approached via a good track up Glen Bracadale in a distance of 2 miles. Trout average ½ lb. and catches of 20–30 fish are frequent. Standard

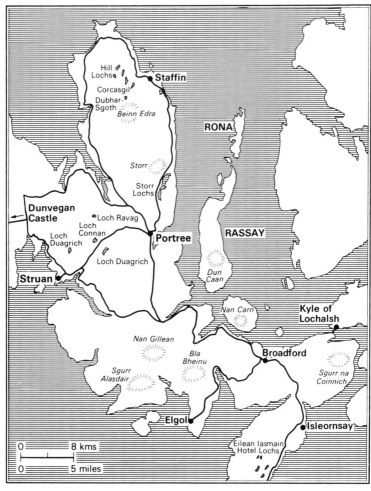

Map 46   *Skye*

pattern flies work well and this water is set amongst magnificent scenery. A lovely loch to fish.

LOCH RAVAG   23/380450
Permission: Ullinish Lodge Hotel, Struan, Isle of Skye.
Tel: Struan (047072) 214

Ravag lies to the north of Loch Connan and may be approached via the minor road which runs eastwards from the A863 near Caroy (309429) or from the B885. Weed has always been a problem on Ravag but Ullinish Lodge has put in hand an improvement scheme to improve access. The fish are already there for the loch holds a good stock of wild brown trout.

LOCH CORCASGIL 23/452643
LOCH DUBHAR-SGOTH 23/456640

Permission: The Gamekeepers Cottage, Staffin, Isle of Skye.

Loch Corcasgil lies to the south of craggy Quiraing (543m) and is a walk of 2 miles from the Portree-Staffin road. The loch is at the foot of Beinn Edra (611m), 400 yards long by 100 yards wide. The trout average ¾–1 lb. and there are also *ferox*. Fishing is from the bank and the water is deep near the edge so it is easy to cover the fish. Trout tend to move closer in during the evening and on a good day baskets of 10 fish can be taken. Loch Dubhar-sgoth is to the south and the trout are smaller but fight just as well, and you can expect a basket of 4–6 fish averaging ½–¾ lb. These lochs are not fished very often due to the long walk involved. Don't be put off, it's worth it and the scenery is superb.

LOCH LEATHAN 23/505515
STORR LOCH 23/500505
LOCH FADA 23/493495

Permission: Portree Angling Association, Masonic Buildings, Portree, Isle of Skye.

29   *The Storr Lochs, Skye.*

These three interlinked lochs are known as the Storr Lochs and lie to the north of Portree, east of the A855 road. They are 2½ miles long by up to half a mile wide across Loch Leathan. The Storr (719m) and the Old Man dominate the western horizon and this is one of the most scenic lochs in the north. Both boat and bank fishing are allowed and the average weight is just under 1 lb. Sample baskets from 1981 included 4 fish weighing 3 lb. and several 2 lb. fish are taken each season, and some of 3 lb. were also landed. The best fish for 1981 was a trout of 3 lb. 9 oz. and the record for the loch is 12 lb. Baskets of 10–15 fish are not uncommon – it depends upon the weather and the lochs fish well throughout the entire length. Particularly good is the area round the island in Loch Leathan, the bays on the eastern shore of Storr below Arimishader, and round the island on Loch Fada. Over 800 trout are taken most seasons and the Storr Lochs are top quality trout fishing is perfect surroundings. Highly recommended. Best flies include Black Pennell, Woodcock and Yellow, Grouse and Claret, Teal and Green, Butchers and Zulus.

THE HILL LOCHS OF NORTH SKYE   23/460690
Permission: Portree Angling Association, Masonic Buildings, Portree, Isle of Skye.

There are 14 lochs here, controlled and administered by the Portree Angling Association. Fishing is from the bank only and most of the lochs are within easy reach of the road. About 300 trout are taken each season and Loch Mealt, adjacent to the road at Elishader, holds char which average ½–¾ lb. Baskets of 10–12 fish can be expected but watch out for the bigger ones, fish of 1½–2 lb. have been taken recently. Dark patterns of fly work best. A very beautiful area to fish and worth a visit.

LOCH AN IASGAICH   32/673142
Permission: Fearann Eilean Iasmain Hotel, An t-Eilean, Sgitheanach, Skye.
Tel: Isle of Ornsay (04713) 266

This is a small loch in the south of Skye, near to Drumfearn. Leave the Broadford–Isle Ornsay road by the telephone kiosk. The loch is a short walk into the hills and contains trout which average ½ lb. Bank fishing only and you can expect excellent baskets of hard-fighting little trout. Lovely views of the Cuillin Hills to the north-east.

LOCHAIN DUBH 32/676207

Permission: Fearann Eilean Iasmain, Hotel, An t-Eilean, Sgitheanach, Skye.
Tel: Isle of Ornsay (04713) 266

There are 3 small interlinked lochs here to the west of the A581, past the junction to Skulamus. They contain trout which average ½ lb. and the occasional sea trout. Good baskets of small fish and marvellous scenery. Easily accessible from the road. Use small dark flies and spend an hour or so enjoying yourself.

LOCH BARAVAIG 32/685098

Permission: Fearann Eilean Iasmain Hotel, An t-Eilean, Sgitheanach Skye.
Tel: Isle of Ornsay (04713) 266

Approach from the A851 by the small roadside loch south of the

Map 47 *Mull*

village. You must ask permission before crossing the farm land to
the loch and the walk is an easy 20 minutes. This is the best of the
south Skye lochs with good natural feeding for the trout. The
trout average ½–¾ lb. and fight hard. Fishing is from the bank
and there were plans to stock the loch in the 1982 season. A really
delightful place to fish.

ISLE OF MULL
LOCH POIT NA H-I   48/315230
Permission:
Callum Campbell, Fidden Farm, Fionnphort, Mull.
Tel: Fionnphort (06817) 213;
Peter Bonnetti, Achaban House, Fionnphort, Mull.

This is a small triangular-shaped loch near Fionnphort and the
ferry to Iona. It is a shallow loch and contains brown trout and
occasional sea trout. The average weight of trout is ½ lb. and
baskets of 8–10 fish are taken frequently. The best trout caught
during 1981 weighed 1½ lb. and both boat and bank fishing are
available. The best fishing area is in the vicinity of the small island
and where the water leaves the loch on its short run to the sea at
An Caolas. Standard loch fly patterns work well.

LOCH ASSAPOL   48/405205
Permission:
A. Campbell, Argyll Arms, Bunessan, Mull;
James McKeand, Scoor House, Bunessan, Mull.
Tel: Fionnphort (06817) 297;
D. Cameron, Assapol, Bunessan, Mull.
Tel: Fionnphort (06817) 258

Assapol is 1½ miles south-east of Bunessan and is the largest loch
on the Ross of Mull. Beautiful, remote and peaceful, Assapol is
about three-quarters of a mile long by 500 yards wide and contains brown trout, sea trout and grilse. Both boat and bank fishing
are available and is free to Scoor House guests until mid July.
Trout average ½ lb., sea trout 2 lb. and grilse 5 lb. Sample
catches from the 1981 season will probably send you rushing to
the telephone to book, but do remember a lot depends upon the
weather and conditions vary year to year. First weekend in May,
2 rods, 17 sea trout averaging 2 lb. with best fish at 4½ lb. Two

weeks in August, 3 rods, 78 sea trout averaging 1 lb. with a best fish of 3½ lb. and 40 brown trout. The best brown trout caught during the past two years weighed 7½ lb., best sea trout, 4½ lb. and the heaviest grilse, 10 lb. Brown trout fishing is best in May and June and then again towards the back end when most of the larger fish are caught. There can be a good run of sea trout at Easter, but the best month is July. This is an exciting loch in perfect surroundings and highly recommended. Best flies include Peter Ross, Invicta and Greenwell's Glory. Mr McKeand will show you the best places round the loch to use them. Get there if you can, it's worth it. The best sea trout taken in 1985 weighed 4 lb. 12 oz. and a salmon of 6 lb. 8 oz. was also landed. The early sea-trout runs of 1986 produced more than 50 fish.

LOCH ARM   48/419217

Permission: James McKeand, Scoor House, Bunessan, Mull.
Tel: Fionnphort (06817) 297

This is a small hill loch to the east of Bunessan and is approached from the A849 by following up the Bun an Leiob. The walk takes about 40 minutes – depending upon how often you stop to marvel at the panoramic view and beauty of the surroundings. The average size of trout is ½ lb. and baskets of 8–10 fish may be expected. The best fish caught during 1981 weighed 2 lb. 2 oz. and fought like a 5 lb. fish. Bank fishing only. Use size 14–16 flies, Mallard and Claret, Invicta and Black Pennell are good ones to start off with. Splendid fishing in splendid setting.

LOCH AN TORR   47/450530

Permission: W. R. Fairbairns, Cuin Lodge, Dervaig, Mull.
Tel: Dervaig (06884) 275

Loch an Torr is on the north side of the B8073 Tobermory–Dervaig road and easily accessible. The loch is in a pleasant setting with a forest to the west and mountains to the south. Both boat and bank fishing are allowed but outboard motors are prohibited. Loch an Torr contains brown trout, some rainbow trout and the occasional sea trout. 1981 was a good season for the loch with trout of up to 3½ lb. and sea trout of 5 lb. being caught. The whole area of the loch fishes well and standard patterns of loch flies will suffice.

THE MISHNISH LOCHS
LOCH CARNAIN AN AMIS
LOCH MEADHOIN
LOCH PEALLACH 47/480526

Permission:
Tobermory Angling Association, c/o A. Brown & Sons, 21 Main Street, Tobermory, Mull.
Tel: Tobermory (0688) 2020;
W. R. Fairbairns, Cuin Lodge, Dervaig, Mull.
Tel: Dervaig (06884) 275;

The Mishnish Lochs are a series of 3 interconnected lochs adjacent to the B8073 Tobermory–Dervaig road. They are easily accessible and their differing characteristics make for interesting fishing. Boat and bank fishing are available and the lochs cover an area nearly 2 miles long by 300 yards wide to 50 yards wide. Peallach holds the largest fish but tends to be weedy and a good fish is hard to control. This varies in depth between 2 and 10 feet and trout of up to 2 lb. are taken. The best drifts on Loch Meadhoin are round the margins, but they can also be a bit weedy. Loch Amis is the deepest of the three and can produce excellent baskets of ½–¾ lb. trout. The hardworking Tobermory Angling Association stocks these lochs every two years with up to 5,000 5 inch trout and growth rate is good, there being an abundant supply of shrimps, snails and caddis for the trout to feed upon. The best basket during the 1981 season consisted of 15 fish weighing 12½ lb. and another catch had 3 fish weighing 5 lb. 1980 produced a 3½ lb. fish and 1981 a trout of 2¾ lb. Best flies are Soldier Palmer, Butchers, Teal and Green, Peter Ross, Dunkeld, Wickham's Fancy, Ke-He, Black Pennell and Zulus. Well worth your time and recommended. Best basket taken during 1986 (June) was a catch of 30 fish weighing 38 lb. and the heaviest trout caught up until June 1986 weighed 3 lb. 8 oz.

LOCH FRISA 47/480490
Permission: W. R. Fairbairns, Cuin Lodge, Dervaig, Mull.
Tel: Dervaig (06884) 275

This is the largest freshwater loch on Mull and is nearly 5 miles long by half a mile wide. Frisa is a deep loch which drops to 200 feet near the middle. High winds can make this a dangerous water and do listen to local advice if you are warned to stay off the loch. Nevertheless, Frisa is a very beautiful loch and is full of hard-fighting ½–¾ lb. trout which are of a Loch Leven strain, pink-fleshed and well-shaped. There are the occasional sea trout and salmon to be caught as well, depending upon water levels in the outlet burn. Boats are available from the Forestry Commission at Salen and Glenbellart House Hotel also has a boat on the loch. During the 1981 season guests from the hotel had 33 trout in one outing with the fish averaging between ½–1 lb. Catches of 10–15 fish are frequent and another Glenbellart Hotel basket during 1981 produced 40 trout. Best flies are Dunkeld, Black Zulu, Peter Ross, Soldier Palmer, Mallard and Claret, Connemara Black and, of course, the Black Pennell. Fish near to the edge. Remember the warning about the weather. Have a good day.

LOCHAN NA GUALINE DUIBHE   47/527524
Permission: Tobermory Angling Association, c/o A. Brown & Sons, 21 Main Street, Tobermory, Mull.
Tel: Tobermory (0688) 2020

This loch lies 3 miles to the south of Tobermory and is easily accessible from the main road. Bank fishing only, in a pleasant woodland setting. The loch was stocked by the association in 1978 and the average weight of trout is ½ lb. Can be dour and average baskets amount to 2–3 fish. Fishes best during the early months of the season. Standard loch pattern flies.

AROS LAKE   47/520538
Permission: Tobermory Angling Association, c/o A. Brown & Sons, 21 Main Street, Tobermory, Mull.
Tel: Tobermory (0688) 2020

One mile south of Tobermory, Aros contains both brown and rainbow trout. Fishing is from the bank only and since the loch is surrounded by trees access is limited to clearings from which to cast. There are rearing cages in the loch and some trout escape. The largest rainbow caught weighed 9½ lb. and several trout of 3–5 lb. are taken. An average day should produce 5 fish weighing 3 lb. Reservoir type lures seem to be necessary.

ISLE OF ISLAY
LOCH GORM   60/230660
Permission: Brian Wiles, Islay House, Bridgend, Islay, Argyll.
Tel: Bowmore (049681) 293

Loch Gorm is the largest loch on Islay and both boat and bank fishing are available. Bank fishing is good and should it be too

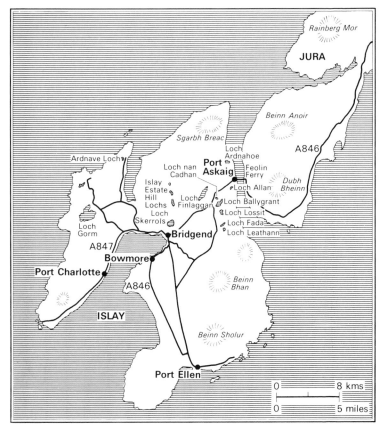

Map 48   *Islay*

windy to use the boat concentrate on the dozens of little bays round the loch. Eilean nan Uan in the western bay is a particularly good bank fishing area and in the vicinity of the feeder burns in the north-east bay can also be very good. The trout average 1 lb. and fight hard, and the best basket taken during the 1981 season accounted for 39 fish including a trout of 2 lb. When using the boat be cautious, since there are hidden shallows and underwater boulders. Take a few spare sheer pins for the outboard just in case. An excellent loch and standard pattern loch flies will bring results.

ARDNAVE LOCH 60/285728

Permission: Brian Wiles, Islay House, Bridgend, Islay, Argyll.
Tel: Bowmore (049681) 293

Ardnave is approached from the B8017 from Bridgend and is a
small loch where boat and bank fishing are allowed. The trout
average 1 lb. but do not give themselves up easily and you will
have to work hard for your fish. An average basket would be 2–3
fish and the best fish recently weighed 3 lb. 2 oz. Great fighters
and rise well to standard loch fly patterns. A lovely loch to fish
and a challenge.

LOCH SKERROLS 60/340638

Permission: Brian Wiles, Islay House, Bridgend, Islay, Argyll.
Tel: Bowmore (049681) 293

Loch Skerrols is in a woodland setting to the north of Bridgend.
Boats are available and bank fishing is not allowed. This loch
provides excellent sport and it is as well to book in advance. The
trout average ½ lb. and baskets of up to 20 fish are often taken.
An average day is likely to account for 8–10 fish and the heaviest
during 1981 was a trout of 1½ lb. Best fishing area is at the north
end of the loch and favourite flies include Black Pennell, Coch-y-
Bonddu and Soldier Palmer. Good fishing in attractive
surroundings.

LOCH FINLAGGAN 60/385674

Permission: Brian Wiles, Islay House, Bridgend, Islay, Argyll.
Tel: Bowmore (049681) 293

Finlaggan is a long, narrow loch between Port Askaig and
Bridgend and is approached via the road to Finlaggan Farm, at the
north end of the loch. There are 2 boats available and bank fishing
is also allowed. A lovely loch complete with island and ruined
castle, and superb scenery. The south end fishes best and the trout
average ½ lb. with baskets of 12 fish being taken frequently. Fish
of up to 1 lb. can be caught and standard loch fly patterns will do.

LOCH BALLYGRANT 60/405662

Permission: Mrs K. McPhee, The Port Askaig Shop, Port Askaig,
Islay, Argyll.
Tel: Port Askaig (049684) 663

This loch lies close to the Port Askaig–Bridgend road and is in a
woodland setting. The main part of the loch is circular and about

500 yards across. A narrow bay extends to the north-east and this can give good sport. Two boats are available and results are better from the boat than from the bank. A favourite area to fish is in the vicinity of the island in the north-west corner and trout average ½–¾ lb. with the occasional 1 lb. fish – to catch you unawares. Baskets of 15–20 trout are taken, particularly in May and June which are the best months. Use Black Pennell, Grouse and Claret, and Zulus.

LOCH LOSSIT   60/407652
Permission: Mrs K. McPhee, The Port Askaig Shop, Port Askaig, Islay, Argyll.
Tel: Port Askaig (049684) 663

Both boat and bank fishing are available on this small loch and good results come from either method. May and June are the best months and the trout average ½–¾ lb. The best areas to fish are round the three small islands and down the eastern shore. Standard loch fly patterns work well.

LOCH NAN CADHAN   60/403668
Permission: Mrs K. McPhee, The Port Askaig Shop, Port Askaig, Islay, Argyll.
Tel: Port Askaig (049684) 663

This small loch lies to the north of Loch Ballygrant and the trout average ½–¾ lb. It is easily accessible, adjacent to the Port Askaig–Bridgend road. The finger-like bays at the south end of the loch are the best fishing areas and standard loch fly patterns will do. Good baskets are often taken and you may expect up to 10 fish for your day out.

LOCH FADA   60/410638
Permission: Mrs K. McPhee, The Port Askaig Shop, Port Askaig, Islay, Argyll.
Tel: Port Askaig (049684) 663

The name Fada means 'long' and this loch lies to the south of Ballygrant and the A846 Port Askaig—Bridgend road. It involves a 15 minute walk over the moor and is half a mile long by 100 yards wide. Weed can be a problem but baskets of 8–10 trout averaging ½–¾ lb. are considered average. Fish are caught all round the loch and the best cast to start with should include Black Pennell, Grouse and Claret, and Silver Butcher.

LOCH LEATHANN   60/410634
Permission: Mrs K. McPhee, The Port Askaig Shop, Port Askaig, Islay, Argyll.
Tel: Port Askaig (049684) 663

Loch Leathann, 'the broad loch' involves a longish walk over the moor but is well worth a visit. Approach from the same point as for Fada. The trout average ¾–1 lb. and fish of up to 3 lb. have also been taken on Leathann. There is a boat available and bank fishing is also allowed although thigh waders would be useful here. This loch has a reputation for being dour but the fish are of excellent quality. The best area is the bay in the north-east corner and standard loch fly patterns will produce results – perhaps.

LOCH ALLAN   60/425678
Permission: Mrs K. McPhee, The Port Askaig Shop, Port Askaig, Islay, Argyll.
Tel: Port Askaig (049684) 663

This loch is to the south of Port Askaig and one boat is available for anglers. Bank fishing is not very productive. Trout average ½–¾ lb. and standard loch fly patterns work well. Baskets of up to 8 fish may be expected and the best area to fish is where the feeder burns enter the loch in the south-west and north-west corners. Easily accessible and an attractive water to fish.

LOCH ARDNAHOE   60/420715
Permission: Brian Wiles, Islay House, Bridgend, Islay, Argyll.
Tel: Bowmore (049681) 293

This is a deep loch to the north of Port Askaig and is 550 yards by 350 yards in extent. Fishing is best in the shallow water close to the shore and both boat and bank fishing will produce good results. The fish average ½–¾ lb. in weight and 6 fish is normal for a day. There are some heavier trout and fish of 1 lb. are sometimes caught. Black Pennell, Cinnamon and Gold, Blae and Black are good flies to try. Magnificent views over to Jura and a lovely loch to fish.

THE ISLAY ESTATE HILL LOCHS   Sheet 60
Permission: Brian Wiles, Islay House, Bridgend, Islay, Argyll.
Tel: Bowmore (049681) 293

The Islay Estate has good fishing on a number of hill lochs

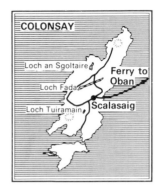

COLONSAY

Loch an Sgoltaire
Loch Fada
Loch Tuiramain

Ferry to
Oban
Scalasaig

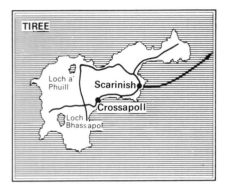

TIREE

Loch a'
Phuill
Loch
Bhassapol

Scarinish
Crossapoll

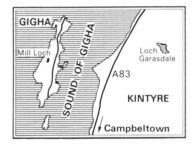

GIGHA

Mill Loch

SOUND OF GIGHA

Loch
Garasdale

A83

KINTYRE

Campbeltown

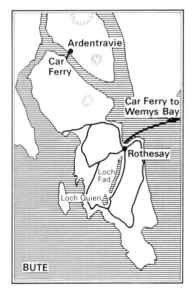

Ardentravie
Car
Ferry

Car Ferry to
Wemys Bay

Rothesay

Loch
Fad

Loch Quien

BUTE

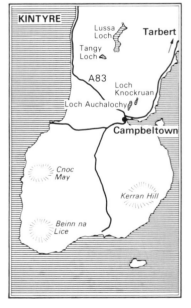

KINTYRE

Lussa
Loch

Tarbert

Tangy
Loch

A83

Loch
Knockruan

Loch Auchalochy

Campbeltown

Cnoc
May

Kerran Hill

Beinn na
Lice

0   8 kms

0   5 miles

Map 49 *Kintyre and Islands*

throughout the estate. Most involve a good tramp, but the visitor
will be more than rewarded by the superb scenery and gentle
peace of the surroundings. The islands abound with birdlife and
wild flowers and the walk over the moors is a delight in itself.
You will return refreshed and probably with a nice basket
of ½ lb. trout for your trouble. What angler could ask for
more?

ISLE OF COLONSAY
LOCH FADA	61/385957
LOCH AN SGOLTAIRE	61/387975
LOCH TUIRAMAIN	61/392953

Permission: Isle of Colonsay Hotel, Colonsay, Argyll.
Tel: Colonsay (09512) 316

The island of Colonsay is a beautiful, peaceful place and offers a
complete escape for 'tired' anglers in search of relaxation amidst
perfect surroundings. There is a choice of accommodation ranging
from a first-class hotel to well-equipped, traditional cottages.
Loch Sgoltaire is the best loch and the average weight of fish 1 lb.
Fishing is from the bank and the west shore produces the best
results. The area of the islands is the place to head for. Fada is a
long, narrow water of almost three separate sections. An average
basket from Fada would be 4 fish weighing 5 lb. Fada has a boat
as well, and fishing from the boat is most effective since the loch
becomes weedy as the season progresses. Loch Tuiramain has
trout averaging ¾ lb. and a good basket would consist of 4–6
fish. Bank fishing only. Standard loch fly patterns work well.
Something for every member of the family on this lovely island
and well worth considering for an away-from-it-all holiday.

ISLE OF GIGHA
THE MILL LOCH	62/645505

Permission: Gigha Hotel, Gigha, Argyll.
Tel: Gigha (05835) 254

The Mill Loch on the Island of Gigha, off the west coast of Mull
of Kintyre, is a delightful water on a delightful island. The loch is
stocked every two years with ¼–½ lb. rainbow trout and fishing
is from boat only. The growth rate of fish is excellent and they
average 3½ lb. in weight – when caught. Use standard pattern
flies and crossed fingers to try. Just the place to escape from it all;
quiet, remote, beautiful and a good trout loch close by – sounds
about perfect.

ISLE OF TIREE
LOCH BHASSAPOL   46/973470
Permission: The Factor, Argyll Estate Office, Heylipol, Scarinish, Isle of Tiree, Argyll.
*Tel:*Scarinish (08792) 516

Loch Bhassapol, on the lovely, warm, romantic, Atlantic-washed island of Tiree, is a first-class trout loch. It is strictly private and fishing is syndicated but is available from time to time and visitors should inquire at the estate office. The loch contains brown trout and the occasional sea trout. The average weight of fish is 1 lb. and a reasonable basket should produce up to 6 fish. The south end is the best area to fish and along this shore the water is not deep and wading easy. Boats are available but bank fishing is very good. The heaviest fish caught during the 1981 season weighed 3¾ lb. and two rods had 26 fish in three hours to the dry fly. In spite of these baskets, the trout do not give themselves up and are very informed and selective about what they eat. Fish in the evenings for the best chance and use Grouse and Claret, Greenwell's, Light Blue Dun, Silver Butcher and Wickham's Fancy. A perfect loch.

LOCH A'PHUILL   46/956420
Permission: The Factor, Argyll Estate Office, Heylipol, Scarinish, Isle of Tiree, Argyll.
Tel: Scarinish (08792) 516

This loch is also syndicated and the fishing is strictly private. However, there may be day lets from time to time and visitors should inquire at the estate office. The loch contains brown trout and the occasional sea trout and the average weight of fish is 1 lb. A good basket would hold 3–4 fish and trout of up to 3 lb. are caught. One rod, fishing for a day during the 1981 season, had 18 trout and when conditions are right the fish rise well. Dry fly does not work so effectively here but other standard pattern loch flies all produce results. The most productive area is along the feeding bank about 150 yards out from the shore. If water levels are low then wading down the bank can be every bit as good as fishing from the boat. Visit it if you can.

ISLE OF BUTE
LOCH QUIEN   63/065595
Permission: The Bute Estate Office, Rothesay, Isle of Bute.
Tel: Rothesay (0700) 2627

Loch Quien is easily accessible and is to the west of the A845 road from Rothesay. It is 1,000 yards long by 500 yards wide and the loch is stocked with both brown and rainbow trout. The average weight is 1 lb. and the best fishing area is in the vicinity of Quien Hill near to the small island. There are boats available to the visitor and bank fishing is also allowed. Standard loch fly patterns work well and Loch Quien is a pleasant loch which produces good results throughout the season.

LOCH FAD   63/075610

Permission:
Hills D.I.Y. Shop, 62 Montague Street, Rothesay, Isle of Bute.
Tel: Rothesay (0700) 2880;
At the loch

The loch is three-quarters of a mile long by 350 yards wide and is easily accessible. Boat and bank fishing is allowed and the loch is being used as a fish farm from which it is being developed into a major new fishery. The Rothesay Seafoods, who own the loch, release fish from their fish farm into Fad and the present average weight of trout is in the order of 6–12 oz. with the occasional larger fish of over 1 lb. being landed. Use standard pattern flies.

KINTYRE
TANGY LOCH   68/692280

Permission:
A. P. MacGrory, Main Street, Campbeltown, Kintyre.
Tel: Campbeltown (0586) 52132;
Tangy Farm at the loch

This is a small water on the west coast of Kintyre and is approached via the A83. The loch is a walk of about half an hour east of Tangy Farm and both boat and bank fishing are available. Trout in Tangy average ¾ lb. and an average basket should produce 4–6 fish. The best fishing area is in the vicinity of the island at the eastern end of the loch and along the north shore. Fish it early in the season since weed can be a problem later on. Best cast, Black Pennell, Grouse and Claret, and Kingfisher Butcher. Good sport in attractive surroundings.

LUSSA LOCH   68/710300

Permission: A. P. MacGrory, Main Street, Campbeltown.
Tel: Campbeltown (0586) 52132

Lussa loch is 2 miles long by half a mile wide and is in a pleasantly wooded situation. It is easily accessible and both boat and bank fishing are allowed. Fishing is managed by the Kintyre Protection and Angling Club and visitors will find the members are a very welcoming group and always ready to help and advise. Most of these waters are not overfished and offer excellent sport. The trout on Lussa average ½–¾ lb. and a reasonable basket would hold 6–10 fish although larger catches are taken each season. Best flies include Blae and Black, Grouse and Claret, and Coch-y-Bonddu.

LOCH AUCHALOCHY   68/726226
Permission: A. P. MacGrory, Main Street, Campbeltown.
Tel: Campbeltown (0586) 52132

This loch is to the north of Campbeltown and is an easy half hour walk from the road. It fishes best early in the season and the average weight is ½–¾ lb., a days fishing generally producing up to 6 fish. The most favoured areas to fish are in the shallows at the north end and both boat and bank fishing are available. From time to time Auchalochy produces trout of up to 2½ lb. and the flies that tempt them are Cinnamon and Gold, Peter Ross and Wickham's Fancy.

KNOCKRUAN LOCH   68/733228
Permission: A. P. MacGrory, Main Street, Campbeltown.
Tel: Campbeltown (0586) 52132

Loch Ruan, as it is known locally, lies to the east of Auchalochy and fishing is from the bank only. Trout average ½ lb. and it is approached by the same route. If things are a bit quiet on Auchalochy, Ruan can often provide sport and it is a very pleasant loch to fish.

LOCH GARASDALE   62/765510
Permission: The Sawmill Office, Largie, Tayinloan, by Tarbert, Kintyre, Argyll.

This is a scattered loch half a mile long by 700 yards wide to the east of Ballochroy on the A83 Tarbert–Campbeltown road. Two boats are available and the loch contains brown trout with an average weight of ½–¾lb. and in spate conditions sea trout run up the Ballochroy Burn. An average basket would consist of 6 fish and the standard loch fly patterns work well. The best fishing areas are in the south of the loch where the feeder burns enter and down the east shore.

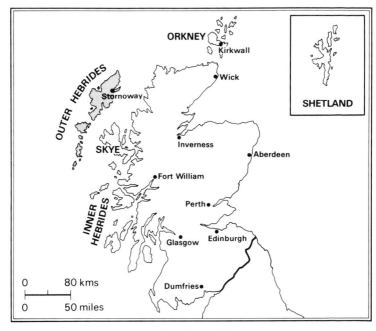

Map 50 *Outer Hebrides*

12 Outer Hebrides

It is just not possible to describe all the trout fishing available in the Outer Hebrides. Have a look at a map and you will see what I mean. Benbecula is mostly water and all the lochs contain trout which range from small three to the pound fish right up to fish of over 5 lb. I hope that the lochs that I have described will help you to begin, no doubt you will soon discover your own favourites. Wherever you go you will be enchanted and ensnared by the magic of the islands. Time seems to pass more slowly here, if you know what I mean. On some of the small crofts, crops are still harvested by sickle and scythe and the smell of peat fires lingers in the soft evening air. In the spring and early summer, the machair of South Uist bursts into a riot of colour and you will stand on some deserted beach and marvel at the beauty and serenity of the view. There are few more lovely places to spend time fishing, from the magnificent fish of the machair lochs of South Uist to the little trout-filled lochans of Lewis, the Outer Hebrides will provide you with a memorable and excellent fishing experience.

ISLE OF LEWIS
LOCH LANGAVAT   8/215440
Permission: Not required

Loch Langavat lies to the north of Carloway on the A858. Turn left just past the village. Langavat is half a mile long and there are two long bays at the south guarded by a small island and a further bay running northwards. It is an easy walk from the road and trout of up to 4 lb. have been caught. Catches during 1981 included baskets of 3 fish weighing 5 lb., the average weight being 1¼ lb. Not a loch for the beginner but if you do catch a fish you will remember its strength and quality for a long time. Fish the peninsula separating the two finger-like bays at the south end and a good north-east wind seems to 'move' the fish. Large dark patterns of fly are best.

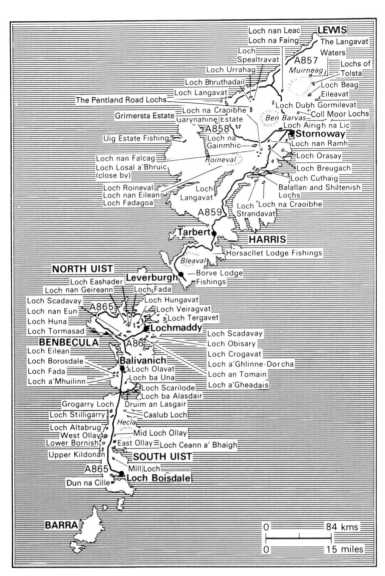

Map 51 *Outer Hebrides*

THE PENTLAND ROAD LOCHS

LOCH CEANN ALLAVAT	8/276390
LOCH AIRIGH SEIBH	8/260386
LOCH AN TUIM	8/255358
LOCH ALMAISTEAN	8/220396
LOCH BORADALE	8/214414

Permission: None required

The Pentland Road runs across Lewis from Carloway in the west to near Stornoway in the east. The moor to the north, in the vicinity of Beinn Bragar (261m), Beinn Rahacleit (248m) and Beinn Choinnich (210m), is scattered with trout lochs and de-serted, ruined shielings. Eastwards from Pentland Road, to the A858, lies a further, astonishing array of good fishing.

The principal waters are noted above and all contain trout which vary in size from modest 6 oz. fish to Ceann Allavat, which has produced trout of up to 2 lb. Most of these remote waters are rarely fished so information is sparse. Certainly, you could stumble into one for the glass case here, so always be prepared for that violent, heart-stopping tug.

LOCH NA GAINMHICH 8/285295

Permission: Not required

This loch is one mile long by 400 yards wide and is a fifteen minute walk from the A858 south of Lochganvich. Inquire in the village regarding boats since one might be available from time to time. The best areas to fish are round the north-east and north-west shores. The southern bay is also good and most of the larger trout are caught here. Trout average ½–¾ lb. with the odd one of over 1 lb. They fight very well and an average day should pro-duce 4–6 fish. Most popular flies include Blue Zulu, Teal and Green, and Teal and Black. Several other small lochs lying to the south all contain trout in the ½ lb. class and offer great sport if things are quiet on Gainmhich.

LOCH NAN RAMH 8/327300

Permission: Not required

Loch nan Ramh is a small loch 6 miles from Stornoway by the side of the A858. Trout average ¾ lb. and a days fishing might account for 3–4 fish. The most productive area is along the road-side bank. Pay particular attention to the area around the large rock. Flies to try should include Teal and Green, Mallard and

Claret, Silver Butcher and Invicta. Bank fishing only and waders are really required to cover the water properly. Take care as there are areas down the roadside bank where the mud is soft and dangerous. Sample catches last year were as follows: two trout weighing 1 lb. 14 oz, two trout weighing 1 lb. 10 oz. and 1 trout weighing 1¾ lb. This loch fishes very well in the late evening and the trout are great fighters.

EAST ARNISH WATERS
LOCH AIRIGH AN SGAIRBH 8/408310
LOCH MOR A'CHROTAICH 8/410305
Permission: None required

These lochs lie to the east of the A859 Stornoway–Balallan road and involve an easy walk over the moor. An Sgairbh is known locally as Pipers Loch and a Chrotaich as the Frying Pan. Trout average 10 oz. On an Sgairbh, concentrate on the west shore, by the small island; on a'Chrotaich the north-west shore produces best results.

LOCH URRAHAG 8/325480
LOCH BHRUTHADAIL 8/316460
LOCH SPEALTRAVAT 8/313454
Permission: Not required

These lochs are situated near Bragar on the A858. The end of Urrahag touches the road 2 miles south from the Lower Barvas junction. The two main lochs are separated by a causeway, the southern section being known as Bhruthadail. Spealtravat is joined to them by a short stream and the series is over 2 miles long. Urrahag is the most productive and the trout average ½ lb. with the occasional ¾ lb. fish. There are similar sized trout in the other lochs and the water tends to be rather coloured, but they fight well and an average basket should produce 6–10 fish. Sample catches from 1981 included 6 trout between 6–12 oz. and 13 trout between 6–12 oz. An inflatable boat would be an advantage on Urrahag since larger trout are frequently seen but always out of reach. Who says trout are stupid? Standard loch fly patterns work well.

LOCH DUBH GORMILEVAT 8/365435
Permission: Not required

To the west of the A857 Stornoway–Lower Barvas road,

Gormilevat is a three-quarters of a mile walk over the moor. Park the car near to where the Barvas river comes down the hill and then turns north to follow the road. Walk out from here. The trout in this loch are of excellent quality and average 2 lb. in weight. Fish of 4–5 lb. are also sometimes taken. Bank fishing only and take care round the outlet in the north-east corner – there is a dangerous bog there. Best flies are large, dark patterns or reservoir lures and fish them deep since trout seldom rise to flies on the surface. Recent catches included a fish of 3 lb. one of 2¾ lb. and a fine basket of 3 trout weighing 6¾ lb. Not a beginner's loch but hard to resist the challenge.

WEST ARNISH WATERS
LOCH NAN SGIATH 8/362303
LOCH FAOILEAG 8/358298
Permission: None required

An easy walk to the west of the roadside Loch Breugach brings you to these two delightful waters. Park at the north end of Breugach and walk out past the ruined croft. You will pass a small, triangular-shaped lochan and should stop for an experimental cast. Although very weedy, trout of up to 2 lb. have been taken here. Mid-way between Breugach and Sgiath, as you bear south-west, there is another small, dour loch – worth a throw: fish of up to 2 lb. have been caught. Trout in Sgiath and Faoileag are of excellent quality and average 10–12 oz. and fight well.

LOCH BREUGACH 8/375300
Permission: The Sports Shop, 6 North Beach Street, Stornoway. *Tel:* Stornoway (0851) 5464

This loch is on the A859 Stornoway–Balallan road and easily accessible. The angling association has carried out improvements to the loch but it still has a reputation for being dour. Both boat and bank fishing are available and best bank fishing areas are the two points on the north shore. Dark pattern flies work well and the average weight of fish is ¾–1 lb. with the odd larger trout of up to 1½ lb. Try a cast with Grouse and Claret, Black Pennell, and Silver Butcher.

LOCH ORASAY 8/390280
Permission: Not required

This is a beautiful loch to the south of the A859 Stornoway–

Balallan road. It is easily accessible from the B897 which runs down the east bank and Orasay is a popular venue. Evening fishing produces the best results and trout average ¾–1 lb. and Orasay also contains char. The northern half of the loch round the west shore and amongst the scattered islands are the best fishing areas and trout of up to 2¾ lb. were taken last season. Even larger fish can be had in Loch Crogavat which is joined by a small stream to Orasay in the south-west corner. Trout of up to 5 lb. have been caught here. Best flies to use include Peter Ross, Teal and Red, and Butchers.

LOCH AIRIGH NA LIC   8/400343
Permission: Not required

This loch is just outside Stornoway and contains brown trout and the occasional sea trout. Trout average ½ lb. and a reasonable day should produce up to 6 fish. The best area is at the east end of the loch and flies to use are Silver Butcher, Kingfisher Butcher, Dunkeld and Peter Ross. The loch is rather spoiled by the proximity of the town rubbish dump. Fish it for sea trout when the river swells, then walk out into the hills and moors for better sport.

LOCH NAN LEAC   8/430485
LOCH NA FAING   8/424487
Permission: None required

Drive north-west from Stornoway along the A857 Barvas road and park at 389453, by the bridge over the Cliastul Burn. Nan Leac and na Faing are a three-mile hike north across the featureless moor. You must take a compass, otherwise, should the mist descend, you could spend days walking round and round in ever-decreasing circles – fishless.

Both lochs contain trout which average 1 lb. in weight with heavier fish of up to 3 lb. occasionally taken. On nan Leac, the most productive area is along the south-east shore, by the remains of the old crofts. On na Faing fish the south-west shore as well, round to the single island and the ruined crofts on the outlet burn. Bank fishing only.

COLL MOOR LOCHS
LOCHAN A'SGEIL   8/434435
LOCH AN TUIM   8/425435
LOCH FADA CAOL   8/437444

LOCH AN TOBAIR	8/435456
LOCH NA FOLA	8/444454
LOCH NAN LEAC	8/446458
LOCH AN FHEOIR	8/452460

Permission: None required

Follow the B895 north from Stornoway to the community of Coll. Just before the church, turn left, past the school and Lighthill. This peat road will lead you out (clutching compass) onto the moor.

Lochan a'Sgeil has the largest trout and fish of up to 4 lb. have been caught, but they have a reputation for being dour. The other waters have a good supply of 6–8 oz. fish with the odd trout of up to 1 lb. But an Tobair contains very silvery fish with some of up to 1½ lb. These lochs provide an excellent day out, fishing and walking, in a very lovely setting.

LOCHS OF TOLSTA

LOCH MOR A'GHOBA	8/485472
LOCH IONADAGRO	8/513466
SOUTH BEAG SGEIREACH	8/500468
LOCH SGEIREACH MOR	8/490455
LOCH NAN GEADH	8/484464
SOUTH A'CHITEAR	8/480468

Permission: None required

These lochs lie to the west of the B895 North Tolsta road and getting to them will exercise your lungs, legs and map-reading skills. All contain trout in the 6–8 oz. class. South Beag Sgeireach (unnamed on the map), however, can produce trout of up to 3 lb. although they do not give themselves up easily. Similarly, south a'Chitear (unnamed on the map) has produced trout of up to and over 3 lb. in weight.

THE LANGAVAT WATERS

LOCH LANGAVAT	8/525545
LOCH BEAG EILEAVAT	8/512540
LOCH MOR EILEAVAT	8/514535
LOCHAN VATALEOIS	8/520538
LOCH SGEIREACH NA CREIGE BRIST	8/545535
LOCH EILLAGVAL	8/528523
NORTH EILLAGVAL	8/525528

Permission: None required

Starting point for the Langavat Waters is north of New Tolsta, at the end of the B895 road from Stornoway. There are dozens of lochs out on the moor and the principal ones have been listed above. All contain wild brown trout which average 6–8 oz. and these lochs are rarely fished. Consequently, for the angler who is prepared to walk for more than an hour over the moors, there could be the odd surprise. For instance, Creige Brist has produced fish of up to 5 lb.; narrow (unnamed on the map) North Eillagval has trout of up to 3 lb. and Loch Beag Eileavat has fish which average ¾ lb. and the odd larger trout of up to 2 lb., particularly in the east section of the loch. Park at 541501, drag on the climbing boots, have a good day – you will not meet another soul.

THE GARYNAHINE ESTATE FISHINGS   8/237317

Permission: Garynahine Estate Office, Isle of Lewis, Hebrides. *Tel:* (08502) 209

The Garynahine Estate lies to the west of Stornoway, on the A858 and has more than 30 excellent trout lochs available for guests and visitors. Andrew Miller Mundy is the factor and he is always ready to help and advise about the availability of fishing. The estate also has salmon and sea-trout fishing on the famous Blackwater River and when rods are not taken up by Lodge guests they are available to day fishermen. A very lovely place to fish which also offers first-class stalking and shooting and superb accommodation.

LOCH ROINEVAL   13/235225
LOCH NAN EILEAN   13/233235
LOCH FADAGOA   13/245235

Permission: The Factor, Soval Estate, Balallan, Isle of Lewis. *Tel:* Balallan (085183) 223

These are three of many lovely lochs in the vicinity of Roineval (218m) and are approached from Balallan on the A859 Stornoway–Tarbert road. The lochs lie to the north of Roineval and are full of trout which vary in size from ½ lb. to 1 lb. Baskets of 20–30 fish are taken frequently and no one loch is particularly better than another. This is a perfect area for the angler and a day out in the hills here will be one to remember for many a year to come. Good sport in superb surroundings. Best flies include Black Pennell, Teal and Green, March Brown and Greenwell's Glory. Well worth a visit.

LOCH NA CRAOIBHE   13/300277
LOCH NAN FALCAG   13/300270
LOCH LOSAL A'BHRUIC   13/290275
Permission: Not required

These lochs involve a walk of about half an hour from Achmore to the south of the A858 Stornoway–Garynahine road. There are dozens of other waters nearby, all of which hold trout, and this is a most attractive and pleasant area to fish. The three named lochs are linked and the trout average between ¾–1 lb. Loch na Craoibhe is the best loch and the east side is the place to fish, but all the small bays hold their fair share of trout and should be carefully fished. An average basket on na Craoibhe will consist of 6–8 fish and much greater numbers will be caught on the other lochs. Standard loch fly patterns will do. At the end of the day, it will be hard to leave.

LOCH LANGAVAT   14/155130–225220
Permission:
Grimersta Estate, Grimersta Lodge, Callanish, Isle of Lewis.
Tel: Callanish (08502) 262;
The Factor, Soval Estate, Balallan, Isle of Lewis.
Tel: Balallan (085183) 223

Loch Langavat is the largest loch in the Hebrides and is 8 miles long by about half a mile wide. It is situated amongst some of the finest scenery in all of Scotland and contains salmon, sea trout and brown trout. Brown trout are caught all over the loch, but some places are more productive than others. A good area on the north-west shore is off the promontory (185197) near the junction with Loch Coirigerod. The fish here average 1¾ lb., have pink flesh and fight like demons. The walk out is a bit of a demon too, and it takes about one and a half hours to get there. Approach over the track from the B8011 Stornoway–Uig road. Loch Coirigerod is full of small trout and baskets of 40 trout are caught here. Further up Langavat in Boathouse Bay (224208) is not so productive an area for trout although salmon are caught here during the early months of the season. Morsgail Bay, below Scalaval Sandig on the west bank, is also an excellent salmon lie and at the end of the season produces first-class trout. Probably the best trout fishing on Loch Langavat is in the vicinity of the Dyke, halfway down/up the east shore. It gets its name from an old dry-stone wall which used to run from Arivruach on the A859 right out to the loch. This wall has long since disappeared but the line is a good route to follow out to the loch from that side. Where the Dyke meets the loch is a great place for trout and many really large trout have been caught here and trout of up to 4 lb. are not unusual. To the south of the Dyke are a number of delightful bays known as the Aline Bays and these are also a good area to fish. The south end of the loch should be fished carefully and it holds good trout as well as grilse. Watch out if you are on the wrong side of the river Langadale and it starts to rain heavily. It can become unfordable within an hour and present you with a really daunting walk back to the car. Loch Langavat is a perfect loch in perfect surroundings and well worth a lot of your time. Ask the estate if there is a boat available – from time to time there may be one – but don't worry if there is not, you will do very well from the bank. Standard loch fly patterns do well too.

GRIMERSTA ESTATE

Permission: David Whitehouse, Fishery Manager, Grimersta Estate, Isle of Lewis.
Tel: Callanish (08502) 262

The Grimersta system is available to angling clubs and other interested parties during the early months of the season – April, May and early June. David Whitehouse reports good catches of salmon, sea trout and brown trout during 1986.

LOCH STRANDAVAT   14/255195

Permission: Not required

This is a long, narrow loch adjacent to the A859 Stornoway road and south of Balallan. The setting is superb, with the hills of Harris to the south and Roineval to the west. The loch is easily accessible and fishing is from the bank only. Wading is safe and easy and the trout average ½ lb. with the odd heavier fish of up to 1 lb. occasionally being taken. Best flies are Teal and Green, Silver Butcher and Black Pennell and an average basket would consist of 8–10 fish. Fish the narrows below Sullanan Ard. A sample basket taken last summer held 13 trout with the heaviest fish weighing 12 oz.

LOCH CUTHAIG   14/275215
LOCH NA CROIBHE   14/285220

Permission: Not required

These lochs are to the north of Balallan on the road from Stornoway and are approached via a peat track which begins just past Balallan school. Loch na Croibhe is the smaller of the two and has an ill-deserved reputation for being dour. The trout average ¾ lb. and tend to leave it to the last moment before taking the fly, so make sure you give them plenty of time. The best area to fish is down the west shore. A basket last year included a trout of 1¼ lb. and fish of over 2 lb. have been caught. Loch Cuthaig, to the west of the peat track, has fish which average ½–¾ lb. and a good basket would hold about 6 fish. A basket during the 1981 season consisted of 9 trout with a good fish of just over 1 lb. Flies to use on both lochs are Silver Butcher, Dunkeld, Teal and Green, and Grouse and Claret.

LOCH NA CRAOIBHE   14/300182
Permission:
D. J. Smith, No 1 Shiltenish, Balallan, Isle of Lewis;
Claitair Hotel, Shiltenish, Balallan, Isle of Lewis.
Tel: Balallan (085183) 345

This is an excellent loch in magnificent surroundings and is best approached from the B8060 Balallan–Kershader road. There is a ten minute walk from the road to the loch and the trout average ¾ lb. The west and south shores fish best and a good cast to start with could be Black Pennell, Teal and Black, and Bloody Butcher. Fishing is from the bank only and trout of up to 2 lb. are caught. A good day should account for 4–6 trout and sample baskets from 1981 included 8 fish with a heaviest trout of 1¼ lb. Re-seeding nearby seems to have improved the fishing on this loch and it fishes best early on in the season. Well worth your attention.

LOCH KEOSE   14/366223
LOCH NA MUILNE   14/362225
LOCH NAM BREAC   14/368234
Permission:
The Sports Shop, 6 North Beach Street, Stornoway, Isle of Lewis.
Tel: Stornoway (0851) 5464;
J. Smith, 3 Keose Glebe, Keose, Isle of Lewis.

Keose is a very lovely loch and lies 10 miles south of Stornoway and is approached from the A859 south of Soval Lodge. The loch is three-quarters of a mile long by 250 yards wide and has two islands the southern of which is a bird sanctuary. The other island off the north-west shore is a perfect spot for a picnic and anglers may land on it. The local angling club have been improving the loch over the years by the addition of lime and trout now average about ¾ lb. Fishing is best near the margins and you should arrange to drift down the bank about 10–20 yards out. Black Pennell and Black Spider produce good results and these trout fight very well indeed, out of all proportion to their relevant size. A recent catch included 37 trout in 2½ hours fishing and there are quite a few fish of 1 lb. and over in the loch. The other two lochs mentioned, to the west of the main loch, are not fished as much as Keose but hold good trout and can offer excellent sport also.

UIG ESTATE FISHINGS   13/056333
Permission: Uig Estate, Uig, by Stornoway, Lewis.
Tel: Timsgarry (08505) 286

The Uig Estate offers salmon, sea trout and brown trout fishing and is situated in the south-west of the island. There are over 70 hill lochs in this area and visitors should inquire at the Uig Hotel for further details. At the time of writing this property is changing ownership but it is a very lovely area full of interest and there are excellent trout lochs. Worth visiting.

HARRIS
THE BORVE LODGE ESTATE FISHINGS
                                                  18/031947
Permission: Tony Scherr, Borve Lodge Estate, Borve, Harris.
Tel: Scarista (085985) 202

Borve is at the southern end of Harris and the estate has many lochs and lochans all containing small brown trout eager and willing to jump straight into the frying pan; but there are also larger fish to be caught. Many of the hill lochs will not have seen an angler for years and each new water is an exciting adventure into the unknown. Borve is an area of stunning beauty and well worth a visit. Sea trout are the principal interest but the brown trout provide great sport as well.

THE HORSACLIET LODGE FISHINGS   14/141965
Permission: Neil Macdonald, 7 Diraclett, Harris.
Tel: Harris (0859) 2464

The Horsacliet Lodge fishings are beautifully situated amongst the hills of South Harris and offer the visitor salmon, sea trout and brown trout fishing. Fishing is usually let with the Lodge, but from time to time day lets may be available. The Lodge may be available through C. J. Lucas, Warnham Park, Horsham, West Sussex and it makes a delightful centre for a Hebridean holiday. The best trout loch on the estate is Loch Drinishader which is just over one mile long by 250 yards wide. There are many lovely bays and islands throughout its length and both boat and bank fishing are available. The trout are pink-fleshed, prawn fed and average ½ lb. and fight very well indeed. During 1979 135 trout were caught, 1980 accounted for 132 and 1981, 222. The best fish recently was a trout of 2½ lb. Flies to use include Blue Zulu, Black Pennell and Invicta and the loch fishes well all over. Drinishader may be available for day lets also, and visitors should contact Neil MacDonald.

BENBECULA
LOCH EILEAN IAIN	22/786535
LOCH BOROSDALE	22/783528
LOCH FADA	22/793530
LOCH A'MHUILINN	22/785523

Permission: Department of Agriculture and Fisheries, Area Office, Balivanich, Benbecula.
Tel: Benbecula (0870) 2346

These lochs are to the south of Balivanich and contain trout which average ½–¾ lb. with the exception of a'Mhuilinn, which holds very much larger fish indeed. As per usual, getting them onto the bank is the problem. A'Mhuilinn is a narrow water and easy to cover. Wading is safe from either north or south bank and this is a small loch where the angler quickly gets the feel of the water. Trout of over 2 lb. are caught from time to time and the approach to these waters is a pleasant walk south of the B892 at Aird. Standard loch fly patterns work well on all the lochs and an average basket should account for 6–8 fish.

DRUIM AN LASGAIR 22/805495
Permission: Department of Agriculture and Fisheries, Area Office, Balivanich, Benbecula.
Tel: Benbecula (0870) 2346

This is a small loch at the end of a farm road and anglers' should request permission from the local farmer before using it. Turn left from the A865 and onto the B891 just to the north of Greagorry. This loch is easily fished from the bank and the best areas are along the west and north-eastern shores. The loch becomes weedy the further down you go and the best results come from the top end. Standard loch fly patterns will do and trout average ¾–1 lb. This is a pleasant loch to fish and easily accessible.

LOCH OLAVAT   22/815545
Permission: Department of Agriculture and Fisheries, Area Office, Balivanich, Benbecula.
Tel: Benbecula (0870) 2346

Loch Olavat is a roadside loch south of Gramsdale and the northern end of the loch touches the A865 road. The loch is one mile long by half a mile wide and the best fishing areas are in the vicinity of the islands and along the north bank and eastern shoreline. Loch Olavat holds good stocks of ½–¾ lb. trout and also a few larger fish. Standard loch fly patterns work well.

LOCH BA UNA   22/818528
Permission: Department of Agriculture and Fisheries, Area Office, Balivanich, Benbecula.
Tel: Benbecula (0870) 2346

With care, Ba Una can be reached via a peat track and it is possible to drive to the lochside. This track is to the left of the A865 one and a half miles south of the garage at Gramsdale. This is a most attractive loch and the fish average ½–¾ lb. with several fish of 1–1½ lb. being caught occasionally. Wading is easy and comfortable and the best areas to fish are along the north and east shores. The east shore is backed by a steep bank but there are rocky points and patches of shingle from which to cast. Baskets of 8–10 trout are often taken and this is a good loch for a family outing.

LOCH SCARILODE   22/847523
Permission: Department of Agriculture and Fisheries, Area Office Balivanich, Benbecula.
Tel: Benbecula (0870) 2346

Take the same route as for Ba Una turning onto the peat road south of Gramsdale on the A865. Park the car at Ba Una and walk eastwards. This is an easy walk of about half an hour and Scarilode is a beautiful loch surrounded by steep hills with rowans clinging to the sides. This is not a large loch but it is deep and difficult to fish. The angler has to do a fair bit of clambering and scrambling to get to the best places and the area where the track comes down to the waters edge is a good place to start. Left and right of this bay can be very good. At the far end of the loch, near to where the feeder burn enters, there is a natural ledge underwater. This is a good casting spot – don't go too far though. However, the best area is from the headland by the bay on the right-hand side of the loch. A promontory juts out into the water and it is possible to wade a short distance to the left of it. Again, do be careful, the water deepens quickly. The Scarilode trout average ¾ lb. with many heavier fish also being taken. They fight very well indeed, are pink-fleshed and rise like bullets. Standard pattern loch flies will do and I highly recommend this lovely loch. The walk out isn't really too bad – time passes quickly amidst such beautiful surroundings.

LOCH BA ALASDAIR 22/857495

Permission: Department of Agriculture and Fisheries, Area Office, Balivanich, Benbecula.
Tel: Benbecula (0870) 2346

Ba Alasdair is a large scattered loch to the east of the B891 Sheiling–Craigastrome minor road. The loch can't really be seen from the road but if you park at (862490) and walk over the small hills to your left, you will come to this beautiful loch within about ten minutes. The first part of Ba Alasdair is an excellent sea trout loch and below Druim na Lice (25m) and joined by a short stream to Ba Alasdair is a perfect brown trout loch. Cross Ba Alasdair at the narrows at the southern end and climb up past the pan-shaped little lochan halfway up the hill. Over the next rise is the main body of water. On your way try a few casts in these small lochs, the pan-shaped one and the lochan to the south-west of it. This last mentioned loch has some very big fish, but they are hard to catch. Still, it's worth a try and the best area is near the small islands. The large loch at the top of the hill is full of good fish which average ½–¾ lb. and fight hard. The hillside slopes sharply to the water's edge at the southern end but there are several bays where it is possible to wade safely. My favourite spot is from the first small island. It is possible to cross over to it and, with care, scramble through the undergrowth to the far end. From here there is a headland where casting is just possible. Cast out to your left towards the other bank. There are good fish waiting. The far north end has much easier wading and good fish can be caught here as well. Work round the north shore and on your way south you will come upon one of the most attractive bays in the world. Surmounted by a grand promontory, heather and rowan clad, this is a perfect spot. Climb down to the rock ledge to fish – or don't bother, just sit and watch, it's beautiful. Take along the usual flies.

NORTH UIST

LOCH SCADAVAY	18/880660
LOCH OBISARY	22/900620
LOCH CROGAVAT	22/924627
LOCH A'GHLINNE-DORCHA	22/915625
LOCH AN TOMAIN	22/920610
LOCH A'GHEADAIS	22/915595

Permission: Lochmaddy Hotel, Lochmaddy, North Uist, Hebrides.
Tel: Lochmaddy (08763) 331

To the south of the A865 Lochmaddy–Benbecula road lie dozens of named and unnamed lochs all holding trout of ½–¾ lb. Be cautious, however, since there is always the possibility of much larger fish and it's generally when concentration lapses that they 'take'. Scadavay is a lovely loch covering a vast area and full of attractive bays and corners where trout lie. Turn left at the road junction before the sea and follow the B894 out towards Drim Sidinish to Loch Obisary. This beautiful loch lies close to Eaval (347m) and the sea and a track runs round the north shore which leads to the other lochs named above. They are all good trout lochs holding excellent quality, hard-fighting trout and lie in perfect surroundings. This area is almost another world of peace and beauty and it would take days to explore it properly and a lifetime to tire of its ever changing majesty. Trout fishing almost becomes of secondary importance, but, just in case, take along the standard pattern loch flies.

LOCH EASHADER   18/805727

Permission: The Secretary, North Uist Angling Club, 19 Dunossil Place, Lochmaddy, North Uist.

This is one of the best trout lochs on North Uist and is easily accessible from the A865. A good track leads from the main road to the loch and the average weight of trout is ¾ lb. Much larger fish are taken and the loch can be fished from the bank where wading is safe and comfortable. The north-east shore fishes very well and it is possible to wade out five or six yards from the bank. Fish down this bay past the remains of the old wall. The other good area is from the headland on the south shore below the

30   *The end of a perfect day for Richard McNicol and Bruce Sandison.*

whins. Dry fly can produce good results on Eashader and in a wind all the standard loch fly patterns work well. Highly recommended for a super day out amidst lovely scenery.

LOCH NAN GEIREANN   18/845725
LOCH NA CEARDAICH   18/853725
Permission:
Department of Agriculture and Fisheries, Area Office, Balivanich, Benbecula.
Tel: Benbecula (0870) 2346;
D. J. MacDonald, 8 Clachan Sands, Lochmaddy, North Uist.
Tel: Lochmaddy (08763) 227

This is a large loch covering an area of 2 miles by half a mile and it lies to the south of the A865 at the top of North Uist. Na Ceardaich is an offshoot from it on the east side. The shoreline wanders in and out of dozens of bays over a distance of nearly 6 miles and Nan Geireann contains salmon, sea trout and brown trout. The best trout fishing area is in the large bay close to the road and enclosed by Aird Reamhar island whilst the salmon lie further down the loch in the largest bay on the west shore. A good sea trout lie is near to the chambered cairn on the east bank. Trout average ½–¾ lb. and good baskets are taken to standard loch fly patterns. Na Ceardaich also holds good brown trout and should not be missed. Walk out to the trout fishing area on the track that leaves the main road at Garry Skibinish.

LOCH SCADAVAY	18/855695
LOCH NAN EUN	18/845675
LOCH HUNA	18/814665
LOCH TORMASAD	18/820650

Permission:
Lochmaddy Hotel, Lochmaddy, North Uist, Hebrides.
Tel: Lochmaddy (08763) 331;
The Secretary, North Uist Angling Club, 19 Dunossil Place, Lochmaddy, North Uist.

These lochs all lie to the north of the A867 Lochmaddy–Benbecula road and cover an area of several square miles. They present an endless panorama of perfect bays and headlands and island-dotted lochs. The brown trout are in the ½–¾ lb. range and a day out here will be very rewarding – or perhaps several days, since there is so much water to cover. Not, however, Loch a'Bharpa adjacent to the road – it's a trout farm and fishing is prohibited. Standard loch fly patterns and a packed lunch.

LOCH HUNGAVAT	18/872724
LOCH VEIRAGVAT	18/880720

Permission:
Department of Agriculture and Fisheries, Area Office, Balivanich, Benbecula.
Tel: Benbecula (0870) 2346;
D. J. MacDonald, 8 Clachan Sands, Lochmaddy, North Uist,
Tel: Lochmaddy (08763) 227

These lochs are to the north of Lochmaddy a short walk west of the A865. Good baskets of ½–¾ lb. trout are caught and fish rise well to all the standard loch fly patterns. Fishing is from the bank only but trout are taken all round, so fish anywhere with confidence. Great area for eagles – look to the north.

LOCH FADA   18/870710

Permission:
Department of Agriculture and Fisheries, Area Office, Balivanich, Benbecula.
Tel: Benbecula (0870) 2346;
D. J. MacDonald, 8 Clachan Sands, Lochmaddy, North Uist.
Tel: Lochmaddy (08763) 227

Loch Fada is 1½ miles north of Lochmaddy and visitors should leave their cars at Blashaval on the A865. The boat is moored at the end of the north-eastern arm of the loch (884711) and fishing from the boat is best, since the most productive areas are round the many small islands which cover Fada. The trout average ½–¾ lb. and great sport can be had, particularly in June and July which are the best months for all the Uist lochs. A very pleasant loch to fish and the standard patterns of loch flies will do fine.

LOCH TERGAVAT   18/925735
LOCH NA CRICHE   18/923730

Permission:
Department of Agriculture and Fisheries, Area Office, Balivanich, Benbecula.
Tel: Benbecula (0870) 2346;
D. J. MacDonald, 8 Clachan Sands, Lochmaddy, North Uist.
Tel: Lochmaddy (08763) 227

Loch Tergavat is the larger of these two lochs and contains good trout. There is a boat available on the loch which is joined to Loch na Criche by a small stream – Loch Tergavat that is, not the boat, if you see what I mean. Approach via the A865 from Lochmaddy and turn right to Lochportain. About 2 miles from the junction, as the road begins to head due south, you will see the lochs on your left. Trout average ¾ lb. and standard loch fly patterns will tempt them. A very attractive setting and pleasant to fish.

LOCH AN DUIN   18/890740
THE DEADMANS LOCH   18/892746
LOCH AN ARMUINN   18/902748

Permission:
Department of Agriculture and Fisheries, Area Office, Balivanich, Benbecula.
Tel: Benbecula (0870) 2346;
D. J. MacDonald, 8 Clachan Sands, Lochmaddy, North Uist.
Tel: Lochmaddy (08763) 227

Three and a half miles north of Lochmaddy, turn right to Lochportain and Loch an Duin is on your immediate left. The boat is moored here and the loch stretches north in a long, narrow scatter of bays and points. Loch an Duin and Deadmans are joined together and accessible by boat but Loch an Armuinn must be fished from the bank. These lochs are beautifully remote and peaceful and hold better than average trout. However, nothing is that simple and they are also harder than average to catch. It's worth trying though since trout of 3–4 lb. have been caught here along with good baskets of smaller fish. Standard loch fly patterns work well. A perfect place to fish, much loved of anglers and eagles.

LOCH AN T-SAGAIRT   18/949725
LOCH NA COINTICH   18/964720
UPPER LOCH AULASARY   18/937724
Permission: D. J. MacDonald, 8 Clachan Sands, Lochmaddy, North Uist.
Tel: Lochmaddy (08763) 227

Loch an t-Sagairt is a roadside loch 3½ miles north of Lochmaddy, to the left of the minor road through Lochportain. Upper Loch Aulasary is to the west of t-Sagairt and Na Cointich is to the east of the road. All these lochs are fished from the bank and contain goodly numbers of ½–¾ lb. trout with the odd heavier one being taken occasionally. These larger fish tend to feed deep and rarely rise to flies on the surface. A sinking line is a good spare to carry on the islands and can often be used to good effect on these lochs. Again, just a perfect place to fish and marvellous surroundings.

SOUTH UIST
CASLUB LOCH   22/825415
Permission: Lochboisdale Hotel, Lochboisdale, South Uist.
Tel: Lochboisdale (08784) 332

After crossing O'Regans's Bridge, the causeway between Benbecula and South Uist, take the second road on the left to Lochcarnan. Just past Holmar, by the cattle grid, you will see the east end of Caslub. A boat is moored here and Caslub fishes best from the boat. The water is brackish and trout average 1 lb. with good numbers of 2 lb. fish also taken when the trout are on. Concentrate round the islands and, when the tide is on the turn, park the boat and, from the bank, fish the narrows where the loch empties into sea-loch Sheilavaig – look out for excellent sport!

UPPER LOCH KILDONAN 22/735280

Permission: Lochboisdale Hotel, Lochboisdale, South Uist.
Tel: Lochboisdale (08784) 332

Upper Kildonan is three-quarters of a mile long by one-third of a mile wide and lies to the west of the A865 at Kildonan. Trout average ¾ lb. in weight and both boat and bank fishing are allowed. Good baskets come from this lovely loch and sample catches during the 1981 season included 21 fish weighing 17 lb. 4 oz., 7 fish at 5 lb. and 12 fish weighing 8 lb. The best trout weighed 2 lb. and an average basket should account for 8–10 fish. There are several islands in the northern part of the loch and a feeder burn enters in the long bay to the east. These are the best areas to fish, though trout can be caught all over. Flies to use are Black Pennell, Peter Ross and Zulus.

LOWER LOCH BORNISH 22/734294

Permission: Lochboisdale Hotel, Lochboisdale, South Uist.
Tel: Lochboisdale (08784) 332

This is a superb loch to the west of the A865. Follow the minor road out to Bornish church and leave the car there. The loch is behind the church. Trout on this machair loch average 1 lb. 2 oz. and trout of up to 3½ lb. are not uncommon. Fish under ¾ lb. must be returned to the water and an average day should produce a basket of 2–3 fish. There is one boat on the loch but Bornish is an easy loch to wade and excellent results are achieved bank fishing. The Black Pennell does most of the damage and baskets taken during the 1981 season included 12 fish weighing 12 lb., 7 fish weighing 9½ lb. and 9 fish weighting 11 lb. This is a first-class loch and well worth a visit.

WEST LOCH OLLAY 22/740327

Permission: Lochboisdale Hotel, Lochboisdale, South Uist.
Tel: Lochboisdale (08784) 332

This is an island-dotted machair loch west of the A865, three-quarters of a mile long by half a mile wide. One boat is available and bank fishing can also be quite good. West Loch Ollay is a dour loch that will test the skill of the most expert angler. But it can produce really spectacular results – such as 12 trout weighing 25 lb. The average is 1½ lb., but if you catch a fish you consider yourself lucky – or skilful? Include a Black Pennell and try round the islands at the southern end. The 1981 season produced trout of 3 lb. 7 oz. and 3 lb. 9 oz. Go thou and try to do likewise. Don't be too disappointed if you don't, it's a lovely loch to fish.

MID LOCH OLLAY   22/755315
Permission: Lochboisdale Hotel, Lochboisdale, South Uist.
Tel: Lochboisdale (08784) 332

Where our Yorkshire terrier fell into a particularly smelly peat bog – they are like that, terriers. Lovely loch, with excellent trout averaging 1 lb. in weight. Best fished from the boat and the place to concentrate is down the middle, past the island – fingers crossed.

LOCH CEANN A'BHAIGH   22/766303
Permission: Lochboisdale Hotel, Lochboisdale, South Uist.
Tel: Lochboisdale (08784) 332

Park by the telephone box at 766298 and make for the east end of the loch – this is the most productive end. Fish average ¾ lb. with the odd one of up to 2 lb. In the autumn, there is also the chance of a salmon or sea trout, so be aware.

MILL LOCH   22/747270
Permission: Lochboisdale Hotel, Lochboisdale, South Uist.
Tel: Lochboisdale (08784) 332

Park at 744272, near the small island with the Dun. There is a good boat although bank fishing is every bit as productive. Mill Loch is a loch for all seasons, giving excellent sport with 1–1½ lb. wild brown trout throughout the season and great sport with salmon and sea trout in the autumn. Another plus is the fact that Beinn a'Mhuilinn and Sheaval provide welcome shelter from high easterly winds and the loch fishes best in winds from the north and north-west.

LOCH DUN NA CILLE   31/745190
Permission: Lochboisdale Hotel, Lochboisdale, South Uist.
Tel: Lochboisdale (08784) 332

This is a large loch lying to the south of Kilpheder. Park at the end of the loch, on the B888. The most likely spots are along the south-west shore, by the islands, and down the north-west shore. Na Cille has a twofold reputation: for trout of up to 3 lb. and more – and for being very dour. You pays your money and . . .

LOCH ALTABRUG   22/745346
Permission: Lochboisdale Hotel, Lochboisdale, South Uist.
Tel: Lochboisdale (08784) 332

Ten and a half miles north of Lochboisdale on the A865, turn left
and follow the minor road through Stonybridge. Loch Altabrug is
on your right and is a long straggle of water with a length of
nearly 2 miles. One boat is available and bank fishing is also
allowed. The trout average ¾ lb. and baskets of 8–10 fish are
often caught. The best fish during the 1981 season weighed
1½ lb. and other sample baskets had 5 fish at 4½ lb., 21 fish at
17½ lb. and 10 fish weighing 7½ lb. After July Altabrug becomes
weedy so fish it early in the season. Black Pennell, Peter Ross and
Zulus should do the trick.

EAST LOCH OLLAY   22/765313
Permission: Lochboisdale Hotel, Lochboisdale, South Uist.
Tel: Lochboisdale (08784) 332

East Loch Ollay is adjacent to the A865, 10 miles north of
Lochboisdale. East Loch Ollay contains brown trout and the occasional salmon and sea trout. Good baskets of trout are taken and
catches of 10–15 fish are frequent. The average weight is ¾ lb.
and the best fishing area is in the bay to the east where the feeder
burns enter. Sample catches last season included 17 trout weighing
15 lb., 12 trout weighing 9 lb. and this peaty loch fishes best at the
end of the season. Best flies are Black Pennell and Peter Ross.

LOCH STILLIGARRY   22/765380
Permission: Lochboisdale Hotel, Lochboisdale, South Uist.
Tel: Lochboisdale (08784) 332

This machair loch is to the west of the A865. Park the car on the
minor road and walk down to the loch. The boat is moored at the
northern end. Bank fishing is also allowed and can be good but
best results usually come from the boat. Loch Stilligarry is half a
mile long by some 500 yards wide and its main features are the
many islands which are scattered throughout its length. The best
place to fish is round these islands and trout average 1 lb. 3 oz.
The quality of the trout is really excellent and they fight very well
indeed. The 1981 season saw baskets of 5 fish weighing 5 lb., 4
fish weighing 8½ lb. and the best fish weighed 3 lb. 2 oz. Black
Pennell, Grouse and Claret, and Peter Ross are good flies to use.

GROGARRY LOCH 22/762395

Permission: Lochboisdale Hotel, Lochboisdale, South Uist.

Tel: Lochboisdale (08784) 332

Leave the A865 at its junction with the B890 and travel west onto the machair. Loch Grogarry is to the south of this road and is half a mile long by about 300 yards wide. There are excellent trout here and all fish under ¾ lb. must be returned to the water. The average for the loch is 1 lb. 2 oz. and the best fish caught during 1981 weighed 3 lb. 9 oz. Bank fishing is not very good and best results come from the boat. An average basket should net you 4 perfect fish and catches taken during the 1981 season included 11 fish weighing 13¼ lb., 6 fish weighing 6 lb. and 6 fish weighing 8 lb. The fish are dramatic and so are the views to Hecla (608m) and Beinn Mhor (606m). Perfect fishing. Best flies are Black Pennell and Peter Ross.

Select Bibliography

Bartholomew, J., *Fishing Map and Gazeteer*.

Highlands and Islands Development Board, *Game Fishing Guide to the Highlands and Islands* (Inverness: H.I.D.B).

Kennedy, J., *70 Lochs – A Guide to Trout Fishing in South Uist* (Balivanich, Benbecula: Uist Community Press).

MacKinnes, Hamish, *West Highland Walks* (London: Hodder & Stoughton).

MacLeod, N., *Trout Fishing in Lewis* (Stornoway: Essprint, 1977).

Murray, W. H., *The Scottish Highlands* (Edinburgh: Scottish Mountaineering Trust, 1976).

Poucher, W. A., *The Scottish Peaks* (London: Constable, 1979).

Scottish Tourist Board, *Scotland for Fishing* (Edinburgh: S.T.B.).

Shetland Anglers Association, *A Guide to Shetland Trout Angling* (East Voe, Scalloway: Shetland Litho).

Weir, Tom, *The Scottish Lochs* (London: Constable).

Alphabetical Index of Lochs